TELLING AIRCRAFT TAILS

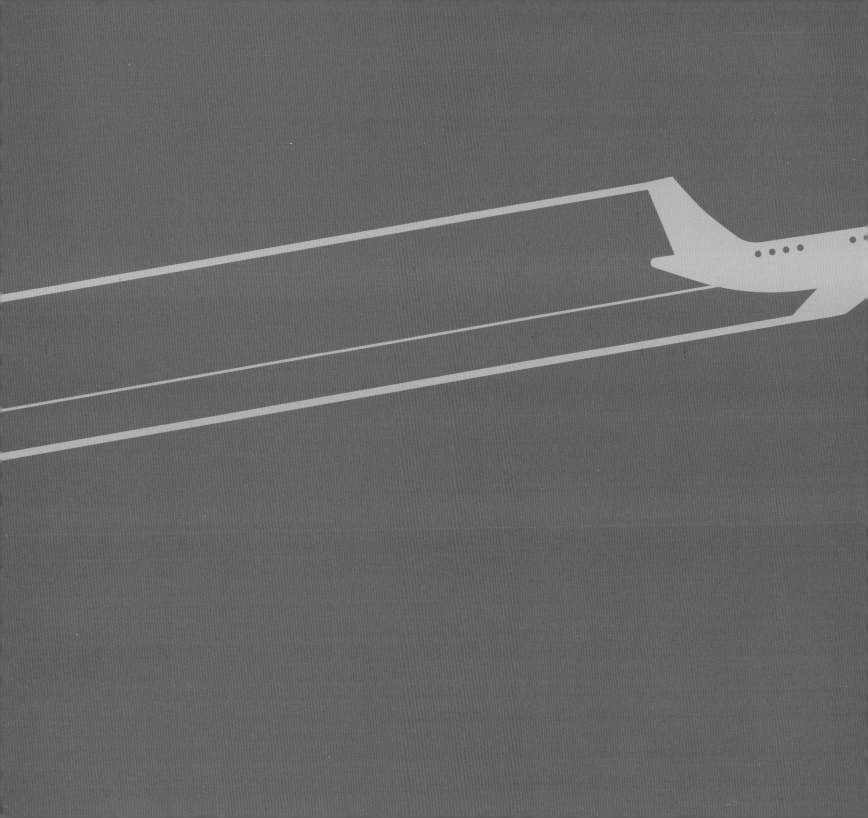

TELLING AIRCRAFT TAILS

A HISTORY OF BRITAIN'S AIRLINES IN 40 AIRCRAFT

GUY HALFORD-MACLEOD

The History Press

Front cover images:
   Top: British Aircraft Corporation One-Eleven
   G-AVGP (The Aviation Photo Company)
   Middle: Boeing 737-200 G-BMOR (The Aviation
   Photo Company)
   Bottom: Canadair C-4 G-ALHG (The Aviation Photo
   Company)

Back cover image: Super Trader G-AGRH (Keith Bunyan
   via Geoff Goodall)

First published 2021

The History Press
97 St George's Place, Cheltenham,
Gloucestershire, GL50 3QB
www.thehistorypress.co.uk

British Library Cataloguing in Publication Data.
A catalogue record for this book is available from the British Library.

ISBN 978 0 7509 7012 9

Typesetting and origination by The History Press
Printed and bound in India by Thomson Press India Ltd

CONTENTS

INTRODUCTION

Over the years, reading about and researching the history of Britain's airlines, I came across one recurring theme: aircraft registrations that looked familiar. I would recognise a specific airliner from some previous incarnation in a new role with a different owner. Here were aircraft being passed on from one hopeful to another: maybe the original owner had been taken over by another airline; or had just changed its name; just as probably, an airline had gone bust and some other airline had taken over its aircraft. The aircraft tail colours, with or without the registrations – not all airlines painted them on the tail – reflect these changes.

Handley Page Hermes G-ALDM, for example, had three different owners. Handley Page, an old established aircraft manufacturer based at Radlett in Hertfordshire, built twenty-five Hermes after the Second World War, and BOAC, the British Overseas Airways Corporation, bought most of them. What is the significance of the letters G-ALDM seen painted on the tail? They are the aircraft equivalent to a car's number plate. The letter G stands for Great Britain, the country where the Hermes was registered. The four letters ALDM were reserved to that particular aircraft, and stayed with it, no matter who owned the aircraft in subsequent years.

The story of G-ALDM mirrors the development of civil aviation in post-war Britain. BOAC preferred American-built airliners and did not really want to buy the Hermes, which had a number of technical shortcomings. After they were delivered BOAC was anxious to be rid of the aircraft as soon as possible; some of them never actually entered service with the corporation. This particular Hermes flew BOAC's African scheduled services for a short while in the early 1950s, and was then sold in 1956 – at a loss to BOAC – to another British airline, Britavia. It used the airliner to carry troops to British military garrisons abroad, in Africa and the Middle East, under a concession granted by the government to the privately owned British charter airlines that compensated them for the denial of rights to fly scheduled services; these had already been given as a monopoly to the nationalised air corporations, BOAC and its sister organisation BEA, British European Airways.

The Aviation Photo Company

7

David Welch

Tony Eastwood Collection

When the trooping concession ended, the aircraft was sold to another British charter airline, Air Safaris, which used it to fly holidaymakers to the sun in the Mediterranean for a few years, before that airline went bust in the early 1960s; after that G-ALDM, now well past its prime, was scrapped.

It was the same aircraft throughout, with the same registration, but it flew for three very different airlines, on very different services. Government policy, an unwilling buyer, a bit of coercion, financial losses, politics, U-turns, holiday charter flights, small independent airlines going bust; that is the very stuff of Britain's airlines and their history.

In the 1970s the sequencing of registrations began to change, as Britain's regulatory authority, the Civil Aviation Authority, now allowed aircraft owners to apply for out-of-sequence or 'vanity' registrations. Some of the listings towards the end of this book become a bit raggedy! One of the pioneers of personalised registrations was Sir Freddie Laker, proprietor of Aviation Traders Engineering Limited, who built a small turboprop airliner in 1957 that he called the Accountant. Serendipitously he was able to register the prototype G-ATEL as those letters were next on the list when he applied.

The choice of forty aircraft is obviously personal and was influenced by many factors: their histories, their survival into the twenty-first century – many at museums around the United Kingdom – even mundane matters such as the availability of photographs and slides. Also I wanted to write about as many airlines as possible. The subject listing of the aircraft accords more or less with the entry into service in Britain of each type. If you want to check a particular airline in the text, there is an index at the end of the book.

The Brabazon Committee: because the name occurs in the text especially in the early post-war years, this is just to remind you that the Brabazon Committee was established by Winston Churchill during the war years with a remit to come up with ideas for what Britain's aircraft manufacturers should build in the way of civil aircraft once the war was over. The Committee, reporting early in 1943, recommended the production of suitable so-called 'interim' conversions of the Lancaster and Halifax bombers and Sunderland flying boats, followed by development of five new types.

In a series of reports issued between August 1943 and March 1945, the Committee expanded on its first recommendations, and proposed the development and production of new types of aircraft, now increased to seven:

Type 1   A multi-engine aircraft for a London–New York direct service;

Type 2A   A twin-engine aircraft carrying thirty-six to forty passengers for European and other medium-stage services;

Type 2B   A twenty-four-seater aircraft, powered by four gas turbine engines, for European and other short- to medium-range services;

Type 3   A four-engine aircraft with accommodation for twenty passengers in sleeping berths, or forty passengers by day, for use on Empire services;

Type 4   A jet-propelled aircraft for express services;

Type 5A   A fourteen- to twenty-seater aircraft for feeder services;

Type 5B   An eight-seater, twin-engine aircraft for feeder, taxi and charter services.

In addition, the Committee recommended the development and production of the Avro Tudor, derived from the Lincoln bomber, to replace the Avro York. Late in 1944 the Vickers Viking, developed from the Wellington bomber, was initiated by the Ministry of Aircraft Production and later endorsed by the Committee, to be joined later by the Handley Page Hermes as back-up for the Tudor.

The Ministry of Civil Aviation accepted the recommendations for the seven new Brabazon types, but recognising that the Type 1 proposal was for a very large aircraft that would take years to develop, the Committee subsequently modified the Type 3 proposal to allow for a somewhat smaller transatlantic aircraft to be designed, to be known as the Type 3A; the original shorter-range 'Empire' aircraft then became the Type 3B, for which the contender was a variant of the Tudor with a longer fuselage, the Tudor 2. The importance of the North American market was pointed up by the fact that there were now three transatlantic designs, the Type 1, Type 3A and Type 4, all of them to different timescales and specifications. Twelve types – the seven Brabazon designs, the two Tudors, the Hermes, the Sunderland flying boat conversion and the Viking – were launched in 1945.

ACKNOWLEDGEMENTS

As always, I am extremely grateful for the help I have received from so many people and institutions. There are a lot of photographs in this book, and my first big thank you goes to Moray Pickering and his Aviation Photo Company who provided me with the bulk of the photographic material. I found the resources of ABPic, the aviation photographic website run by Air-Britain, truly invaluable, and I salute the generosity of its many contributors: Steve Aubury, Kenneth Colbran, Shaun Connor, Howard J. Curtis, Stewart Davidson, Dietrich Eggert, Ken Elliott, Chris England, Barry Friend, Martin Harrison, Arno Landewers, David Lunn, Ralf Manteufel, Dave Marshall, Peter Maurice, Ian McFarlane, Tony McGhee, Brian Nichols, Roger Richards, Steve Ryle, R.A. Scholfield, Charlie Stewart, Ian Tate, Bill Teasdale, Robin A Walker, Jonathan Walton and Dave Welch. I also acknowledge with gratitude the images from the Britten-Norman Aircraft Preservation Society, the J. Exton Collection (courtesy of J.S. Davidson), Colin Higgs and the Peter Keating Collection © A Flying History Ltd., Ron Roberts (courtesy of Barry Friend), Tom Gillmor and The Royal Aeronautical Society via the Mary Evans Picture Library and aviation-images.com, the A.J. Jackson Collection (now in the care of Brooklands Museum), the Air-Britain Archive (including the Peter Berry Collection), Keith Bunyan (courtesy of Geoff Goodall), Tony Eastwood, High Life in Scotland, the Orkney Photographic Archive, the R.N. Smith Collection, the Science Museum and the Smithsonian Institution.

I want to thank the following: the Civil Aviation Authority, for providing online the registration histories of the aircraft I write about; *Air-Britain Aviation World* and *Propliner*, for publishing such useful accounts of the activities of both airlines and airliners; The *FlightGlobal* Archive; and friends in the industry who helped me out, especially Brad Burgess, Malcolm Coupar, David Dorman, Jonathan Hinkles, Jeremy Instone, Terry Liddiard, Malcolm Simpson, Bob Wealthy and Allan Wright. And finally, big thanks to Amy Rigg at The History Press and my wife Johanna for their encouragement during this book's long gestation.

1: DE HAVILLAND DH.84 G-ACIT

De Havilland: a great British aircraft manufacturer. Before the Second World War other aircraft builders supplied Britain's Imperial Airways exclusively with ever more ambitious airliners and flying boats to connect the outermost reaches of the British Empire and Commonwealth, but de Havilland stayed closer to home, and built commercial aircraft that sold to a wider airline base. Imperial Airways relied on the flying boats built by Short Brothers and on landplanes from Handley Page and Armstrong Whitworth, but those manufacturers had little success selling their products to other airlines: de Havilland did. Not only that, but de Havilland also built airliners for Imperial Airways in the pre-war years, adding its products to the heterogeneous mix that dawdled along the Empire's air routes, a complicated web of short-stage sectors with numerous aircraft changes, cross-European train journeys, long days, overnight stops and early starts; all of which required a certain hardiness of spirit.

De Havilland built hundreds of DH.4 and DH.9 bombers during the Great War, many of which were demilitarised after hostilities ceased; when converted, they could carry mail, freight or up to three passengers. Britain's first international airline, Aircraft Transport and Travel, used DH.4s and DH.9s on its regular services between London Hendon and Paris Le Bourget that started on 25 August 1919; passengers wore helmets, goggles and other flying clothing. De Havilland formed its own commercial unit, Aeroplane Hire Service, using single-engine DH.9s and its successor the

DH.50, which carried up to four passengers; its chief pilot Alan Cobham became famous for his long-distance air-route surveys using de Havilland aircraft. When demand for these charters diminished around 1923, the company transferred the remaining aircraft to its School of Flying. De Havilland already manufactured trainers, the DH.60 Moth and Gipsy Moth, and went on to build the legendary DH.82A Tiger Moth, of which more than 8,000 were made. Although these open cockpit biplanes did much to generate interest in private flying, de Havilland recognised that as they progressed private flyers wanted more in the way of comfort, less of the heavy-duty flying gear.

The DH.80A Puss Moth, a high-wing monoplane with a cabin seating the pilot and two passengers, tried to address this issue. As domestic airlines began to establish themselves in the early 1930s, de Havilland went one stage further and built the DH.83 Fox Moth, which first flew in 1932. It could carry four passengers in an enclosed cabin and was the first British aeroplane that could 'support itself financially in the air', powering along five adults on a mere 130 horsepower (hp) provided by de Havilland's own Gipsy Major engines. Ted Hillman, an Essex-based coach operator with a pragmatic approach to airline costs and operations, used Puss Moths and Fox Moths for charter flights and he later started a regular thirty-minute service between Romford and the seaside resort of Clacton-on-Sea. When Hillman wanted to expand his low-cost service to Paris, he approached de Havilland for

The Aviation Photo Company

an aircraft that could carry twice as many passengers as the Fox Moth. De Havilland had a suitable design, a twin-engine bomber it was developing for the Iraqi Air force, and the DH.84 Dragon was born.

The Dragon could carry eight passengers. It cruised at a speed of 109mph, sipping just 13 gallons an hour and cost £2,900 ex-works; Hillman bought four off the drawing board, successfully introducing the type on airline services to Paris in April 1933. With its attractive economics, even better than the Fox Moth's, and the added benefit of twin-engine safety, the Dragon proved popular with many airlines. In Britain, savvy entrepreneurs realised that the immediate future of airline operations lay not in competing with the well-organised and funded railways whose mighty networks already encompassed the mainland but in serving some of the remoter regions within the British Isles, those not served by the railways, especially the many islands round Britain's coastline, from the Scillies in the south-west to the Orkney and Shetland Islands off Scotland's north coast. Dragons were soon flying to Jersey in the Channel Islands, the Isle of Wight, the Isle of Man, across the Severn between Cardiff and Bristol, and in Scotland. Before the airport was built in Jersey, these Dragons had to land on the beach at low tide at St Aubin's Bay.

Hillman was friendly with a busman in Scotland, John Sword, whose Midland Bus Company had recently been bought out by Scottish Motor Traction. Sword enthusiastically started flying both air taxi and regular services out of Glasgow's Renfrew airport, so enthusiastically indeed that his new employers told him after a couple of years that he really had to choose between buses and planes; he chose to stay with the buses. But before that he had bought Dragons, one

Author's Collection

of which could be converted for air ambulance use. After Sword quit aviation, in 1934, his Scottish island routes were taken over by a new airline, Northern and Scottish, formed by an Englishman, George Nicholson.

Other Englishmen were active elsewhere in Scotland. Eric Gandar Dower bought Dragons to fly between Aberdeen and Scotland's Northern Isles. Captain Fresson developed services from Inverness to Caithness and Kirkwall in Orkney. When Fresson's airline, Highland Airways, needed a larger aircraft than the four-seat Monospar it had been using, he bought his first Dragon, G-ACIT, taking delivery at Edinburgh on 30 July 1933; its first flight to Kirkwall was on 2 August. Fresson went on to pioneer air service within the Orkneys, and on to Shetland.

High Life Scotland

The aircraft, named *Aberdeen*, is seen with other members of the fleet at Inverness' Longman Field, a short step away from the railway station and town centre. Fresson used G-ACIT to inaugurate an Aberdeen–Kirkwall service in May 1934, and even after its place on the airline's scheduled services had been taken by more modern aircraft, the airline retained G-ACIT for charter work; its excellent slow-speed performance helped get it in and out of tiny Scottish airstrips and fields. Writing to *Flight* magazine in 1962, Fresson seemed to remember G-ACIT fondly:

That aircraft meant a lot to me as it was the first Dragon I purchased and delivered for Highland Airways in July 1933, and it had the honour, along with myself, of carrying the first

airmail service to be regularly operated in Britain at ordinary letter rates. G-ACIT also had the distinction of being the first Dragon to land on Fair Isle, midway between Orkney and Shetland.

During the early part of the war I was detailed to fly Admiral Somerville to that island on important radar siting. It was a hazardous landing as there was only 300yd available, and if one overshot there was a 200ft drop over the cliffs into the sea. When the rest of our fleet had been dispatched overseas at the beginning of the war, G-ACIT was retained to fly the official Scapa airmail and operate the Orkney air service for VIPs and Service personnel, with myself as pilot.

It flew on constant service throughout the war in all weathers. I well remember one occasion with a load of 1,000lb of urgent mail, piled to the roof, I was rounding the high cliffs of Hoy in a 70 m.p.h. gale and snow blizzard, with overcast almost touching the sea, flying at a hundred feet or so, when a terrific squall all but turned G-ACIT on to its back. The mail tumbled all over the cabin, to make matters worse and recovery more difficult. It was touch and go, but I came out right way up, kissing the gigantic wave tops. I stayed that night in Kirkwall!

In all I flew G-ACIT well over 1,000hr and had many difficult trips. I became very attached to that aeroplane.

Poor Fresson received a further battering when his airline, by then renamed Scottish Airways after it had been amalgamated with Northern and Scottish, was absorbed in 1947 into the new British European Airways (BEA), following the nationalisation of civil aviation after the war. Despite all his experience, his services were soon dispensed with and his request to buy G-ACIT was turned down. His callous treatment at the hands of the Labour government reflected the antagonism of the new administration towards any civil flying ventures that were independent of the nationalised air corporations.

Instead G-ACIT was occasionally used by BEA's new chief executive Peter Masefield as a company hack, before being transferred in 1949 to the Airways Aero Association, a flying club for the three air corporations, and was named *Orcadian*.

The Aviation Photo Company

The Aviation Photo Company

Below: Author's Collection

In 1951 the Dragon was sold to Air Navigation & Trading at Blackpool for sightseeing flights, and subsequently spent many hours flying holidaymakers round the ten-minute circuit, giving everyone a view of the tower and the beaches.

G-ACIT was withdrawn from service in June 1959. In 1962, and by now almost thirty years old, G-ACIT was again on the sales lists and caught the eye of the same Peter Masefield, now chairman of Britain's light aircraft manufacturer, Beagle. Succumbing surely to nostalgia, he bought and used the aircraft as a company runabout for a couple of years, repainting it in Beagle's corporate bronze colours.

G-ACIT eventually passed to the Historic Aircraft Museum at Southend in 1971, and in 1983 the Science Museum bought it at auction for £28,000; the aircraft is kept at Wroughton together with many of the museum's other aircraft, and has been repainted in Highland Airways colours, but there is a handsome 1:24 scale model on view at the Science Museum in London. The Scottish Museum of Flight at East Fortune has an Australian-registered Dragon on display.

Science Museum

2: SHORT BROTHERS SUNDERLAND G-AGER

The Short Brothers go back to the very start of aviation, obtaining the British licence from the Wright Brothers to build six Flyers, the first of which flew in England in 1909. They went on to build balloons, airships, seaplanes, motor boats, mooring buoys, even lightweight bus bodies, for they were early researchers in the use of duralumin, which was light, resistant to corrosion and not liable to water soakage. The company launched the first of its all-metal flying boats, the twin-engine Singapore, in 1926; the design was developed as the Calcutta with three engines, seating fifteen passengers, and by 1930 Imperial Airways was using four of them. Better known as Imperials, the airline, privately backed but receiving subsidies from the state, was Britain's 'chosen instrument', vigorously developing routes within the British Empire and Commonwealth, and European routes with perhaps less panache. Passengers to India, the Middle East and Africa started their journey by coach from Imperials' London terminal to Croydon, and continued by air to Paris or Basel in Switzerland, followed by an overnight train journey to a Mediterranean port, Genoa, later Brindisi, then by flying boat to Alexandria, where a train connected passengers to Cairo; there they resumed the flight eastwards to Karachi or south to Khartoum and Cape Town.

The Kent, larger and faster than the Calcutta, joined the fleet in 1931. With four engines, it flew at 130mph with a range of 450 miles; they were used on a modified routing from Brindisi via Athens to Haifa in Palestine for onward connections to Karachi and points east.

Imperials faced competition on its routes to the Far East from the Dutch airline KLM; the latter used faster landplanes, Fokkers and modern Douglas DC-2 monoplanes, and their passengers did not need to change aircraft once they boarded at Amsterdam. In contrast the British had had no end of difficulties obtaining rights to fly over some of the countries on the routes to the Far East, hence the long train journeys! Imperials admired the sleek Douglas airliner, but thought it was too small for their requirements, for as well as carrying passengers Imperials had to carry mail, which became all the more pressing after the British and Commonwealth governments agreed under the Empire Air Mail Scheme of 1934 to carry all air mail at a non-surcharged rate, leading to a surge in demand. A much larger and faster air transport was needed, a significant step up from the existing biplanes in the fleet. The trouble was, a significantly larger landplane would require significantly upgraded facilities along the route, a daunting and expensive prospect given that many of the landing fields were prone to challenging weather conditions like the monsoon; if it rained, the ground became soft, not good for a 20-ton airliner landing on a small set of wheels. The solution seemed to be to use flying boats, which could land safely on water at much higher weights. The British were not alone in thinking along these lines: the Americans, French, Germans and Italians all designed and manufactured large flying boats for the same reasons. Shorts designed an impressive new class of flying boat, the Empire

Author's Collection

or C-Class, which could carry up to twenty-four passengers and a ton of mail at 160mph over 750 miles within the tall, two-deck fuselage. G-AEUE, pictured on page 23, joined Imperials in 1937 and survived the Second World War; it was finally withdrawn and broken up in 1947.

As the Empires entered service this coincided with the easing of some of the restrictions placed on Imperials' routings. Passengers could now fly directly from the new marine base at Southampton over France and Italy, although the Empires still needed to refuel in Brindisi and the Greek islands. The route to South Africa, along the Nile and then down the coast to Durban, was well suited to flying boat operations. Likewise the Empires could fly all the way to Singapore with little change to the existing routes but with an enormous saving in journey time, down from eleven days to five.

Imperials was not the only British operator to be enthusiastic about the enduring and reliable flying boats built by Short Brothers at Rochester in Kent. The Royal Air Force had used more than thirty armed Short Singapores for extended operations in Gibraltar, Aden, the Persian Gulf, Colombo and Singapore. As Imperials drew up its plans for the Empire class, the Royal Air Force was looking for a long-range armed flying boat, and accepted Short's proposal for a design not dissimilar to the C-Class that became known as the Sunderland. Empires and Sunderlands were parallel designs; Sunderlands came along later and were built to more stringent military specifications. During the war they were used by the Royal Air Force and Royal Australian Air Force for ocean patrols. They escorted convoys, hunted U-boats, transported personnel and equipment, and performed the first air-sea rescues; 749 were built, the last one in 1946.

Imperials had been somewhat diffident about air services to Europe, aside from its prestigious Paris service, and as a result a second privately owned airline, British Airways, had been formed in 1936 to develop European routes; it also received government subsidies. With the war against Germany looming, the government felt it had to have more control over its two 'chosen instruments'; it bought them both out and merged them, forming the first of Britain's state-owned air corporations, British Overseas Airways Corporation, better known as BOAC. A truly hapless airline, BOAC was officially established, suitably enough, on 1 April 1940, as the war in Europe was escalating and just before Italy joined the German axis. There was a belated recognition in the Royal Air Force that the service had insufficient transports, in fact almost none, so BOAC was co-opted to participate in numerous military operations, many of them on the front line. The extreme heroism of BOAC crews stands in sharp contrast to the many inadequacies of the new corporation and its management; BOAC was severely handicapped by a shortage of suitable equipment and operations staff. Not until 1943 when General Critchley took over as director-general did the government finally relent and give the new corporation some priority in obtaining new aircraft, recognising that the corporation would not take off as a transport wing of the Royal Air Force; instead the RAF was allowed to establish its own Transport Command.

BOAC's operations in the Far East and to Europe had been severely curtailed once hostilities started, but the corporation maintained flying boat services from Poole in England to West Africa; and also from South Africa through the Middle East to India and Australia, the so-called Horseshoe Route. The Empires in the fleet diminished in number as the war progressed; there had been thirty at the start, sixteen remained at the end. To make good the attrition from losses in action and other operating accidents, BOAC was allowed to take Sunderlands from the production line, twelve in 1943 and a further twelve in 1944. Austerely outfitted with bench-and-mattress seating for sixteen passengers on the lower deck, the Sunderlands had a range of 2,000 miles, cruising at 165 mph. G-AGER was the first to be delivered, on 8 January 1943; it was used on the Poole to West Africa service before transferring in October 1943 to the new service between Poole and Karachi, extended in 1944 to Calcutta.

Civil Sunderlands were painted in grey and green camouflage, with large red-white-and-blue national markings under the registration letters. The picture illustrates one of the many problems of flying-boat operations: the laborious passenger-handling arrangements requiring mooring buoys, pontoons and launches. Maintenance was just as tricky and time-consuming. Meanwhile, airfields around the world were

being constructed with hardened runways suitable for the new four-engine landplanes that American manufacturers were bringing to the market. Runways may have been just as difficult to find in bad weather, but at least they stayed put, unlike the ocean waves that flying boats had to land on.

With the end of the war, BOAC desperately needed all the aircraft it could get to consolidate and enhance its route operations. The Empires continued to operate the Horseshoe Route until it closed in 1947. Sunderlands were refurbished to full airline standard, with twenty-four seats on two decks, and given a new class name, Hythe. They were also given individual names; G-AGER became *Hadfield*. The Hythes were used to extend the eastern routes to Australia, and from Calcutta to Hong Kong and later Japan. Short Brothers went on to develop the design of the Sunderland; later classes of flying boats, the Sandringham and Solent, continued in service with BOAC until November 1950, when the corporation terminated its flying boat services.

But G-AGER had a longer life. Early in 1948 BOAC sold it and two other Sunderlands to Wing Commander Barry Aikman, who needed the flying boats to fly for his new airline, Aquila Airways, which was participating in the Berlin Airlift of 1948–49. Berlin, isolated in the middle of the Soviet Zone of post-war Germany, was occupied by the four victorious powers, America, the Soviet Union, Great Britain and France, each of which had its own sector. The only feasible way for the three western powers to get supplies to Berlin's inhabitants, around 2 million living in the bombed-out remains of the city, was to use the railways, autobahns and canals crossing the Soviet Zone. As the Cold War became reality, the Soviets closed down all overland access in June 1948. Some quick thinking, and deft use of a slide rule by the RAF's Air Commodore Waite in Berlin, suggested that Berlin's western sectors

A.J. Jackson Collection

could be supplied by air, a daunting task as it was estimated that Berliners needed 4,000 tons of supplies daily; coal as well as foodstuffs. One requirement was salt, not an easy commodity to fly in an aircraft, but flying boats were already treated to prevent corrosion, so RAF Sunderlands began flying salt from Hamburg to the Havelsee in Berlin. The RAF was underequipped and undermanned for the massive airlift, BOAC had its own equipment problems, and the British government was forced to turn to the newly formed privately owned airlines that had started up after the war, airlines such as Aquila. Aquila was unique as it was the only airline with flying boats; its Sunderlands were quickly dispatched to help out the RAF. As well as salt, Sunderlands, with their capacious fuselages, were good for carrying bulky loads such as light bulbs and cigarettes. The flying boat operation ended that winter, but it had provided Aquila with an excellent source of revenue during the airline's first year of operations, around £54,000. The two other Sunderlands and *Hadfield* had been bought for £14,000, so there was a solid financial cushion for Aquila's next phase.

The government grudgingly allowed the private airlines to take over routes that the state-owned airlines did not wish to operate. One route that nobody had thought about much except Barry Aikman was that to Madeira, a small and very rocky Portuguese island in the Atlantic that had no airport but a considerable tourist trade; its mild climate made it a popular winter destination for British holidaymakers. With considerable backing from the Portuguese authorities, Aquila started a flying-boat service in 1949 from Southampton to the port of Funchal in Madeira, with a stop at Lisbon. The Portuguese generously allowed Aquila to carry passengers between Lisbon and Funchal as there was no other air service available, and despite the difficulties of operation, Aquila

The Aviation Photo Company

maintained a regular service to Funchal until the airline closed down in 1958. Aquila tried other routes as well, to Mediterranean islands, Las Palmas in the Canaries, Montreux in Switzerland, and performed charter flights worldwide, but the Funchal service always remained the heart of the business.

It was a slick operation: Aikman wrote in *Aeronautics* magazine in 1953:

Aquila has now developed a procedure whereby passengers leave their hotels 15 minutes before take-off time. Baggage weighing is done separately at each of the major hotels. While the baggage is loaded passengers have their breakfast at the hotels where they have been staying. Because the flying boat can moor up near the centre of the town it takes only five minutes from hotel to launch, less than that by launch to the flying boat and then five minutes to settle the passengers and get under way.

Think about that the next time you are waiting in a queue to get through security.

Aquila upgraded its equipment as larger and faster flying boats emerged from Short Brothers, but G-AGER remained in service until 1956. Its role in the fleet changed; with most of its interior stripped out, it was used mainly for freight carriage, including fresh fruit from the Mediterranean. Occasionally seats were installed and it could be used for shorter sectors, such as the Lisbon–Funchal service. It was not very comfortable! Apart from the lack of insulation, the ceiling of the top deck was quite low; and a passenger could not stand upright. By the time G-AGER was withdrawn it had flown 1¼ million miles.

The island of Madeira had to wait until 1964 before an airport was constructed, its runway jutting out into the Atlantic like an aircraft carrier. The Solent Sky Museum has preserved a Short Sandringham that was used by the Australian airline Ansett to fly between Sydney and Lord Howe Island for more than twenty years, and there is an RAF Sunderland at the Imperial War Museum at Duxford.

3: AVRO YORK G-ANTK

Imperial Airways relied on its flying boats to serve its main Empire routes but was fully aware of the advantages of landplanes; historically, landplanes from British manufacturers had helped develop Imperials' services in the Middle East and Africa as well as to Europe. Imperials observed dolefully the success of the Dutch airline KLM, which flew modern Douglas airliners on parallel routes down to Singapore and on to Australia. Indeed, when Shorts had been given the contract for the Empire flying boats, a similar contract had been given to Armstrong Whitworth, another trusted Imperials supplier, for a large four-engine, high-wing landplane intended for overland routes to India. But while Shorts delivered, Armstrong Whitworth was distracted by demands for its Whitley bomber that the Royal Air Force needed as part of Britain's rearmament programme.

Design and development of the Ensign class was protracted and the aircraft did not enter service with Imperials until late in 1938; even then the aircraft was unsatisfactory and underpowered, but it was the only large landplane that the United Kingdom had and proved its worth during the early stages of the war ferrying personnel to and from France; later, having been given more powerful American Cyclone engines, the remaining aircraft were dispatched to the Middle East, flying between West Africa and Cairo, and then between Cairo and India, the route for which they had been designed. Ensign G-ADSR is shown in flight in pre-war days.

When war broke out, the immediate need was for fighters and bombers, and for training aircraft to school the pilots and navigators. Avro, whose origins through its founder Alliott

The Aviation Photo Company

Verdon Roe went back to the earliest days of pioneering British aviation, contributed both trainers and bombers in large numbers: the Anson, more than 7,000 of which served in flying, navigation and air gunnery training roles in Britain and the Commonwealth; and the outstanding Lancaster bomber. Air transport aircraft were not a priority. Britain acquired American-built Liberators and the smaller twin-engine Lockheed Lodestars for some immediate transport needs, but was otherwise forced to rely on BOAC for longer-range transportation tasks, and depended for essential air services within the British Isles on the domestic airlines such as Scottish Airways and its DH.84 Dragon G-ACIT. It says much for the foresight of Avro's chief designer, Roy Chadwick, that he began designing a large, long-range, four-engine transport plane as early as 1941, using the Lancaster bomber as its basis, but substituting a boxy, voluminous fuselage to produce the York airliner. It also says much for their design that Yorks were still in use more than twenty years later. At first the Yorks entered government service as VIP transports, comfortably fitted out for eight to ten passengers, but by 1944 Yorks were in more general use with RAF Transport Command and BOAC; more than 200 were built.

Yorks distinguished themselves during the Berlin Airlift of 1948–49 as the RAF's major load carriers, carrying 230,000 tons in 29,000 sorties, around 8 tons a flight. BOAC used them to fly up to eighteen passengers and mail to South Africa, Kenya and India; its sibling corporation British South American Airways (BSAA) to its namesake destinations. Skyways, a major British independent airline, bought four Yorks that went on to see service on the Berlin Airlift. The RAF withdrew most of its Yorks after the Airlift, their role taken over by the Handley Page Hastings, and around forty were offered for sale from 1952 onwards. They were bought by the independent airlines and used as freighters and fifty-seat troop carriers, flying military personnel and their families to British garrisons in the Middle East, Africa, the Caribbean and even Fiji in the Pacific. Many a national serviceman had to endure the thirteen-hour flight in a York to Fayid in the Suez Canal Zone, where Britain maintained a number of large military bases. Douglas Whybrow, then a major at the War Office, describes what it was like:

The Yorks were converted freighters with a speed of about 160mph, some with little sound-proofing to take the edge off the lusty roar of the four Rolls-Royce Merlin engines, and all too often with dirt and damage to the interior lining from previous freight flights. The flights were long – anything from ten to thirty hours – and the discomfort astonishing; aircraft seats did not recline, some did not even have headrests and the rules specified that children under two would not be provided with a seat.

Still, it was better than three weeks on a troopship, and entrepreneurs such as Freddie Laker and Harold Bamberg would soon take steps to enhance the comfort and facilities on their Yorks. Yorks were later used by Skyways on its scheduled services, and one writer saw little to criticise:

Not being pressurised, the York has a square-sectioned fuselage which gives a very spacious effect – indeed, there is no doubt that the fuselage *is* spacious. From the point of view of the passenger the York offers an interesting journey because the high wing allows a good view from all windows, and everything on the ground can be seen.

In 1956 the Air Ministry suspended the use of Yorks for trooping flights following two accidents involving Yorks of Scottish Airlines, but permitted their continuing use as freighters. And actually, the York was better suited as a freighter. Its high wing and low-slung fuselage made loading easier, as did the wide doors on the port side. The square cabin allowed the volume to be utilised efficiently, cargo did not mind the noise, and the aircraft carried an 8-ton payload over 1,000 miles. Hunting-Clan had four Yorks and used them on a new and successful cargo service to East Africa that started in 1955. The Air Ministry used civilian Yorks on service cargo flights to Cyprus and the Middle East, and to Singapore and the Far East; in 1956 it awarded the latter contract to Dan-Air Services, a new entrant in this field. Dan-Air had started operations in 1953 flying Dakotas on passenger and freight charter work, and later bought three Yorks from RAF storage at Kirkbride.

G-ANTK was one of them. This York entered service with 242 Squadron Royal Air Force (serial number MW232) in 1946; it was transferred to 511 Squadron at Lyneham in 1947 and took part in the 1948–49 Berlin Airlift, before being withdrawn from use in 1950 after the squadron converted to the Hastings. Dan-Air refurbished it at the company's new engineering base at Lasham in Hampshire and it joined the active fleet in October 1956. After that it frequently returned to its former base at RAF Lyneham to undertake cargo charter flights to Singapore. Flying freight around was an important element in a charter airline's business plan, and did not meet with such a hostile reaction from the British government; every charter airline expected to vary its loadings between passengers and freight from day to day. As Whybrow observed, it could play havoc with the interior trim!

Dan-Air bought three more Yorks, but then lost two in accidents in 1958. G-ANTK was kept working on the Singapore contract until 1959, by which time the RAF began using its newly delivered Bristol Britannias for these freight flights. The next long-term freight contract gained by Dan-Air was from British European Airways (BEA), the third of the three state-owned corporations established after the war. G-ANTK took over a programme of regular freight flights between London Heathrow, Glasgow and Manchester on 1 November 1959, later adding Brussels; there were occasional flights elsewhere in Europe, but by 1961 regular services were flown to Paris, Rome, Milan, Frankfurt and Dusseldorf. Then BEA began introducing its own freighters, Viscounts and the Argosy, on its routes, and by the end of 1961 these had replaced the Dan-Air Yorks.

Dan-Air retired two of the Yorks in 1962, but kept G-ANTK and sister ship G-ANXN flying on ad hoc and Air Ministry flights. G-ANXN was let go early in 1963, with her Certificate of Airworthiness about to expire. G-ANTK still picked up cargo charters within Europe. Here is a sample of her schedule in October 1963: Gatwick to Marseilles (9 October), Paris (10 October), Gibraltar (16 October), Milan (17 October), Dublin to Paris (18 October), Gatwick to Zurich (25 October) and Frankfurt (26 October). Not a high utilisation programme to be sure, but a useful source of revenue on a written down aircraft with an undemanding crewing requirement. Ad hoc flying continued into 1964, including eighteen flights from Gatwick to Marseilles in February and March. The last commercial flight was from Geneva to Heathrow on 23 April, after which G-ANTK positioned back to Gatwick before transferring down to the Dan-Air engineering base at Lasham on 30 April. It was not the last York in service: that distinction fell to Skyways, which eked out its last York for another six months.

Dan-Air stayed active in the freight charter field for some more years, using Bristol Freighters and a Douglas DC-7 until the last Freighter was pensioned off in 1970, by which time Dan-Air was concentrating on its passenger services; it was by now a major charter operator of holiday flights complemented by a growing network of scheduled services.

Even then, that was not the end of it for G-ANTK. The York was donated to the Lasham Air Scouts and used as a bunkhouse for many years. Lasham was and remains a major gliding centre and the scouts are pictured preparing a Slingsby T.21 for take-off, with G-ANTK in the background. I remember seeing it on my infrequent visits to Lasham. The York was later swapped by the Air Scouts for a Comet, and some restoration work was started on G-ANTK before it was donated to the Duxford Aviation Society in 1986, which then spent twenty years working on it before putting it on display in 2006. Another York is preserved in the RAF Museum Cosford in RAF markings.

The Scout Association/Mary Evans Picture Library

Duxford Aviation Society

4: AVRO TUDOR G-AGRG

A.V. Roe, better known as Avro, was busy after the Second World War. As well as building the York and the speedier Lancastrian, both based on the Lancaster bomber, the company was the chosen contractor for one of the five types that had been proposed by the Brabazon Committee, the Type 3, originally a York replacement for Empire routes, but which had been redefined in part for a transatlantic role as a result of the overambitious timescale and engineering effort required for the Brabazon Type 1 Bristol Brabazon, now unlikely to enter service before the 1950s. The Type 3 requirement was further modified: the first version, reclassified as Type 3A, became a 40-seat transatlantic airliner; the second, Type 3B, was intended for the more traditional puddle-jumping Empire routes.

But BOAC needed an aircraft now that it could use on transatlantic routes, and helpfully the Ministry of Aircraft Production suggested that the Avro Tudor design, using the wings and Rolls-Royce Merlins from the Avro Lincoln (a development of the Lancaster) mated to a new pressurised fuselage, would provide an interim solution. If only. The Brabazon Committee accepted the arguments of the Ministry and told Avro to put its major design effort into the Tudor, which with a little tweaking, could also fulfil the Type 3B requirement. BOAC supinely accepted these decisions, taken over the corporation's head. Avro, with limited resources, could not develop the Tudor and the Type 3A simultaneously, and in any case had been told to go ahead with the Tudor. The Type 3A design went through a number of permutations, then curled up and died on the drawing board.

Which was a pity, because what BOAC needed was a transatlantic airliner that could take on the formidable competitors that the American manufacturers were building: Douglas with the DC-6, a pressurised, enlarged, extended-range development of the successful DC-4 Skymaster; Lockheed, which had already built the first of its Constellations during the war; and Boeing with its Stratocruiser. All of them were big, powerful, long-legged and pressurised. Somehow, Brabazon and his team concluded that the Tudor, an airliner not even as big as the wartime Skymaster, and a tail-dragger to boot, would suffice, provided it was luxurious. For me, it evokes memories of the Imperial Airways' Handley Page HP.42 and King George's Daimlers: slow, dignified, old-fashioned, but comfortable. In its final form, the Tudor 1 for BOAC would have carried just twelve passengers, albeit with sleeping facilities; even commentators of the period thought it absurd.

Meanwhile, the Tudor design was adapted for the Type 3B 'Empire' role, with less range but an enlarged fuselage. Interestingly, the fuselage for what became the Tudor 2 and 5 variants was not only longer but wider than the original Tudor 1, which explains why it is more rotund than the sleek Tudor 1, especially around the nose. Government ministers took to calling them the 'fat' and 'thin' Tudors. The Ministry ordered seventy-nine of the Tudor 2s, to be shared with BOAC and its Commonwealth partners Qantas and South African Airways, but there was some rapid walking away from the project, and the orders were revised downwards incrementally to zero, although not before a small number had been built. Instead the Ministry and BOAC sought proposals for a Medium Range Empire and Long Range Empire specification, which eventually emerged as the Bristol Britannia.

The Tudor had a protracted development and it did not enter service in 1946 as planned. BOAC was then allowed to buy Constellations, and later Stratocruisers; unsurprisingly the corporation's enthusiasm for the Tudor, never strong, evaporated, and now under much more robust management, BOAC abandoned its orders for both types of the aircraft, although a number, including G-AGRG, were accepted but never put into service. G-AGRG first flew in June 1946, but it would be two years before it was delivered to BOAC and then only to be used as a training aircraft. Chillingly, BOAC had planned to name the aircraft after famous Tudors and Elizabethans including Anne Boleyn, Lady Jane Grey, Catherine Howard, Mary Stuart, Sir Walter Raleigh, Thomas Cranmer, the Earl of Essex … as I recall, they too all met an untimely end.

The Tudor found two champions, however. The first was Air Vice-Marshal Bennett. A star of RAF Bomber Command during the war and now chief executive of British South American Airways (BSAA), the second of the nation's state-owned corporations and which already flew Lancastrians and Yorks, he became an enthusiast for the type after Avro decided to build a slightly longer version, the Type 4, with a range of around 2,800 miles, and which could carry thirty-two passengers, a more economical prospect than BOAC's configuration; a grateful Ministry, which otherwise would have had a large stock of unsold Tudors on its hands, sugared the pill. Tudors started flying for BSAA in 1947, but the corporation then had to cope with the unexplained disappearance of two of these aircraft within a year of each other, G-AHNP

in January 1948 and G-AGRE in January 1949, which led to the grounding of all of its Tudors; in the end BSAA could not cope and it was forcibly taken over by BOAC.

Before that, in this Shakespearean melodrama bordering on tragedy, the Tudor did have its one moment of glory. During the Berlin Airlift of 1948–49, when every four-engine aircraft was needed to help the RAF bring life's essentials to the Berliners, the 'fat' Tudors proved their worth as fuel tankers. Just seven of them, each carrying 9 tons of fuel, accounted for a significant proportion, 30 per cent, of the 'wet' lift; the rest was brought in by a fleet of forty Lancastrians and Halifaxes. BSAA operated five of the Tudors, and the other two were flown by Bennett's new airline, Airflight, the air vice-marshal having been unceremoniously kicked out of his position at BSAA following the loss of G-AHNP. BOAC also quickly transferred its Tudor 1s to BSAA, two of which were also used briefly on the Airlift, though not G-AGRG. The photograph overleaf shows G-AGRG in Germany, and this aircraft may have been used for flight training and logistical support of the bigger tanker Tudors; G-AKCC, a 'fat' Tudor, is shown in BSAA livery.

Now came along the Tudor's second champion, Freddie Laker. He wanted to replace his fleet of Yorks, but his preferred type, the DC-4 Skymaster, was too expensive at the time, with every aircraft in demand for the Korean War. He did not think much to the Handley Page Hermes, and the Canadian-built C-4, a pressurised DC-4 built by Canadair and re-engined with Rolls-Royce Merlins, was not available. As it happened, he had taken over the remnants of Bennett's fleet so was now the operator of a Tudor 2, which was being used on freight flights from Berlin. Was there anything Laker liked better than a scintillating aircraft deal? In 1953 he bought the entire inventory of Tudors from the Ministry of Civil Aviation, some

The Aviation Photo Company

twenty in all, of all marks and sizes, many of which he scrapped and used for spares. He then set about revamping the Tudor 1s, putting in a handsome forty-two-seat passenger interior into G-AGRG with the intention of using it and the other Tudors on trooping flights and a proposed colonial coach-class scheduled service to Lagos, Nigeria. His sky-high ambitions quickly came down to earth, however. The Air Ministry absolutely refused to countenance the Tudor, with its tainted reputation, on trooping services. Then the licensing authority turned down his unrealistic Lagos application; these colonial coach-class services were meant to be flown by small and obsolete aircraft going the long way round, not large, four-engine airliners with the range to operate across the desert to Lagos. That did not stop him from reapplying in 1959, with the same lack of success!

Laker bounced back from these disappointments. The Treasury allowed him to buy Skymasters, which his airline Air Charter then used on trooping contracts, the most secure source of revenue for charter airlines at the time. As for the Tudors, six of them were rebuilt as Super Trader freighters with a large cargo door cut into the port side; they were able to carry around 5½ tons over distances of 2,700 miles. G-AGRG was converted to a Super Trader. The image shows the as yet unpainted longer nose. It spent a year out of service before emerging at the end of 1955 to join its sisters on Laker's Air Charter contract with the government to fly on a weekly basis to Woomera in Australia in support of the rocket range there. Finally Laker had got a government contract for the Tudors, and it lasted into 1959.

A.J. Jackson Collection

Keith Bunyan via Geoff Goodall

The Super Traders proved reliable and well up to the task of hauling freight over the long distances to Australia and Christmas Island, where the British government was conducting its nuclear bomb testing. It would have been nice to have concluded with a dignified ending for G-AGRG. Alas, the aircraft crashed on take-off at Brindisi, on 29 January 1959, killing two of the crew.

Three months later, on 24 April, Super Trader G-AGRH – seen in this colour photo at Nadi, Fiji, in 1958 – disappeared after leaving Ankara; its remains were found six days later on a mountain peak in Turkey. The circumstances of that crash have not been explained. The remaining Tudors were withdrawn from the service at the end of May, and the contract was taken over by Dan-Air, using Bristol Freighters. Laker's last Tudor flight was from RAF Lyneham to Southend on 1 November 1959.

'I can only conclude that the type was a large-scale failure, and that it never did the work for which it was designed,' wrote aviation historian John Stroud in 1993. It is difficult not to agree. The aircraft was not fit for purpose: it was unsafe, with among other faults the disconcerting habit of rapidly losing altitude when the autopilot disconnected involuntarily; it was poorly assembled – its designer, Roy Chadwick, was killed when the prototype Tudor 2 crashed on take-off as a result of incorrect assembly of the aileron controls; it ruined BSAA, at the time the most proficient of the three state corporations; and the design, testing and production of the aircraft seriously got in the way of Britain's post-war airliner development, something for which the various government departments involved were as much to blame as Avro and the star-crossed BOAC.

5: DE HAVILLAND DH.89 DRAGON RAPIDE G-AGSH

The Dragon Rapide made its first flight in April 1934, the fourth in de Havilland's design evolution of an airliner with acceptable economics. First there was the DH.83 Fox Moth which appeared in 1932. It could carry four passengers in an enclosed cabin – at a pinch, five, on sightseeing flights – powered by a single 130hp de Havilland Gipsy Major engine; the pilot sat outside, behind the cabin.

Next came the DH.84 Dragon which first flew at the end of 1932, also designed for economical short-haul flying, able to bear aloft up to eight passengers on its two 130hp Gipsy Majors. Skipping the DH.85 Leopard Moth, a private tour- ing aircraft, the third de Havilland airliner was the DH.86, a 'fast' four-engine, ten-seat aircraft – at 166mph it outpaced the more sedate DH.84, which cruised at 109mph – built to a specification from the Australian government for an airliner that could fly from Singapore across Java and the Timor Sea to Australia. Four engines promised greater safety, while more powerful six-cylinder Gipsy Six engines gave a higher speed and greater payload. A number of DH.86s were used in Aus- tralia, and Imperial Airways bought twelve, which it used in Europe, on the Trans-Africa route from Khartoum to Nigeria, and for the connection between Bangkok and Hong Kong. Jersey Airways bought six to replace its DH.84s in 1935 on the London–Southampton–Jersey route, G-ACZR being named *La Saline Bay.* Here it is at Jersey Airport, opened in 1937; still a grass field of course, but a step up from West Park beach at Saint Aubin's Bay. A total of sixty-two aircraft were constructed.

Author's Collection

By comparison, 728 Dragon Rapides were built; like its predecessors, this magnificent airliner was designed by Arthur Hagg, its engines by Frank Halford. All four designs were built of spruce and plywood, the fuselage an internally unobstructed plywood box covered with doped fabric. Designed as a succes- sor to the DH.84, the Rapide was a scaled-down, twin-engine version of the DH.86, sharing its fine lines, tapered wings and trousered undercarriage. It could carry between six and eight passengers at a speed of 115mph, powered by two de Havilland Gipsy Queens of 200hp, and was as rugged as the Dragon; later Rapides had cabin heating, a landing light on the nose and flaps to help get the aircraft down on to the ground. The type sold well: by 1936 de Havilland had recorded sales to Aberdeen Airways, British Airways, British Continental Airways, Jersey Airways, Olley Air Services, Railway Air Services and United Airways in the British Isles, and further sales overseas, in Europe, Africa, Canada, the Middle East and Australia; at the outbreak of the war, around 200 had been built.

The Rapide played an important role at the very beginning of the war. All available civil aircraft were drafted into service and twenty-four Rapides were used to supply the British forces in France; they were then used to help evacuate them and the many inhabitants of the Channel Islands after the Germans overran France in 1940. When that was settled, the remaining Rapides provided certain essential air services, mainly in Scotland. The Rapide was also in demand by the Royal Air Force as a navigation trainer and communications aircraft, and Ministry orders gave a significant boost to the Rapide's overall production. A total of 522 Dominies, as the type was named in military service, was built between 1938 and 1946. Most of the later production was by Brush Coachworks at Loughborough, as de Havilland had to concentrate on building the Mosquito twin-engine bomber. Indeed, the services found themselves with too many Dominies towards the end of the war, so later aircraft were sent directly to de Havilland's Repair Unit at Witney and furnished to civil standards for resale as Rapides. G-AGSH was one such aircraft.

Its first buyer was Channel Islands Airways, the holding company for both Jersey and Guernsey Airways (now wholly owned by the railways, which had emerged as the monopoly provider during the war); the airline was back in the air as soon as the war in Europe was over, resuming regular flights to the Islands on 21 June 1945.

G-AGSH entered service in August and operated from Croydon and Southampton to Jersey and Guernsey. The Islanders were very possessive of their airline, even if it was owned by the railway companies, so when the new socialist government of Clement Attlee, voted in after the war on a promise to nationalise public transportation, demanded to take over Channel Islands Airways, the Islanders responded angrily, claiming that they should be allowed to run their own aviation affairs. But the British government was also nationalising the railway companies, so the result was a foregone conclusion; nevertheless the Islanders put up a stiff resistance, prolonging the negotiations for some months. British European Airways (BEA) was established on 1 August 1946, and took over the domestic routes on 1 February 1947. It was not until two months later that BEA assumed control of Channel Islands Airways, after Britain's Home Office had beaten the Islands authorities into submission, telling them to stop being obstinate and reminding them that the government had been generous in paying off the Islands' war debts; this after the Channel Islands had been abandoned in 1940 in the face of the German invasion.

R.T. Riding

On 1 May 1947 G-AGSH was transferred to BEA and continued flying to the Channel Islands. G-AGSH is seen at Jersey airport in the original minimalist BEA markings. Behind it is one of BEA's Dakotas, and some interesting war-surplus vehicles. When BEA took control of the railways' air companies it gained thirty-nine Rapides, and a further six from Channel Islands Airways. Older airframes were quickly disposed of, so that a year later only twenty remained in service, including G-AGSH. They were used in Scotland, to the Channel Islands and the Scillies.

Now named *James Keir Hardie* and repainted in the attractive dark red and silver BEA colours, the Rapide stayed with the airline until 1956; then it was sold to Airviews in Manchester and would have flown that airline's service to the Isle of Wight. Financial problems led to its sale in Ireland the following year, but it was back on the British register as G-AGSH in July 1957, and early in 1958 was sold to Maldwyn Thomas, a Welshman resident in Jersey, who had revived a measure of insular pride in its civil flying when he launched Jersey Airlines in 1948. Actually, he was told he could not use the name Jersey Airlines because it was too close to Jersey Airways; so he registered the company as Airlines (Jersey) and painted Jersey Airlines on his aircraft anyway. Starting cautiously at first with a single Rapide, offering day trips to France, he became a scheduled operator in 1951, flying Saturday-only services to Southampton from both Jersey and Guernsey. Thereafter he extended the network, and the services, both to the United Kingdom and France, buying de Havilland Herons to supplement the Rapides. He was careful not to step on BEA's toes and was rewarded, if that is appropriate, when the state corporation agreed in March 1956 to hand over a number of its services,

A.J. Jackson Collection

A.J. Jackson Collection

Guernsey to Southampton and flights to and from Alderney. BEA also acquired a 25 per cent stake in the airline and released two de Havilland Herons to Jersey Airlines. In return Jersey Airlines stopped flying Jersey–Southampton directly; it could still operate via Guernsey.

G-AGSH was needed for inter-island services, and the image shows it in 1960 painted in Alderney Airlines colours, although this was never a corporate entity. The mutual goodwill between BEA and Jersey Airlines continued; when BEA required a replacement Rapide to maintain its Land's End to St Mary's (Scilly Islands) service, it bought back G-AGSH in 1962, this time naming it *Lord Baden Powell*. It was one of the last three Rapides in BEA service.

A.J. Jackson Collection

The Peter Keating Collection © A Flying History Ltd

On 1 May 1964 BEA replaced the Rapides on the Scilly Islands service with a helicopter operation from a brand-new heliport at Penzance, and G-AGSH flew the last sector from St Mary's to Land's End. The Rapides were disposed of, but did not have to move far. They were sold for £1,000 apiece to British Westpoint Airlines, based in Exeter, and were soon flying back into St Mary's, G-AGSH included. British Westpoint was a West Country airline with a penchant for flying museum-grade aircraft; Dakotas were used on a service to London Heathrow from Newquay in Cornwall, and the Rapides on a number of routes to the Scillies. British Westpoint only made minimal changes to the livery, as shown here by G-AGSH at Bristol Airport.

A.J. Jackson Collection

It did not stay with British Westpoint for very long, being sold on in May 1965 to the RAF Sport Parachute Association, with whom it remained for ten years.

Now it is in the care of the Shuttleworth Trust, still flying, as graceful and elegant as ever, a wonderful tribute to those amazing people at de Havilland, who built such a practical and beautiful transport.

Right: The Aviation Photo Company

Below: Dave Marshall

6: DE HAVILLAND DH.104 DOVE G-AROI

De Havilland's post-war Dove was built in response to the Brabazon Committee's recommendations for a small land-plane for UK and colonial feeder services. The Committee was looking for a Rapide replacement, but it was difficult to specify that requirement precisely and so two versions were proposed, one larger, one smaller. Miles Aircraft was selected to develop the larger fourteen-seat Marathon, and de Havilland the smaller eight-seat Dove; the Marathon used four de Havilland Gipsy Queens, the Dove two. Many great designs sprang from the fertile minds of the Miles family, but despite their amazing contribution to the war effort and British aviation, the company had not accumulated sufficient resources to develop what was an ambitious all-metal airliner design; furthermore, the government unhelpfully vacillated over the design and payment. Following the harsh winter of 1947 and subsequent production problems, the company was forced into receivership in 1947, followed by liquidation in 1948. Sir Frederick Handley Page, at the Ministry's urging, took over the aviation assets, with the promise that fifty Marathons would be bought for the two airline corporations. In the end he settled for forty, most of which were dispatched to the RAF.

Despite appearances to the contrary – Marathon G-ALUB at London Airport in 1951 is painted in full BEA livery – BEA walked away from the aircraft and never took delivery; the corporation had abandoned the inter-island services that Captain Fresson had pioneered before the war in the Orkneys and Shetlands, and found that a small number of Rapides sufficed for the remaining routes of that nature: Glasgow to Barra, Land's End to the Scillies, Guernsey to Alderney. BOAC persuaded one of its associated feeder airlines, West African Airways Corporation, to accept six, but they were quickly returned and replaced by de Havilland Herons, which looked like a stretched Dove with four engines. Handley Page went on to design and build the Herald, based on an earlier design for an enlarged Marathon.

In terms of numbers sold the Dove was the most successful of the Brabazon designs, even if it only got a passing grade in its intended role! Both the Marathon and Dove were sleek, attractive aircraft, with retractable tricycle undercarriages; the Marathon had excellent short-field performance as well.

The Aviation Photo Company

The Dove was continuously developed during its twenty-year production run – it first took to the air in September 1945 – so that by the end it was flying further, faster, higher and carrying a bigger payload; it could carry eight passengers, or eleven if no toilet was fitted, and six luxuriously in executive configuration, for more than 500 miles at 179mph. A total of 542 Doves were built, the last one in 1967. The Dove was expensive to buy, more than twice as much as an 'as-new' Rapide, and had higher operating costs, so it struggled as a feederliner; its economics worked better when bought second-hand. Just nineteen were sold new to British airlines, and a further seventy-eight to airlines in the colonies and overseas, Chile, Japan, overseas Portuguese territories and the Belgian Congo. But the Dove excelled in other roles. Air forces liked them the best. More than 200 Doves went straight into military service and were used as navigation trainers and for communications, including the Royal Air Force, which bought forty; in those far-off days British air attachés at some embassies were issued with Doves, called the Devon in RAF service and Sea Devon when used by the Royal Navy. Argentina bought seventy, split between the air force and government organisations. Towards the end of the production cycle, Doves became popular as business aircraft, breaking into the American market; seventy-five were sold in the United States and smaller numbers in Canada, Mexico and Venezuela during the 1950s. Riley Aeronautics in California went on to modify the Dove in 1963 with Lycoming engines, a rebuilt cockpit and Boeing-style fin and rudder assembly, which sold in small numbers in America and the UK.

The Dove had a successful afterlife. American executive Doves were sold to third-level airlines, and in Britain both Cambrian Air Services and Channel Airways made good use of second-hand Doves on their networks. 'I found the Dove a very attractive aircraft with plenty of room for eight passengers,' wrote Squadron Leader West about Cambrian in *Aeronautics*. 'Their comfortable Doves are doing plenty of work.' Many military Doves saw further use as civilians, including G-AROI, which started life with the Royal Navy. When the Senior Service wanted to upgrade its communications fleet and 'admiral's barges', it sold two of its Sea Devons to Overseas Aviation in a deal that saw the Navy acquire three of Overseas' larger four-engine Herons. Whatever Overseas intended to do with its Herons and Doves – this was an airline that up until then had specialised quite successfully in medium- and long-haul charter flying – was thwarted by Britain's opinionated licensing authority, which was unimpressed by the airline's grandiose plans for domestic and international scheduled routes: Overseas was granted just one licence, Gatwick to Manchester via Sywell in Northamptonshire. Not surprisingly, Overseas' plans needed a rethink, and six months after they had been purchased, both ex-Navy Doves were sold on to Derby Aviation late in 1961.

G-AROI never entered service with Derby, but it was converted to a Mark 5 with more powerful Gipsy Majors and then at the end of 1963 sold to a local building firm, Frank H. Wright (Construction) Ltd, which joined the elite group of British companies flying their own private executive planes.

At least sixty British companies used the Dove, including J.C. Bamford, David Brown, Dunlop, Ferranti, Forte's, Fox's Glacier Mints, GKN, Lec Refrigeration, Leyland Motors, the National Coal Board and the Nuclear Power Group. Wright's advertised G-AROI for sale in May 1965: 'Eight seats. Long range tanks. Recently re-upholstered. Absolute mint condition.'

It was quickly bought by Metropolitan Air Movements, a small charter firm based at Biggin Hill, which had operated two of the larger Herons for Pressed Steel, but now concentrated on oil support flying in Libya with Doves.

G-AROI, however, had a different career path because although it initially received the Metropolitan fleetname, it moved on after further signwriting to British Westpoint at the end of May. That was because Metropolitan was in the process of taking over the management, and subsequently ownership, of British Westpoint; we looked at this airline in the section on the Rapide G-AGSH, and I like the continuity of de Havilland types. G-AROI did not immediately operate in the West Country, however, spending most of that summer flying at weekends between Gatwick and Sandown in the Isle of Wight, with some departures from Heathrow. Despite its new backers, however, British Westpoint was fading fast. The winter season was always difficult for independent airlines as money still flowed out but not a lot came in; there was precious little flying.

The Aviation Photo Company

The Aviation Photo Company

The Aviation Photo Company

G-AROI spent the winter mostly on the ground, operating only a few charters. In April 1966 it resumed the airline's Exeter–Gatwick service, but flew the last British Westpoint service from Gatwick to Exeter on 29 April, a sad finale for a classy airline.

The Dove did not remain unemployed for long. British Eagle, after a long and tiresome battle with Britain's new and somewhat naïve licensing authority, had finally been granted some better – I hesitate to use the word worthwhile – frequencies on its fledgling Glasgow–Heathrow scheduled services, to the extent that one morning and one evening return service could now be flown. In May 1966 BAC One-Elevens were put on the route, and a feeder link to Dundee was introduced, timed obviously to coincide with the London flights. British Eagle bought G-AROI, wittily naming it *Eaglet*, and used it twice a day to fly the thirty-five-minute sector between Glasgow and Dundee's Riverside strip, with a twenty-five-minute connection at Glasgow. Riverside was not ideal; as its name implies the grass runway could get waterlogged, but it was handy for Dundee.

The service continued for a year and a half, but by the end of October 1967, British Eagle was asking for a subsidy of £1,000 a week, which Dundee council refused to countenance. So the service was terminated and *Eaglet* placed in storage at Leavesden. Time was running out for British Eagle as well. Just one year later the airline stopped flying in November 1968 after receivers had been appointed, following a string of misfortunes, including the loss of major contracts and some hostile decisions by the licensing authority instigated by BOAC.

As often happens when they are suddenly put out of work, former employees got together to see whether anything could be salvaged from the wreckage. Most of British Eagle's larger transports subsequently went to other airlines, but a team of

The Aviation Photo Company

four headed by the Mulligan brothers started less ambitiously, buying G-AROI and using it to fly charters for their new airline, Fairflight Charters, from Fairoaks in Surrey. The airline's name should not be confused with AVM Bennett's Fairflight that flew Tudors during the Berlin Airlift! The Dove was bought in November 1968, but its first flight took place in May 1969 after the award of the airline's Air Operator's Certificate.

There seemed to be plenty of business for the aircraft, flying day-old chicks to France, Ford car components to Germany, executive charters and standing in for other Dove operators. Fairflight moved from Fairoaks to Biggin Hill in 1970, where the aircraft is seen lurking behind the fence, and acquired other Doves as oil charter business began to increase in connection with the discovery of oil in the North Sea; G-AROI began visiting airports such as Aberdeen, Norwich

Ken Elliott

and Stavanger in Norway. By 1972 it had acquired an attractive blue and gold livery.

By 1973 Fairflight had four Doves, flying around 800 hours a year, and had just acquired its first Heron, which was used for overnight newspaper delivery contracts. It began buying speedier twin-engine Piper Navajos for its longer-haul contract work. By 1977 the oil business in Scotland had grown to such an extent that the company formed Air Ecosse as a subsidiary to handle the increasing demand for work out of Aberdeen, especially oil-rig crew exchanges to and from the Shetland Islands. Air Ecosse went its own way, acquiring Brazilian-built turboprop Bandeirantes and boxy Short 330s, developing scheduled services and flying for the Post Office.

Jonathan Walton

Fairflight, meanwhile, began disposing of its de Havilland types so that by October 1977 G-AROI was the last remaining Dove in the fleet, still flying the occasional charter in the company of two Herons.

Fairflight's operations were being run down as the emphasis switched to Air Ecosse and its turboprop activities. By early 1980 it was 'time' for the de Havilland aircraft, the Herons going to Thailand, and after its ten-year stint, G-AROI, photographed by Brian Nichols in its final colours, was sold in Denmark to a parachuting club; it flew on there before being withdrawn in 1987. The aircraft was broken up but parts of it remain in storage. The Dove outlasted Air Ecosse by a few months; that airline suspended operations in January 1987. Two years later what remained of Fairflight's flying operations were taken over by Gill Aviation, based in Newcastle.

There are a number of Doves in museums, two of them in the red-and-black livery of the Civil Aviation Authority (Civil Aviation Flying Unit) – one of many government organisations around the world that bought Doves for calibration and transport duties – one at Duxford, seen here in the company of a Comet, Hastings and Vulcan, the second at East Fortune in Scotland. The de Havilland Museum has an executive Dove that started off with Hawker Siddeley Aviation (into which grouping de Havilland was absorbed in 1960), which then became British Aerospace, and whose current *nom du jour* is BAE Systems. The North East Land, Sea and Air Museums in Sunderland has an interesting Dove that was used by Hunting for survey work, and the Newark Air Museum also has an exotic and very early Dove that was used by Iraq Petroleum for pipeline patrol work before seeing further use in Israel.

Brian Nichols

Author's Collection

7: DOUGLAS DC-3 DAKOTA G-AMPZ

In the British Isles, England, Scotland, Ireland and Wales, American-built Dakotas provided the wings to get our nation aloft after the Second World War. More than 300 Dakotas helped get Britain airborne again, more than any other type, and by some margin. Dakotas could carry 32 passengers or three tons of freight over 1,000 miles at 160 mph. BOAC was issued with Dakotas starting in 1943, and by VE Day had received fifty-nine; during the war it also used the Dutch airline KLM's Dakotas, and others provided by the RAF. BOAC operated its Dakotas from Hurn (Bournemouth) to neutral countries in Europe and to the Middle East, India and the Far East. Later in the war Britain's other 'national' carrier, the RAF's No. 110 Wing, 46 Group, flew transport services to those European countries that had been liberated; 110 Wing flew more conveniently out of Croydon, so had to use Dakotas as none of the other larger and heavier transports could use Croydon's grass runway. By the summer of 1945 its operations were quite intense: four times a day to Paris, three times a day to Brussels, twice daily to Naples, and daily services to The Hague, Hamburg and Berlin, Copenhagen, Oslo, Frankfurt and Prague, Guernsey and Jersey, with other less frequent services to Marseilles, Rome and Athens.

BOAC continued using Dakotas after the war was over but transferred around twenty to BEA in 1946 to allow the new corporation to take over from 110 Wing, and disposed of the rest, mainly to its overseas subsidiaries in Aden, Malaya and Hong Kong. England's Railway Air Services used three Dakotas when it was allowed to resume services. One of them crashed spectacularly on to the roof of a house in Ruislip in December 1946, fortunately with no loss of life, but the other two passed to BEA, which eventually had fifty Dakotas in service, mainly on domestic UK and internal German flights; the Vickers Viking was the flagship for international services. A number were refurbished for BEA by Scottish Aviation for further use as 'Pionairs', with standardised cockpits, up to thirty-six seats, and a removable galley and toilet at the rear. Pionairs outlasted the Vikings that were bought to replace them, and they remained the mainstay of Scotland's air services through the 1950s and into the early '60s, after which they were replaced by the much larger Viscount. Scottish Airlines also flew Dakotas on its charter and scheduled services, but sister company Scottish Aviation was better known for overhauling and upgrading Dakotas at its Prestwick facility.

In Ireland, after some false starts with other types, Aer Lingus settled down with a fleet of nineteen Dakotas, in due course replaced by Fokker Friendships and Viscounts; the last Dakota was sold in 1964. And in Wales Cambrian was a champion Dakota and 'Pionair' user, acquiring the first of ten in 1954 to fly alongside its de Havilland Doves and Herons. Cambrian's last Dakota flight was from Paris to Cardiff on 31 October 1968, flown by the company's handsomely refurbished G-AHCZ.

More than 1,900 Dakotas passed through the hands of the RAF, although many were transferred to Allied and Commonwealth air forces; by 1946 a few were even being made available to British independent airlines. Transport Command had to rely on its Dakotas throughout the Berlin Airlift; they and the Yorks were the service's main load carriers until joined by the first of the newly delivered Handley Page Hastings in November 1948. Indeed, RAF Dakotas flew in stocks of the new German currency, the Deutsche Mark, which had been introduced in June 1948 in the western zones and largely provoked the stand-off with the Soviets that led to the blockade of Berlin; one of these Dakotas was serial KN442, which had been delivered to the RAF in March 1945. The RAF's forty Dakotas on the Airlift were joined by sixteen supplied by the independent airlines and three from BOAC, but the civilian aircraft were withdrawn by the end of November. A shortage of spares and lower productivity led the independents to concentrate on larger four-engine aircraft: Halifaxes, Lancastrians, Tudors and Yorks. The US Air Force also discontinued use of its Dakotas; they took the same amount of time to unload in Berlin as the DC-4 Skymasters, which however carried three times more payload.

The RAF's Yorks and Dakotas were largely stood down after the Airlift was over and stored at bases including Silloth and nearby Kirkbride in Cumbria. Some sixty Dakotas were then sold to British carriers, including seven to Mr Wilson and his Liverpool-based airline Starways in 1952, one of them being KN442. Starways and its sister company Cathedral Touring Agency were best known for their pilgrimage flights, to Lourdes in France and Santiago in northern Spain, which were flown out of Glasgow, Belfast and Liverpool.

Pictured is G-AMPZ, as KN442 had become, after delivery from RAF Kirkbride to Liverpool, its new registration barely visible below the fin. Maybe its woebegone appear-

R.A. Scholefield

ance was just too dispiriting, for in the end it never entered service with Starways, which made do with just five; instead it and sister ship G-AMRA were sold on, both finally passing in 1954 into the hands of Transair, a go-ahead airline based at Croydon that had initially used Ansons after the war to carry mail and newspapers to France, Dublin and the Channel Islands, but had now graduated to Dakotas. Transair had also entered the inclusive-tour market, still highly seasonal and concentrated at the weekend, unlike newspaper flying. Transair converted G-AMPZ itself, with thirty-two red leather seats, purple carpets and extensive sound proofing. The airline had some blue-chip clients including BEA and Air France and was one of the first airlines to fly holiday charters to Majorca.

The government was badgering the independent airlines to 'consolidate'; there were just too many of them, and Airwork, an independent airline with excellent political connections, began doing just that. It started in 1956, taking over Transair but keeping its operations entirely separate and retaining its founder, Gerald Freeman. At the beginning of 1958, Airwork acquired a substantial shareholding in Freddie Laker's Air Charter and his engineering companies at Southend; Laker was left in charge. Later in 1958 Morton and Olley, third-level airlines with a lot of history – Morton had bought out aviation pioneer Olley but kept the name – were taken over by Airwork. All these airlines went their own sweet way, little was done to integrate their operations and engineering functions; instead Airwork became a holding company and sold off its fleet of piston-engine aircraft.

Author's Collection

While all this was going on, G-AMPZ was on its travels. In West Africa a major crisis developed in 1955 when the fleet of West African Airways Corporation – Bristol Freighters and de Havilland Doves – was grounded, and Herons and leased Dakotas had to be acquired in a hurry. Having used Dakotas in the short term, the corporation developed a liking for them and began leasing some on a long-term basis, so early in May 1957 G-AMPZ went out to Nigeria and for the next three years flew on the route network, returning to the UK in 1960 after Nigeria achieved independence.

The aircraft came back to find its parent had changed: G-AMPZ was not exactly a stepchild, but part of a larger family. There were many changes in British aviation in 1960, which saw a new framework for air transport regulation and airworthiness licensing introduced, followed by the merger of two of the country's biggest independents, the Airwork Group and Hunting-Clan Air Services. The two airlines had cooperated with each other over many years; their merger was no surprise and just what the government wanted. This time Airwork decided there had to be a new name, the different 'brands' had to go, all were now to be identified as part of British United Airways with an austere red-white-and-blue livery, blue lines, red lettering and the Union Flag on the tail. So G-AMPZ received the new colours, and despite their drabness, the Dakota pictured on the next page still looks good in the pale English sunshine.

The aircraft spent most of its time back in service in the UK flying newspapers to the British forces stationed in Germany. A more extensive repaint followed two years later, in 1962, when the aircraft was transferred to Silver City, which had recently joined the British United grouping after Silver City's parent company, British Aviation Services, sold out to

British United's holding company, Air Holdings. And just a few months later, in May 1962, Jersey Airlines also came under the Air Holdings umbrella. That was a lot for British United to digest.

The Aviation Photo Company

The Aviation Photo Company

G-AMPZ remained in Silver City colours for several months, flying the airline's scheduled services out of Blackpool, the Isle of Man and Newcastle, where it is seen here.

When Jersey Airlines joined the group, bringing its managing director, Maldwyn Thomas, and its own elaborate network of services to and from the Channel Islands, the two divisions were brought together under his leadership; Jersey's name was changed to British United (Channel Islands) Airways in 1963. To further complicate matters, many of Silver City's services were still held in the name of Manx Airways, one of Silver City's constituent members and like Jersey Airlines not a company registered in the United Kingdom. So another 'island' company had to be formed, British United (Manx) Airways. But by this time G-AMPZ had fled the hangar. Handley Page Heralds were being introduced, so Dakotas were disposed of, or sent to join Morton Air Services, which used them mainly for freight work including the carriage of newspapers.

G-AMPZ went to Indonesia and was used by the Pan American Indonesia Oil Co. for several years. Possibly not unconnected to the nationalisation of oil companies in Indonesia in 1965 and the Indonesian 'Confrontation' with Malaysia and Britain, the Dakota was back at Gatwick later that year, looking for a new home. It eventually found one, going to Iceland in July 1966 to join Flugsýn, an airline that among other things hauled fish around. Flugsýn's operations began to run down towards the end of the decade, and the Dakota was back on the British register as G-AMPZ in 1969; it went to two Norfolk aviation families, the Wrights, who had started Anglian Air Charter in 1950, and the Cramptons, who ran Norfolk Airways. They had decided to cooperate in order to take advantage of the coming oil and gas boom and called their joint airline Rig-Air. G-AMPZ was its first acquisition, arriving in Norwich in November 1969.

The Aviation Photo Company

Despite the airline's name, its early business was run-of-the-mill charters, newspapers and car parts, with a sudden boom in mid-1970 when the country was put through a national dock strike. In July of that year, the three operators, Anglian, Norfolk and Rig-Air were combined into one airline, Air Anglia, with additional backing from Norwich Union. G-AMPZ was retitled, the seats were put back in, and it now began flying oil support flights, mainly rig crew changes between Aberdeen and Sumburgh in the Shetlands; it also flew Air Anglia's scheduled service linking Norwich, Edinburgh and Aberdeen.

An important route from Norwich to Amsterdam was started late in 1971, and to Jersey in 1972, which year also saw the introduction of the Dakotas' successor in the Air Anglia fleet, the Dutch-built, turbine-engine Fokker Friendship.

The Aviation Photo Company

Charlie Stewart

Air Anglia had cooperated with Jersey-based Intra Airways on the Jersey route, and in April 1973 sold G-AMPZ to this aspiring airline. Air Anglia went on to develop its east coast and Amsterdam links, buying more Friendships and their jet-powered successor, the Fokker F28. With its stunning mustard yellow livery, articulate business plan and modern equipment, it represents the very best in the history of Britain's airlines.

Intra had started from nowhere in 1969 with one Dakota, flying charters to the south coast and France, newspapers from Gatwick, flowers to the mainland, and took over the Jersey–Staverton scheduled service in March 1971, adding Cambridge in 1972 and acquiring more Dakotas along the way.

The Aviation Photo Company

The Aviation Photo Company

G-AMPZ became a pure freighter again, flying between Jersey, Guernsey and Bournemouth, a route that was so successfully exploited that it spawned a specialist operator, Express Air Freight, associated with the Hunting Group and which used Intra's Dakotas. After a brief marriage to and quickie divorce from Intra in 1980, Express went on to find greater glory as the freight airline Channel Express; and Intra achieved a reasonable divorce settlement as well, retaining its new married name, Jersey European, and eventually finding a wealthy backer who went on to transform the airline into the major operator Flybe, which folded in 2020. Intra was an important seedling in the field of British civil aviation.

But that was all in the future. G-AMPZ spent five years with Intra/Express Air Freight before being sold on to an Irish airline, Clyden, with whom it entered service in 1978.

The picture shows it with its British registration taped over its new Irish marks, EI-BDT. It led much the same sort of life as it had under its British owners, flying between Dublin and Manchester for the Post Office (this time Irish), hauling fish to France, performing sub-charters for English operators, doing some survey work. But An Post went on strike in 1979 for eighteen weeks, and there was a business downturn in Ireland; EI-BDT was parked up late in 1980 and Clyden put up the shutters in January 1981. The Dakota languished for a year, before finding a new owner in 1982. This was Aces High in England, a company that provides aircraft for film producers, and which was filming a BBC series called *Airline*, all about a plucky pilot who starts his own business after the war with a Dakota; G-AMPZ, now back with its original registration, was not one of the stars, however!

The Aviation Photo Company

Instead G-AMPZ moved to its next home in Southend in May 1982, having been sold on to Harvest Air, a company that had just been awarded a major contract by the Marine Directorate of the Department of Transport to provide emergency pollution-control services, for which its experience in aerial spraying suited it well. It joined another Dakota and a fleet of eight Britten-Norman Islanders, located around the country, on call for emergencies; the two Dakotas were based at Exeter and Kinloss in Scotland.

G-AMPZ was modified with the addition of two 10ft spray booms located under the tail and looks smart in its yellow and black chequerboard livery; a Pollution Control Islander is in the background.

Harvest Air was owned by a colourful character, Nigel Brendish, who enjoyed stunt flying his modified de Havilland Canada Chipmunk G-IDDY; he flew the Channel inverted on one occasion. He was killed on 25 September 1987 in an accident flying with a friend in a Cessna 150, and his business had to be closed down; so the two Dakotas had their spray gear removed and in June 1988 joined the Janes, Andy and Hilary, to fly freight services on behalf of Lynx Express between Blackpool and Belfast. The Janes did not believe in spending money unnecessarily and certainly did not repaint the aircraft, so the image serves both airlines, but was taken in 1986 so under Harvest Air ownership.

That was its role for the next ten years, with the occasional freight charter shared with its sister ship G-AMRA. Flights over the Normandy beaches during the summer of 1994, the fiftieth anniversary of the D-Day landings, added authenticity to the occasion. In 1998, to commemorate the fiftieth anniversary of the Berlin Airlift in which G-AMPZ had participated, the Dakota was painted in RAF Transport Command livery complete with its military serial KN442.

Its service with Air Atlantique continued into the new millennium, still operating pleasure flights, and then suddenly it was over. G-AMRA had undergone extensive maintenance and rebuilding to keep the Dakota operation flying, but G-AMPZ was sold in 2001 to a German operator, Air Service Berlin, for sightseeing flights out of Berlin.

Author's Collection

G-AMPZ did not stay long with the Janes, replaced by a Short 330; it joined Mike Collett's Air Atlantique in 1990 and his ever-expanding fleet of propliners, which included two Douglas DC-6s and nine DC-3 Dakotas. Collett was never afraid to operate older airliners and assembled a large fleet for commercial use as well as a heritage collection of aircraft for his various museum enterprises. The Dakotas were used on post office and express parcels work as well as passenger charters, and from 1987, for pollution control. When that contract was extended in 1989, up to four Dakotas were on standby; by 1996 that number had grown to seven. G-AMPZ took over as the 'passenger' Dakota in May 1991, flying enthusiasts to air shows up and down the country and to the Continent.

The Aviation Photo Company

Sprayed Mercedes-Benz silver all over, the Dakota was later registered D-CXXX and settled down to a new life in Germany. To mark the sixtieth anniversary of the Berlin Airlift in 2008, D-CXXX reprised an earlier role but this time wore an American 'star-and-bar' and was named *Rosinenbomber*, to honour the memory of the American pilots who had cheerfully dropped sweets (*rosinen*) to the young Berliners waiting for them on the approach to Berlin's Tempelhof airport. Two years later disaster struck, when the port engine failed on take-off from Berlin's Schönefeld Airport. Unable to gain height, the aircraft crashed in a field nearby, at the site of the new Brandenburg Airport; there were no fatalities, but the aircraft was severely damaged, the starboard wing torn off, the fuselage battered and crushed from the belly landing. That may be the end of its sixty-five-year flying career as it has not been repaired yet, despite efforts by Air Service Berlin.

Bill Teasdale

8: VICKERS VIKING G-AGRP

Of all the aircraft manufacturers that responded to the challenge of post-war airliner development in Britain, I think Vickers comes closest to winning the accolade. The company ticked all the right boxes. It was first in its field, its technology leapfrogged that of the Americans, it built products that were sold worldwide, it efficiently harnessed the many elements of Britain's manufacturing industry to help produce its aircraft and in so doing overcame the problems of scale

it even helped launch British European Airways (BEA), the other British state-owned airline, and was responsible for that airline's most golden years. It is all the more to be regretted that Vickers in its later years flew off course, even if its airliner products were still technically superb.

Vickers successfully designed and built a large bomber, the Vimy, during the Great War but that aircraft did not enter service in time to see action. Instead the aircraft is best remembered for its post-war exploits conquering the world: with Captain Alcock and Lieutenant Whitten-Brown, who were the first to fly across the Atlantic non-stop in June 1919; and a few months later the Australian brothers Ross and Keith Smith used a Vimy to complete the first flight between England and Australia. Vickers quickly adapted the design for commercial use after the Armistice, developing the Vickers Commercial. This used the wings of the Vimy, to which was added a commodious ten-passenger fuselage; even if the type failed to gain much support from the airlines, the RAF used derivatives of the original Vimy bomber transport design, the Vernon, Victoria and Valentia, into the Second World War.

Vickers-Armstrong responded to the Air Ministry's call to start mass producing bombers in the build-up to the Second World War by designing the twin-engine Wellington, an innovative design using a 'basket weave' geodetic form of construction that allowed a robust, fail-safe design with a high strength/weight ratio. More than 11,000 Wellingtons were built; they were used intensively at the beginning of the war in Europe with Bomber Command, later seeing further action in the Western Desert. Coastal Command adapted the design for submarine-hunting, while others were used in the Middle East as troop carriers, adapted to carry eighteen fully equipped troops.

As the Brabazon Committees elaborated their designs for Britain's future airliner requirements, Vickers pragmatically offered an interim design for short-haul services that could be built immediately, using the wings of the Wellington to which was added a stressed-skin fuselage capable of carrying twenty-one passengers. The Viking first flew on 22 June 1945, only a few days after the end of the war in Europe, and the Ministry of Aircraft Production ordered a large quantity

for European services. Initial deliveries of the Viking were to BOAC's British European Airways Division, the forerunner to BEA, and included in June 1946 G-AGRP, only the eighth Viking to be built. This was one of the initial batch of nineteen that had fabric-covered geodetic wings just like the Wellington bomber. *Aeronautics* magazine described the joys of geodetic construction: 'Everything waves quietly about, and all the time you can feel the very cross section of the atmosphere. Yet the supple airframe absorbs most of the bumps, transmitting to the passengers only a restful, springy motion.' But Vickers planned to introduce stressed-skin coverings for the wings, which BEA preferred for ease of maintenance, and the bulk of Vikings built were to this later formula; they were also slightly longer than the original nineteen. Viking designations, applied retroactively, were thus: Viking 1A, the original version; Viking 1,

aviation-images.com/Mary Evans Picture Library

Author's Collection

same as the Viking 1A but with the wings reskinned; and the Viking 1B, built with stressed-skin wings and a fuselage longer by 28in, known as the 'long nose Viking', a misleading title as it was actually the fuselage that was longer! The extra length allowed BEA to fit twenty-four seats. It did not change the appearance of the aircraft, which was endearingly tubby, sitting down on its little tailwheel in the old-fashioned way of many of Britain's interim post-war airliners.

Less than ideal was the main spar that passed through the cabin (see page 57), dividing it into two and requiring the cabin crew to 'hitch up their knickers' as they clambered over the steps. On the plus side, the Viking used the reliable Bristol Hercules engines and was about 30mph faster than the Dakota, with a cruising speed of 190mph and a range of between 800 and 1,000 miles.

BEA needed not only to start operations but recruit and train its staff, so that was what the initial batch of Vikings were used for; G-AGRP was even tricked up with BEA's new 'Key' logo. But then in December 1946 all Vikings were withdrawn from service. Ice building up on the tailplane led to instability in flight, and it was some months before the problem was solved. When services resumed in March 1947, G-AGRP did not rejoin the fleet; by that stage BEA had sufficient numbers of Viking 1Bs so G-AGRP was parked at Langley, near Heathrow, and its certificate of airworthiness allowed to lapse. The aircraft had originally belonged to the Ministry of Supply (successor to the Ministry of Aircraft Production) and was now transferred to the Ministry of Civil Aviation, which sold it on to a travel organiser; but the aircraft did not fly for another five years, when it passed into the fleet of Hunting Air Transport in 1952.

An interesting company, Hunting. The airline was just one of a number of aviation and transport-related companies owned by the Hunting Group. Also under the umbrella was Field Aircraft Services, a maintenance and engineering company; Percival, an aircraft manufacturer; Hunting Aerosurveys; and other long-standing shipping, brokering and oil interests. Hunting had been one of the first charter airlines to take to the skies on 1 January 1946, after the ban on private flying had been lifted, appropriately using a Percival Proctor to fly between Luton and Croydon. The airline quickly moved on to Vikings, buying its first in 1947, a new Viking 1 that was no longer required by BEA; more followed. Hunting was skilled at securing big charter contracts; one such was an exclusive arrangement to fly personnel between the United Kingdom and East Africa in connection with the 'groundnut' scheme; another was the award of the government's first regular trooping contracts, to Britain's military bases in Malta and Gibraltar, during the last days of the outgoing Labour government in 1951. Hunting's bids for these contracts were extremely competitive. One wonders how much they relied on marginal costing; to what extent the aircraft were regarded as an investment; and if losses were born in the short term in the hope of better things to come. The following year the new Conservative government allowed Hunting to start flying restricted low-fare scheduled services to the colonies in Africa, known as Colonial Coach Class, and the airline looked around for additional aircraft, buying G-AGRP in 1952 and converting it to a Viking 1. In October 1953 the Cayzer family, through its subsidiary Clan Line Steamers, bought a half share in Hunting Air Transport, changing the name of the airline to Hunting-Clan Air Transport; a number of other shipping companies had been encouraged by the government to invest in charter airlines.

Hunting and Airwork were allowed to start flying from the United Kingdom to Nairobi late in 1952, and G-AGRP was used to inaugurate the second phase of Colonial Coach services, to Salisbury, Rhodesia, on 26 June 1953. It took three days to get there, with stops at Nice, Malta, Mersa Matruh (Egypt), Wadi Halfa, Khartoum, Juba (all in Sudan), Entebbe (Uganda), Tabora (Tanganika), N'Dola and Lusaka (Northern Rhodesia): there have been a few name changes since then! The aircraft stopped overnight at

Malta, Wadi Halfa or Khartoum and Entebbe, with passenger meals and hotel accommodation included in the price of the ticket. The Vikings flew these services for the next few years, indeed they had to as the government decreed that newer equipment could not be used. It was not until the government finally relented and permitted turboprop aircraft in 1958 that Hunting was able to dispose of its remaining Vikings.

G-AGRP was sold through an intermediary to another charter airline, Overseas Aviation (CI), early in 1958.

There were quite a number of charter airlines charging around the race course by the end of the 1950s. Britain had finally recovered from the harsh vicissitudes of the early post-war years, and people were looking to improve their living standards by buying cars, acquiring expensive gadgets for their houses and taking more holidays, especially holidays abroad. To meet the demand for holidays in the sun, a number of new airlines joined the established carriers

such as Hunting-Clan; it was easy to acquire second-hand aircraft, and there were very few government-imposed restrictions on this particular track. Tour operators and airlines quickly learned that regulations covering holiday charter flights were not onerous, and there was little the men from the ministry could do about it. Overseas Aviation was just one of eleven airlines that set off from the starting gates in the late 1950s; they all started well but ran out of puff before the final furlong. Overseas flew Vikings and Canadair C-4s, and found some of its business in Germany, where the urge to go south towards the sunshine was rekindled post-war; G-AGRP, configured to carry thirty-six passengers, was used on holiday flights from Frankfurt and Berlin throughout 1958. By 1959 more of Overseas' flights were being performed by the bigger four-engine Canadairs, although G-AGRP remained in service throughout 1959 and 1960.

But in 1961, everything changed. The Ministry, goaded into action by its inability to do anything much about the airlines in its charge, introduced new regulations to tighten up its control both of the airlines and the aircraft they flew. Airlines now had to acquire Air Transport Licences for the routes they wanted to fly, and an Air Operator's Certificate to show they could conduct operations safely. Older aircraft were increasingly penalised as their load-carrying abilities were reassessed and their performance re-evaluated, changes that restricted the payload and range of the Viking. By 1961 G-AGRP had been laid up. Overseas took on charge an ever greater number of Canadairs and opened a maintenance base at Gatwick, but operations were sometimes chaotic and as the summer wore on, the airline found itself on the wrong side of its creditors, leading to its abrupt closure on

The Aviation Photo Company

The Aviation Photo Company

15 August 1961. It owed more than £500,000 to the fuel companies, Rolls-Royce, BOAC, the Inland Revenue and many smaller businesses, including the airlines that had performed sub-charters on its behalf. Ronald Myhill, the man behind Overseas, had meanwhile transferred ownership of most of the original fleet, five of the Canadairs and six Vikings (including G-AGRP), to another company with a similar name that he and his wife owned, so when the creditors looked inside the hangar, it was very bare. In the meantime, Myhill was able to sell three of the Vikings for continuing service to Autair, and all five of the Argonauts to Derby Airways. G-AGRP did not join the Autair fleet and it was broken up in June 1962.

The last Viking flew in 1968. In all 163 were built. The RAF took on charge 263 Valetta transports, almost identical to the Viking, and 163 Varsity trainers, modified with a tricycle undercarriage. Viking G-AGRU is on display at Brooklands in BEA colours.

9: BRISTOL B.170 FREIGHTER G-AGVC

Bristol was one of those rare plane makers, like de Havilland, that also made aero engines. The aircraft manufacturer had risen to prominence in the Great War by building the Bristol Scout and Bristol Fighter, and again rose to the occasion in the Second World War, designing and producing the Blenheim bomber and the Beaufighter night fighter, the latter powered by two Bristol Hercules engines that were used subsequently by both the Vickers Viking and Bristol Freighter. But there was also a maverick quality about Bristol's designs. The company did some design work on a big aircraft, the '100-ton' bomber, capable of carrying a 10,000lb bomb load over 5,000 miles, but the Air Staff preferred to stay with the Lancaster. Bristol also designed a rugged, high-wing transport, the Bombay, fifty examples of which were built and served the RAF well in the Middle East during the war. Both projects had a second life.

The Brabazon Committee was seduced by Bristol's proposal for a huge transatlantic airliner, capable of carrying 100 passengers across the Atlantic that had been inspired by the '100-ton' bomber, and gave the project the highest priority; the Bristol Brabazon, as it came to be called, was at the top of the list of recommendations, the Type One. BOAC would have preferred a design that carried twenty-five passengers, and only faintly cheered the project from the sidelines: 'Provided suitable financial arrangements were made, B.O.A.C. would be glad to operate the Brabazon. It was to be regarded as a national experiment.' Telling words, evocative of Concorde. One Brabazon prototype was built and first flew in September 1949, but the

design was overtaken by its slow and difficult development, and, of course, by politics. There were aerodynamic issues that were never resolved; recurrent fatigue cracks limited the life of the prototype, which had only flown 400 hours before the project was abandoned and the aircraft scrapped in 1953.

The Bombay was revisited when Bristol started to look at post-war designs that were less grandiose than the Brabazon, and decided a short-range general-duty transport would be more of a 'bread-and-butter' project; it would have a larger, slab-sided fuselage and more powerful engines than the original Bombay. General Orde Wingate, founder of the famed Chindits, wanted something similar for the Burma campaign to bring equipment to forward airstrips, and suggested it should be able to carry a standard 3-ton army truck, so the design was further refined, and finally two versions were proposed: the Freighter with large clamshell doors and a strong floor; and the passenger-carrying Wayfarer, without the freight doors, able to carry thirty-six passengers. The war ended before the type could be used in the Far East, but the prototype first flew in December 1945, and the second prototype, G-AGVB, a Wayfarer, was used by Channel Islands Airways throughout the summer of 1946, allowing a huge increase in productivity over the airline's de Havilland Rapides; a last hurrah by this independent airline before it was taken over by British European Airways in April 1947.

G-AGVC was the third prototype and first flew in June 1946. It was used intensively over the next two years as the company's demonstrator; G-AGVC set off on a sales tour of

North and South America in August 1946 and did not return until March 1948.

In this rare colour image, the aircraft is in New York with a load of British car exports, Austins, demonstrating the ease of loading; the cars were just driven up a ramp, but not in such numbers! The Freighter could carry two cars and passengers, or three small cars and no passengers. The Freighter never sold in the United States but picked up orders in South America and Canada. On its return G-AGVC was converted so that it could carry two cars and ten passengers, then leased for a new venture to Silver City Airways. Silver City was well financed, backed by mining interests in South Africa and Australia; up until then it had flown Avro Lancastrians, Lancasters converted to carry passengers, on long-range charters.

Smithsonian Institution

Author's Collection

Taking a car to Europe by sea ferry was a lengthy process; not only was there a lot of very tedious paperwork involving HM Customs, who insisted on checking every small detail such as the engine number, but the cars had to be physically craned on and off the ferryboat, one at a time. And many travellers disliked crossing the Channel by sea anyway. Silver City spotted an opportunity and even if it could not do much about the paperwork problem, it was relatively easy to drive cars into the hold of the aircraft, and by choosing airfields close to the Channel, Lympne in Kent and Le Touquet in France, the airline offered a very short flight that minimised the flying cost and so the fare. Commentators wondered why Silver City had not chosen Gatwick, which is closer to London, but Silver City wanted to schedule as many flights as it could into the working day, and the 42-mile sector allowed the airline to perform at least one round trip every sixty minutes, four cars per hour.

Silver City tested the idea with G-AGVC. On 15 June 1948 an Armstrong Siddeley 16hp Lancaster saloon belonging to the airline's boss, Air Commodore Powell, was driven over the grass and up a ramp into the Freighter and then flown over to Le Touquet. The service continued until September, and was deemed promising enough for the airline to launch a regular schedule the following year; it became the mainplane of Silver City's operations, supporting years of profitable and efficient service well into the 1960s.

G-AGVC had its brief moment of glory but was then needed for more urgent purposes, the Berlin Airlift, and Silver City used it alongside another Freighter on flights into Berlin from Hamburg; Airwork also contributed two Freighters. They were handicapped by their slow speed, but were much valued for their ability to carry outsize loads, such as rolls of newsprint and vehicles, and for their ease of loading and unloading; they were able to carry merchandise out from Berlin as well as bringing goods in since they achieved such quick turnaround times. And they carried 4 tons of freight, 1 ton more than the RAF's Dakotas. All the Freighters were reluctantly let go by the following February, before the onset of winter, as they could only fly under visual flight rules, and it would have taken too long to install the Rebecca radio navigation system. G-AGVC returned to Bristol and spent the next two years on experimental work, including aerial top dressing. But 1952 saw the aircraft back in service with Silver City, flying the route it had pioneered in 1948, and it continued as a car ferry until October 1954.

The service operated out of Lympne, a homely grass strip with a small collection of wooden huts off the A20 south of Ashford. *Punch* humorously explained why formalities continued to be a chore:

It has long been the belief of H.M. Customs that the purpose of British motorists in visiting the Continent is to sell their engines for large sums, buy new ones for a fraction of the price and bring back the profits in the form of solid gold bumpers or dummy tanks full of watches. The Customs staff who struggled to frustrate this disreputable traffic at Lympne had to do so in one corner of an English field, whence the sheep were excluded by wire.

The cars were driven on and off by Silver City drivers. The flight lasted around twenty minutes, and then a landing at Le Touquet, where 'the arrival formalities are expeditiously handled', and usually only an hour after first arriving at Lympne the motorist would be on his or her way, hopefully remembering to stay on the right side of the road; those were the early days of continental motoring!

G-AGVC's next role was as a passenger airliner; indeed many Bristol Freighters saw out their golden years carrying people rather than cars. Other intelligent uses of the Freighter were as part of an early containerised cargo operation between the North and South Islands of New Zealand, and to haul beef carcasses from abattoirs in northern Australia to railheads and ports. There were some military users but not the RAF. The design was handicapped by the lack of rear doors for air-dropping supplies; even I realise you could not very well open the front doors in flight! Silver City transferred

G-AGVC in 1956 to Manx Airlines, recently bought out by Silver City's parent company, British Aviation Services; the aircraft was retitled in Manx colours and flew passengers between the Isle of Man, Glasgow and Newcastle.

Manx was later absorbed into Silver City's Northern Division, which now also included Blackpool-based Lancashire Aircraft Corporation and Newcastle-based Dragon Airways, taken over at the same time, and in 1958 G-AGVC was back in Silver City colours, even though Manx remained a legal entity and the actual licence holder.

The Aviation Photo Company

The Aviation Photo Company

G-AGVC might have received another repaint in 1962 had it not suffered a landing accident at Ronaldsway, Isle of Man, on 30 June, which caused it to be written off; the latest signwriting would have shown the name of Silver City's new owner British United Airways, which had taken over the British Aviation Services group in January 1963.

A unique aircraft, the Bristol Freighter. I am not sure why it did not sell in greater numbers; only 214 were built between 1945 and 1958. Peter Brooks in *The Modern Airliner* noted that the design had a high-drag configuration: 'This adversely affects operating economy except with bulky loads carried on very short stages.' The type faced competition from war-surplus Dakotas and Curtiss Commandos, and without a rear cargo door was not able to air-drop supplies. It was never

adopted for a tactical role by the RAF, at the time awash in Valettas and Hastings, neither of which enjoyed the Freighter's versatility but were 'available', always an important factor in the Treasury view. Despite heroic efforts by Silver City to expand the network, car ferry services never thrived away from the core routes, the very short flights to Le Touquet and later Calais and Ostend, which were operated to a punishing schedule. Flying cars across the Channel was a hard way to make money, and eventually succumbed to the new era of drive on, drive off ferries pioneered by Townsend Brothers and Thoresen Car Ferries. To end on a literary note, readers of Nevil Shute's *Round the Bend* will recognise the Plymouth Trader 'George Able Nan How Victor' as a Bristol Freighter, just as competent carrying a bulldozer as flying pilgrims.

10: HANDLEY PAGE HALIFAX G-AHDM

There is something magnificent about Sir Frederick Handley Page, eponymous founder of the aircraft manufacturer that built the first large bombers of the Great War, then produced some iconic airliners for Imperial Airways after it, and went on to build the Halifax, one of three four-engine bomber designs that Britain contributed to the war effort, the other two being the Short Stirling and the Avro Lancaster. Sir Frederick seemed adept at handling the Air Ministry and the civilian and military ministries that followed on after the war, prising contracts out of them over seven decades. In my mind's eye I see him literally striding down the corridors of power; government records indicate a general desire to keep on the right side of him!

More than 6,000 Halifaxes were built, many of them in 'shadow' factories; as the war progressed they were increasingly used for parachuting, troop carrying and delivering materiel by air as well as to tow gliders. At first they had Rolls-Royce Merlin engines, but later versions had the Bristol Hercules; such were fitted to the last 100 Halifaxes built, the Halifax C.VIII, equipped with a large removable ventral pack for cargo and able to carry ten stretchers or eleven passengers within the slender 9ft 6in wide fuselage. The first aircraft did not fly until June 1945, so the variant missed the war in Europe, but some continued in RAF service until the summer of 1948, when the remaining aircraft were placed in storage. Twelve were allocated to BOAC in 1946 and converted by Short Brothers into airliner configuration, with a solid rather than a transparent bomb-aimer nose, ten seats, larger windows for the passengers, a galley, toilet and the class name Halton; passengers had to squeeze by the seats sideways to pass along the aisle.

BOAC needed every aircraft it could lay its hands on after the war, otherwise it is difficult to see why the corporation added this type to its fleet; it was supposed to replace the Dakota as a stopgap until something better came along. The first six Haltons, including G-AHDM, entered service in September 1946, but then had to be grounded almost immediately following failures in the hydraulic system; they also needed anti-icing equipment, so were sent back to the manufacturer.

Haltons did not return to service until June 1947 and were used mainly on the West African service, a twenty-nine-hour odyssey from London to Lagos in Nigeria, stopping

The Aviation Photo Company

at Casablanca, Dakar and Accra. The Lagos service was later superseded by a faster, if hopelessly uneconomical, direct route over the Sahara that imposed payload restrictions on the Halton. The Minister of Civil Aviation complained that the direct route was costing £9,500 a week. There must have been a collective sigh of relief all round when Avro Yorks replaced the Haltons in May 1948.

Not for the last time, Britain's independent airlines were able to take over the corporations' rejects and put them to better use. In any case, a number of charter airlines had already started flying Halifaxes at the same time as BOAC; as freighters they carried around 6½ tons. One enterprising new airline, London Aero and Motor Services (LAMS), bought a fleet in 1946, painted them all-over blue and began flying in fresh fruit from the Continent, a pleasing luxury now that the war was over. Another, Lancashire Aircraft Corporation, got tired of just flying de Havilland Rapides on sightseeing trips around Blackpool Tower and bought Halifaxes, which it flew worldwide from Bovingdon; they carried cargo, fruit and ship's spares, even the ship's crews sometimes, squeezing in twenty. Halifaxes excelled at carrying awkward loads such as ships' propeller shafts, which could be winched up into the bomb bay. Other freight could be loaded into a ventral pannier and hitched under the fuselage. Freddie Laker, young, self-confident, a dealmaker, borrowed £38,000 from a friend and used it to buy all the BOAC Haltons, including G-AHDM, for his new engineering company, Southend-based Aviation Traders. He was not the only one to start his career buying Halifaxes. Harold Bamberg, of Eagle renown, bought his first when he took over short-lived Air Freight and its Halifax G-AJBL in May 1948; he quickly expanded to operate four. Both Laker and Bamberg timed it

right; LAMS lamentably wrong. LAMS ceased operations in June of that year, just as the British government was cranking up its support of the Berlin Airlift.

As one of the guarantors of the western sectors of the beleaguered city, marooned in the middle of the Russian zone and now cut off from its hinterland in Germany's western zones, Britain participated with the Americans in what became a massive, twenty-four-hour operation to supply Berliners by air. The Royal Air Force was Britain's major resource, but to the embarrassment of the post-war Labour government neither it nor the two major state airline corporations, BOAC and BEA, were up to the task; Commonwealth aircrew helped out but in the end, reluctantly, the government had to turn to the charter airlines, the very airlines it had been beating up on for the past three years. The Foreign Office chartered the aircraft, BEA provided some ground support and coordination, and an ever changing inventory of chartered aircraft, 100 in total, took their turns flying up and down the air corridors. The most numerous in the air fleet were the Halifaxes.

Altogether forty Halifaxes were used on the Airlift, carrying 52,800 tons of goods and fuel on 8,100 sorties. Laker could not operate the Haltons himself as at that stage he did not own an airline; instead Westminster Airways took over three, including G-AHDM, and Bond Air Services used another eight of his Haltons plus a further four Halifaxes. Lancashire Aircraft Corporation flew thirteen Halifaxes.

Bond Air Services only carried dry goods in the stripped-out interiors; the others were mainly used as tankers, each one able to fly in 1,300 gallons of liquid fuel. They represented Britain's unique contribution to the Airlift. Britain's Foreign Secretary, Ernest Bevin, had to concede that: 'It is important not only because it is a significant part of our contribution but also because it provides the whole of the wet lift for liquid fuel into Berlin.' He spoiled the effect by adding that he was worried that the independents might make 'excessive profits at the expense of the Crown'.

Some of those profiting from the Foreign Office contracts were his fellow parliamentarians: Air Commodore Harvey; Max Aitken, son of Lord Beaverbrook; and Michael Astor, son of Nancy Astor, Britain's first woman member of parliament. They had clubbed together in 1946 to form Westminster Airways, and did quite well for a time, flying Dakotas and smaller Airspeed Oxfords. The Dakotas were pressed into service for the Airlift, but all civil Dakotas were withdrawn before the end of 1948, and instead G-AHDM became one of Westminster's constituents, flying 176 sorties as a freighter before being converted to a tanker, and flying a further 106; it was joined by a Halifax and two more of Laker's Haltons, one of which was written off after just ten sorties.

The Berlin Airlift came to an end, as far as the civilian airlines were concerned, on 15 August 1949 when the tap for the wet airlift was turned off; business, you might say, dried up. Many operators struggled in the aftermath, not least Westminster Airways. Blaming the Labour government's restrictive policies towards the charter airlines, the MPs decided to close down the airline in December of that year. G-AHDM was broken up the following year.

The Aviation Photo Company

11: DOUGLAS DC-4/C-54 SKYMASTER G-APID

Nobody would claim the Skymaster set the gold standard for civil transport aircraft after the war, but nevertheless its design was aspirational, the one to beat. It was the next step forward in the evolution of airliners. The British recognised this; at least one pre-war design, the Fairey FC-1, shared the same qualities as the DC-4 but due to the outbreak of hostilities it did not progress. Peter Brooks, in *The World's Airliners*, wrote:

The DC-4 and its developments have been to the post-war growth of long-haul air transport what its predecessor, the DC-3, was to the first period of economic expansion. The type's economic characteristics over the longer ranges correspond closely to those of the DC-3 on short stages … Although unpressurised the DC-4 provides its passengers with a remarkably comfortable ride.

All the more odd that after the war so little was achieved by the British in trying to build an aircraft that matched the Skymaster's strengths in design, range, payload, general ability and reliability. First flown before the war, by August 1945 the U.S. military had more than 800 in operation; after the war, Douglas refined the design and sold a small number as the DC-4.

Skymaster, DC-4 and its American military designation C-54 are largely interchangeable, and I usually call the type Skymaster, but it is of note that the ex-military C-54 came with a large cargo door and was around 2 tons lighter than the post-war DC-4. The Skymaster carried forty first-class passengers over 2,500 miles at 200mph, but many were later reconfigured to carry up to eighty-six economy passengers; it was a good load hauler, usually bulking out at 8 to 9 tons, and shouldered most of the burden of keeping Berlin supplied during the 1948–49 Airlift.

Both American and European airlines were quick to deploy Skymasters once the shooting had stopped in Europe. The Dutch government bought eighteen, which were initially operated by the Netherlands Government Air Service before being transferred to KLM; Air France and Sabena were also early buyers. Winston Churchill received one for his personal use, and the RAF were allocated a further twenty-two under Lend-Lease, but they had to be returned after the war was over. BOAC would have liked Skymasters too, but was prevented from buying them by a government that believed air transport was more about building airliners than operating them. So BOAC did the next best thing, which was to charter them in when it could; and in 1949 the corporation persuaded the government to let it buy twenty-two of a developed, pressurised version

licence-built in Canada, the Canadair C-4, known as the Argonaut class.

One airline that BOAC chartered from was Skyways, a new British charter airline that was extremely well connected. Skyways was able to persuade the Treasury to release dollars so that it could buy four Skymasters from KLM in 1947 and use them on oil and trooping contracts as well as to fly some of BOAC's Middle East services. But Skyways' early promise gave way to disappointment, and the Skymasters were sold to Air France for £100,000 each in May 1950; a pity, really, as in June the Korean War broke out and the price of a Skymaster subsequently soared to around £250,000. Prices stabilised after the Korean armistice, and Skymasters began to enter the fleets of British charter airlines. Freddie Laker and his airline Air Charter was an early user, in 1955, followed in 1958 by Starways, based in Liverpool. Although nowhere near new, Skymasters were still reliable and could take holiday passengers to more distant destinations in the Mediterranean; they flew further, faster and carried more passengers than the Dakota and the Viking, obviously, but also compared well with the Ambassadors and Handley Page Hermes that were entering the charter airlines' fleets.

G-APID was built in 1944 as a C-54 for the United States Army Air Force, and in 1950 was passed on to California Eastern Airlines, originally an all-cargo airline but which then participated in the 'Tokyo Airlift' of US military personnel during the Korean War. It was brought on to the British register in 1957 by Independent Air Transport to join its growing fleet of Vikings and Skymasters; G-APID was the second Skymaster to join the company, and a third followed in 1958. The atmospheric picture on page 73 of Independent's G-APID shows the simplicity of open-air maintenance!

Ian McFarlane

Independent was one of the new airlines that sprang up in the mid-1950s to take advantage of the growing holiday market in Britain and on the Continent; Skymasters were used when loads were heavy, but could also fly further afield, carrying freight to the Middle and Far East, and to Africa. The airline was propelled by its managing director, Captain Marian Kozubski, a gentleman with a long and colourful career in British aviation, though not an especially happy one.

Everything seemed to be going fine with Independent, one of a gaggle of young hopefuls. But that all changed when one of Independent's Vikings, carrying two engines to Tel Aviv for El Al, crashed into a house in Southall on 2 September 1958, killing its three crew members and four people on the ground. The aircraft was overloaded and seriously off course, the captain appears to have been exhausted and unaware of his correct location, and previous problems with an engine had been imperfectly addressed. The subsequent public inquiry caused outrage, followed by intense media interest; the commissioner was critical of the company and the way it was run. Kozubski baled out and then focused on his new airline, Falcon Airways. Independent scrabbled hard to keep going, changing its name so that sometimes IAT appeared on its aircraft, sometimes Blue Air, more usually nothing at all.

But it was to no avail; the airline was shut down in late 1959. The most striking outcome of this sorry episode was the realisation that the government had little effective control over the airlines it was supposed to regulate, which led to the establishment in the following year of much stricter regulations concerning the airlines and the aircraft they flew.

But before all this happened, G-APID had found a new owner, another sprightly new entrant charter airline. It was British-owned but initially concentrated on holiday flights from Rotterdam, so its name, Continental Air Services, was appropriate.

The Aviation Photo Collection

The Aviation Photo Company

Like Independent, Vikings made up most of the fleet of Continental but the airline changed course late in 1959 when it was taken over by T.D. 'Mike' Keegan, who renamed it Continental Air Transport and took the opportunity to acquire some of the Vikings and added G-APID. He transferred the operation to his old stamping ground, Southend. Keegan is up there in aviation's Hall of Fame with Laker and Bamberg, a pioneer with a string of airlines to his credit: Crewsair, BKS (his was the initial K), Trans Meridian, British Air Ferries, all of them airlines that under his stewardship had impeccable safety records, surely a tribute to his skill both as engineer and inspirational leader. It is difficult to imagine a greater contrast than the 'general inefficiency of the maintenance organisation' apparent at Independent, and Keegan's scrupulous and painstaking attention to engineering quality control. Keegan had many business interests, buying planes, mending them, leasing them out, and was shrewd enough to see the writing on the wall for the unregulated independents. The dawning era of red tape for the charter airlines would not have appealed to him, and he closed down Continental at the end of the 1960 summer season, retaining the aircraft. He leased the Skymasters briefly to World Wide Aviation, a 1960 start-up; G-APID then spent time early in 1961 with British United, before being operated by Lloyd International Airways later in the same year.

The Aviation Photo Company

Lloyd had only started operations in June 1961, specialising in carrying ships' crews and spares out to the Far East, and whatever freight the captain could negotiate in Hong Kong for the return trip! In between these flights Lloyd operated passenger charter flights, and on one such flight in October 1961 its sole Skymaster was destroyed at Malaga airport in Spain after the refuelling bowser caught fire. G-APID was leased at short notice and its tail painted with the characteristic Lloyd flash, spending the winter with the airline before it was replaced by two Skymasters bought in Alaska.

G-APID was then leased to Starways for the summer of 1962, flying out of Liverpool for this dedicated devotee of Skymasters that owned no fewer than six. Starways flew a scheduled service from Liverpool to London, and also specialised in pilgrimage charters to France and Spain; the company had a robust business model; it was a no-nonsense, low-cost airline. In 1961 it had negotiated a deal to fly for Sabena, the Belgian airline, already a Skymaster user, which at the time needed extra aircraft to fly United Nations troops and supplies around the former Belgian Congo, wracked by civil war following the granting of independence in 1960. Flying in the Congo was not without its excitement: one Starways Skymaster was destroyed on the ground after a rocket attack by a rebel aircraft. Starways sold out to British Eagle in 1964.

G-APID, meanwhile, returned to its owner in 1962, joining Trans Meridian Flying Services, a newly launched charter airline with financial backing from Keegan. Unfortunately the Skymaster suffered a wheels-up landing at Liverpool during a training sortie, so G-APID was sent up to Prestwick to be repaired, only rejoining Trans Meridian in mid-1963.

Like many charter airlines of the day, Trans Meridian flew a mixture of freight and passenger flights on what were

The Aviation Photo Company

The Aviation Photo Company

called ad hoc contracts; that is, they were on a day-to-day basis rather than long term. They included freight flights for the Ministry of Defence, and some passenger work, often for other airlines. By the end of 1964 the company needed a larger freighter for the Ministry contracts and decided to acquire a much bigger aircraft, the Douglas DC-7, for this purpose. The Skymaster would still earn its keep, however; G-APID joining Dan-Air in 1965 for a summer season of charter flying. Dan-Air had been in existence for twelve years, flying a mixture of scheduled and passenger charter services, many of them for inclusive tours (I.T.), and a lot of freight flying. The Skymaster was used mainly as back-up: ad hoc charters, trooping flights, some freight charters, occasional I.T. work, additional capacity for summer scheduled services and flying sub-charters for other airlines. G-APID is seen here at Gatwick, still with the Lloyd fin flash on the tail!

The Aviation Photo Company

By the end of the 1965 season, Dan-Air recognised that the Skymaster was past its best and something else was needed for holiday charter flights. G-APID was returned to Keegan, and in a bold move that assured Dan-Air's future for the next quarter century, instead of merely going one step up the equipment ladder and, like so many other charter airlines, buying turboprops such as the Britannia and Viscount, Dan-Air leapfrogged them by moving straight into the jet age, and bought the first two of many Comets in 1966. And because Dan-Air wanted to stay in the cargo business, it bought a Douglas DC-7 from Keegan to join its Bristol Freighters.

It was time for Keegan to sever his connection with G-APID too. In 1967 he bought out Trans Meridian, returning to his previous role as airline operator, and invested in Douglas DC-7s before moving on to the bigger and much more productive Canadair CL-44, a sensational cargo carrier built in Canada; it had a swing tail and was based on the Bristol Britannia. But G-APID's time was not yet over!

Wing Commander Hugh Kennard was another airline entrepreneur of the early post-war years, up there with the best of them, who started flying after the war from Lympne in Kent. His first airline was called Air Kruise, flying small aircraft – Geminis and Rapides – across the Channel. It was taken over by British Aviation Services, parent company of Silver City, and progressed to bigger aircraft – Dakotas and Bristol Wayfarers – taking holidaymakers on the short hop to Belgium and France, where coaches took them on to their destinations. After the airline was absorbed into Silver City in 1958, Kennard remained as joint managing director until 1960. He then left when Silver City sold out to Air Holdings, the backers behind the newly formed British United Airways. British United then merged the Southend-based operations of Air Charter's Channel Air Bridge with the Lydd-based operations of Silver City under the new name of British United Air Ferries.

British United was somewhat irritated when Kennard announced in 1963 that he was starting another airline, Air Ferry, which would fly Vikings and Skymasters on charter flights out of Manston in Kent, near Margate, with the backing of Leroy Tours. He also wanted to fly car ferry services, and successfully applied for licences out of Manston to Ostend and Le Touquet. It was all too much for British United, already annoyed by the new airline's name, much too close to its new 'brand' for comfort, and then he wanted to compete on the vehicle ferry routes as well! In very short order British United bought out Leroy Tours in late 1964 and found itself in possession of another airline, Air Ferry, to add to its already extensive and variegated menagerie. With what I can only describe as extraordinary aplomb, Kennard merely launched another new airline, Invicta, which would still fly out of Manston, using two Vikings and two Skymasters, and for good measure would get its business from all the other tour operators who had previously used Air Ferry, with the obvious exception of Leroy. Invicta started flying in 1965, and the following year more than doubled its fleet, taking on three more Skymasters and acquiring Air Ferry's Vikings; relations between the two Manston airlines must have become somewhat cordial. One of the Skymasters was G-APID, which received a new coat of paint, swapping the Lloyd flash for the Kentish White Horse.

But it did not enjoy its new livery for very long. In June of that year, 1966, whilst taxiing at Manston with eighty-three passengers on board, its nosewheel collapsed. Invicta gave up on the old aircraft and eventually it was sent back to Luton

and then sold in Spain, where it ended its days as a café, the Aerolandia, near Seville. It was finally broken up in 1978.

G-APID came under the care of eight different British airlines during its ten years on the British register, if nothing else attesting to the optimism and volatility of civil aviation in those early years. But the Skymaster made history for its British owners too, flying for many of the brightest stars in the pantheon of British aviation: Keegan, Laker, Eagle's Bamberg, Dan-Air's Newman, Channel's Squadron Leader Jones, British United's Sir Myles Wyatt, the Kennards, General Critchley and the early Skyways.

The Aviation Photo Company

12: CANADAIR C-4 G-ALHG

Like Britain, Canada had to decide what to do about its aircraft manufacturing industry, which had expanded hugely during the war, after the fighting was over. Victory Aircraft in Ontario had built large numbers of aircraft to Avro designs, Ansons and Lancasters; later renamed Avro Canada it designed and built jet fighters after the war, and the second jet airliner to fly, the C102, which never went into production. Canadian Vickers had built the Canso, a version of the American PBY Catalina flying boat, and was about to develop a version of the Douglas DC-4 Skymaster when it was absorbed into a government-owned aircraft manufacturer, Canadair, based in Montreal.

Canada needed a long-range transport both for its air force and the national carrier, Trans-Canada Air Lines. The less expensive solution was to build under licence a variant of the Skymaster and fit it with British engines, Rolls-Royce Merlins, as these attracted lower import dues; they also gave better performance than the Skymaster's Twin Wasps. The Canadians then went one step further and improved the design, using a shortened version of the pressurised Douglas DC-6 fuselage, which allowed Canadair to offer a pressurised forty-seat airliner, faster by 50mph than the Skymaster. It was everything that the Avro Tudor was not, and BOAC lost no time in buying as many as it could, citing the advantages

of buying Rolls-Royce-engined airliners from a Commonwealth country and so minimising dollar expenditure. Sir Miles Thomas, BOAC's new chairman, tells how he persuaded the Ministry to allow him to buy more than twenty of them by suggesting a 'silly, odd sort of number' rather than a round figure, like twenty-five, which he thought the Ministry would then cut back to an equally round number, like twenty. He asked for twenty-three and was very pleased when his request was only cut back to twenty-two! Canadair delivered the aircraft early, and to their credit, the Argonauts, as the Canadair C-4 was called in BOAC service, stayed at the crease for more than eleven years, a good innings by the standards of the day. They were used on services to the Middle and Far East, Africa and South America, at first in a first-class configuration, later refitted with fifty-four tourist-class seats. They were also among the first BOAC aircraft to be painted with a white roof, which helped to reduce cabin temperature.

As BOAC's huge inventory of new types – Britannias, Comets and Boeing 707s – began to enter service at the end of the decade, it was time for the Argonauts to return to the pavilion. The last flight was by G-ALHG, flying inbound from Abadan to Heathrow on 8 April 1960. The corporation disposed of its nineteen remaining Argonauts – two were lost in crashes, one airframe was retained – with six going to associate airlines, East African and Aden Airways, four to the Royal Rhodesian Air Force, and nine, including G-ALHG, to British charter airline Overseas Aviation, joining that airlines' fleet of six Vikings. It was a big boost in capacity. 'The sort of expansion – a 600 per cent increase in capacity in two years,' wrote Michael Ramsden in *Flight* magazine, 'is probably unparalleled in UK airline history.' As there were fewer than twenty-three flight-deck crews to fly these aircraft, I

The Aviation Photo Company

cannot believe utilisation was anything other than abysmal, squished into the weekends of the peak summer months. The newly acquired sixty-five-seat Canadairs allowed the airline to increase capacity on its holiday routes, many of which were flown out of Germany – where G-ALHG spent most of the summer of 1960 – and also to fly low-fare services between Europe and South Africa, using Lourenço Marques in Mozambique as the entry point; passengers then flew scheduled to South Africa. Long sectors are better for year-round utilisation but demanding on crew hours and engineering.

Overseas' enthusiasm, however, knew few bounds and during the next year, 1961, a further fifteen Canadairs were bought at an advantageous price from Trans-Canada Air Lines, of which nine entered service with Overseas still carrying their Canadian registrations. The Argonauts and Canadairs had their seating configurations increased to seventy, but despite such a huge increase in capacity, Overseas

The Aviation Photo Company

had difficulty in maintaining its operations satisfactorily, so sub-charters and flight delays were frequent; nor was the money coming in, and certainly not enough was going out. Matters came to a head in the middle of August when the fuel companies withdrew fuel supplies, and the operations of the airline came to a halt amidst a welter of unserviceable aircraft, stranded passengers and implacable fuel suppliers, in the middle of the peak holiday period. The creditors got little joy, however, as most of the serviceable aircraft had been transferred to another company, albeit with a similar name, which was not affected by the winding-up process. We have already seen how Viking G-AGRP escaped, and so did G-ALHG, which was sold to Derby Airways along with two others, also former BOAC stock, to operate some of the former Overseas' holiday flights from 1962.

Derby Airways had been negotiating to buy two Douglas DC-6s to enter the inclusive-tour market, and its training

captain and later commercial manager, Captain Cramp, did not think the right decision was made when the company bought the Canadairs instead! 'The decision was a disastrous one insofar as the aircraft were concerned for, cheap as they were, they were very expensive to operate and did not have either the range, capacity or the cargo doors of the DC-6.' He points out that the Merlins needed overhauls at 1,450 hours, with a cylinder block change at 650 hours, whereas the Pratt and Whitneys on the DC-6 had a Time Between Overhaul (TBO) of 3,000 hours and no work required at half life. Undoubtedly the Canadairs did suffer serviceability problems during their time with Derby, but the company put in an extra row of seats and the aircraft operated Mediterranean holiday flights out of Birmingham, Manchester and Cardiff for the next six years.

By 1967 the company, which had changed its name to British Midland Airways, was beginning to invest in turboprop aircraft, a Handley Page Herald to begin with, then the first of many Vickers Viscounts.

The Aviation Photo Company

The Aviation Photo Company

The Canadairs were assumed to have a limited life. That was foreshortened, however, when G-ALHG suffered loss of power as it approached Manchester Airport on 4 June 1967 and crashed in Stockport, with the loss of sixty-nine passengers and three crew members. The aircraft had experienced fuel starvation to its two starboard engines due to inadvertent cross-transfer from the main to auxiliary tanks, a poor design feature involving the cocks controlling the cross-feed, which the subsequent inquiry criticised as 'badly placed, difficult to move and gave no certain impression of what had been selected'. The inquiry commissioner was critical of the design of the seats, which broke loose on impact and caused such injuries that many of those who died had been unable to evacuate the aircraft before it caught fire. He was also extremely critical of the failure of communication between

airlines and the regulatory authorities over such safety issues. BOAC knew about the problem in 1953 and had worked out a solution with Canadair, but that information did not come to light until six months after the crash: 'At the time of the disaster not only did British Midland's pilots and engineers believe inadvertent fuel transfer in the air to be impossible in Argonauts, but the Accident Investigation Branch and the Air Registration Board did not know that it could occur on a significant scale.' It was a bleak indictment of the regulatory system. British Midland withdrew its two other Canadairs, and indeed from inclusive-tour flying, preferring to concentrate on its growing and successful scheduled services.

The accident occurred just one day after a Skymaster of Air Ferry had crashed in the Pyrenees with the loss of eighty-eight lives. There was an angry response and much criticism of charter airlines for flying old and therefore supposedly less safe aircraft. *Flight* magazine got it right, however, in an editorial on 15 June 1967 when it pointed out that financially strong airlines were safer airlines:

What is needed above all else is acceptance of – even awareness of – the fact that safe airlines are financially strong airlines. The safety record of the independents is worse, very much worse, than that of BOAC and BEA. But the question of whether an airline is publicly or privately owned, though it provides many jolly hours of debate for politicians, is irrelevant to safety. The truth is that Britain's airline industry is politically divided, so far as commercial opportunity is concerned, into rich and poor. This commercial division creates and maintains a financially marginal and frustrated sector of the airline industry, and one that finds difficulty in attracting capital. This cannot be good for that very expensive commodity, air safety. If British air transport is to be safe, there must be greater commercial stability for the independents. This means a more liberal and independent licensing policy.

The government did take action, launching a far-reaching review not just of safety standards but also the whole regulatory environment; better known as the Edwards Report and published in 1969, it changed attitudes towards safety and took the edge off much of the hostility that the government, the state corporations and the regulators displayed towards the independent airlines. And indeed, changes in the operat-ing environment and technological advances all made flying that much safer.

Writing of this period, the post-war years, Captain Whitlock commented in his autobiography *Behind the Cockpit Door*:

I had been fortunate enough to enjoy an aviation career spanning only peacetime years, and yet within the first twenty-five years well over a hundred pilots, whom I had known personally, had met their deaths in aircraft accidents; while within the next fifteen years none at all, so dramatic had been the improvements in safety.

13: HANDLEY PAGE HERMES G-ALDG

The Handley Page Hermes was the first modern, British, pressurised, all-metal, four-engine airliner to enter service with BOAC, and for that matter, the independent charter airlines. Twenty-five were built. The design was a parallel development of the Handley Page Hastings military transport, both of which Handley Page proposed to, and were accepted by, the Ministry of Aircraft Production in 1944; Handley Page was already producing Halifax transports and had an inside track to the Ministry, and to the services, for that matter. A new circular fuselage and a single tail unit were married to a conventional two-spar wing centre section attached to the outer wings from the Halifax; Handley Page preferred to use Bristol Hercules engines rather than Rolls-Royce Merlins. In order to speed development, especially of the tail unit, Handley Page built two prototype Hermes, but the first prototype crashed on its maiden flight on 2 December 1945, killing the crew and destroying the aircraft. The company then completed two prototypes to the military Hastings configuration, the first of which flew in May 1946. Work was stopped on the second Hermes after the first prototype crashed, and much thought expended on what to do next. Rebuild it with turboprops? That required a longer fuselage and nosewheel undercarriage, and a more reliable engine than the Bristol Theseus proposed. BOAC had issued a requirement for a Medium Range Empire aircraft, and Handley Page put forward the bigger Hermes with Bristol Proteus turboprop engines; but the Ministries – yes, there were two, as well as BOAC, involved in the decision – chose the Bristol Britannia, so Handley Page persuaded the Ministries to allow it to continue with the revised Hermes project, still with the Hercules piston engines but incorporating the longer fuselage and tricycle undercarriage; it was a shadow project for the Avro Tudor, an aircraft that was really not doing too well in the general scheme of things. Handley Page existed in a parallel universe: the Hermes was not a Brabazon Committee recommendation and all sorts of hurdles had to be overcome, including BOAC's indifference, but Sir Frederick Handley Page knew how to work the system, and in the end the bigger Hermes 4, as it came to be known, was built, and it was bought by BOAC.

The second prototype, G-AGUB, emerged in 1947 with the longer fuselage but retaining its tailwheel. To me it looks almost identical to the Avro Tudor 2.

It was used for intermediate testing, and a year later, in September 1948, the prototype of the definitive Hermes 4, actually part of the BOAC order, took to the air. The Hermes had a protracted and unhappy development, and Sir Frederick found that BOAC was a much tougher customer to satisfy than the Royal Air Force. The initial batch of five Hermes 4s were all overweight, and late in 1949 BOAC refused to accept them for delivery. It is not unfair to compare the Hermes to the Canadair C-4 Argonaut; both had similar dimensions, range and capacity, but the Hermes needed more powerful engines and even after dieting, still weighed 3 tons more than the Canadian aircraft. By this time BOAC was headed up by Sir Miles Thomas, a veteran of wartime production who knew how to navigate within Ministry corridors, and somewhat to Sir Frederick's surprise, Sir Miles carried the day. Two of the rejected aircraft were used for

The Aviation Photo Company

training purposes, briefly, but were then stored. BOAC accepted G-ALDE and the remaining aircraft from February 1950 onwards; G-ALDG arrived in March and was used for route-proving. The Hermes 4 entered service with the corporation on 6 July 1950, replacing flying boats on the African services to Nairobi and Johannesburg, and Avro Yorks on the route to Kano, Lagos and Accra, but it had a short innings. By the beginning of 1952 the Hermes were being replaced by the jet-powered de Havilland Comet and the Canadian-built Argonaut; there was a short reprieve in 1954 when Hermes were urgently needed to maintain schedules after all the Comets had been grounded following a number of crashes, but that lasted only six months. By the end of 1954 the remaining nineteen were cocooned and offered for sale at £198,000 apiece, including G-ALDG. Maybe Sir Frederick had the last laugh as the Hermes remained on BOAC's balance sheet for many years; they were eventually sold with some difficulty to a number of British independents, at a loss of around £100,000 each.

Why nineteen? What happened to the other six? One was lost in a forced landing in the Sahara, but the other five, which were the overweight aircraft BOAC refused to accept, had gone to Airwork in 1952. In its role as the government's 'most-favoured' charter airline, Airwork had secured some of the first big trooping contracts, to the Canal Zone in Egypt, and later to the Far East, and BOAC was strong-armed into releasing four of the early Hermes into Airwork's care. Airwork almost immediately lost two of them in accidents, so a further Hermes was then made available. The sale of the remaining nineteen two years later then became the subject of some controversy.

First, BOAC wanted to do a deal with its 'most-favoured' airline, Skyways, recently reinvigorated under its new chair-man, Eric Rylands. Rylands was happy to cooperate with the corporation; indeed, he had bought a large fleet of Yorks from it and had accepted the role as major subcontractor to BOAC. BOAC was banned from tendering for the large air-trooping contracts now being issued by the government, following its decision to switch from sea to air the carriage of personnel and their families to and from overseas garrisons. The Conservative government thought that reserving trooping contracts for the independents, as well as being much cheaper, was some sort of quid pro quo for not letting them fly regular scheduled services. Sir Miles Thomas had other ideas, however, and proposed to Rylands that Skyways should take over all the remaining Hermes at an advantageous rate, in ex-

A.J. Jackson Collection

change for a 25 per cent stake by BOAC. Thus BOAC would become eligible for government tenders through a surrogate, and also dispose of its fleet, and for good measure, retain some sort of interest in, if not control of, the charter market. Rylands and the Minister quickly agreed, and it was almost a done deal; but then the other charter airlines found out what was going on. Their collective fury was magisterial as in succession their boards stomped in and out of the Minister's office and made their feelings known. The Minister backed down, and Skyways did not get all the aircraft, just twelve of them; the others went to Airwork, which took on G-ALDG, and Silver City, which obtained the other six. Then Thomas had to overcome considerable union resistance among his engineering staff at Heathrow, who refused to prepare the aircraft for sale. The dispute, in time-honoured BOAC fashion, went on for some months before Thomas, who had never wanted the Hermes in his fleet anyway, was able to calm matters down with vague, somewhat Delphic promises. Ironically, Skyways never received any major trooping contracts even though it had the biggest fleet of troopers; instead it had to make do as a subcontractor for Airwork on the Far Eastern flights. It also flew the Hermes as a freighter for BOAC, even though it was not suitable; it only had small passenger doors, for instance. Silver City obtained some trooping contracts that were operated under the aegis of its parent company, British Aviation Services, or Britavia for short. Laker would have nothing to do with the Hermes, flying a mixture of Yorks, Skymasters and Avro Tudor freighters on government contracts instead. Other trooping contractors such as Scottish Airlines fell by the wayside; and Bamberg's Eagle concentrated on using Vikings for trooping services to Malta, Gibraltar, Libya and within the Mediterranean area.

Author's Collection

All Airwork's Hermes were lease-purchased from BOAC, so there was always a time lag before purchase was complete; G-ALDG finally transferred to Airwork ownership in July 1957. It received a sixty-three-seat interior configuration with rearward-facing seats. The Hermes was not comfortable for passengers on the long flights out to the Far East; the journey took three days and included two night stops, and the 1,300-mile range of the aircraft meant there were many refuelling stops en route, six between London and Singapore. The aircraft could become unbearably hot on some sectors as the air conditioning, having been designed for much smaller passenger loads, could not cope; Airwork installed electric fans in the cabin but never upgraded the ventilation system. Mothers with small children still had to hold them on their laps, and food was what you would expect from the lowest-cost tender; many meals, however, were taken on the ground. Passengers enjoyed the night stops, and the aircraft was much quieter than the York or BOAC Argonaut; the alternative was a four-week voyage by troopship, another daunting prospect. The Hermes troopers were eventually replaced in 1959 on the Far East routes by turboprop Britannias, which did the journey in just twenty-four hours.

G-ALDG was put up for sale in August 1959, and after some curious transactions – one of which involved Falcon Airways, which owned the aircraft for less than twenty-four hours – it passed to Britavia in October. Britavia, however, had given up on its trooping tenders so all its Hermes were now painted up in Silver City markings. The Hermes still suffered from its built-in drag factor – at its optimum speed, the aircraft suffered from engine vibration, so it was either flown at a higher speed, which increased fuel consumption, or at a lower speed, which caused the tail to droop and induce drag further – but by the time BOAC passed the aircraft on to the independents the corporation had worked out most of the bugs and the independents inherited some good stock. Silver City continued to operate its Hermes for another three years, a tribute both to the airline's renowned standards of maintenance excellence and the aircraft's strength and reliability. Silver City used the Hermes on short-range sectors including Manston to Le Touquet, which was part of the London to Paris 'Silver Arrow' service with train connections at each end. For a time the company gained a new trooping contract to fly from Manston to Germany in support of the British Army of the Rhine. Furthermore, many tour operators breathed a sigh of relief when they were able to contract inclusive-tour flying with a reliable airline such as Silver City, even if it meant that passengers had to trek out to remote Manston in Kent. In the end spar replacement issues and old age presaged the end of the service life of these aircraft, abetted by changes in Silver City's ownership, for early in 1962 Silver City was taken over by Air Holdings, the parent company of British United.

But it was not quite the end. Sensibly, British United shifted the Silver City operation away from Manston to Gatwick. The 'Silver Arrow' now made more sense, with a straight run from

The Aviation Photo Company

Victoria to the airport station at Gatwick, and the air sector was now operated by British United's Viscounts. The Hermes continued flying inclusive tours for the 1962 summer season, finally being withdrawn from service in September. They were replaced on inclusive-tour work by Viscounts, not the best aircraft for the job, and indeed this was the start of British United's subsequent uncomfortable relationship with holiday flying that the airline never resolved. G-ALDG survived, though, or at least its fuselage did; it was used by British United as a cabin-crew trainer, and when British United became British Caledonian, it was repainted in the new colours. I used to see it outside the maintenance hangar on my occasional visits to Gatwick in the 1970s when I was with Dan-Air. Now the fuselage has passed to the Duxford Aviation Society and been repainted in BOAC colours, all that remains of this significant airliner. Significant? Not to BOAC perhaps, but to the charter airlines that flew it the Hermes was a definite step up the engineering ladder, the first modern, pressurised four-engine airliner to enter service with them and a taste of what was to come.

14: AIRSPEED AMBASSADOR G-ALZO

The Airspeed Ambassador was designed by de Havilland's Arthur Hagg, who had created so many of de Havilland's pre-war masterpieces. He designed it from the inside out, starting with the windows and the high wing to enhance the view for passengers. Airspeed, the company founded by writer 'Neville Shute' Norway, had been taken over by de Havilland in 1940. Wartime production demands of the successful Airspeed Oxford twin-engine trainer required different management skills from those of its original founders; sensing this, Norway had parted ways with the company in 1938. 'In Airspeed the time for the starters was over and it was now for the runners to take over the company,' he wrote in his autobiography *Slide Rule*. 'I was a starter and useless as a runner.'

The Aviation Photo Company

Airspeed spent the war building Oxfords and Mosquito bombers at its Christchurch plant near Bournemouth, and like every other aircraft manufacturer wanted to get back into civil aircraft production after it was over. The company got two chances. First, it converted around 150 Oxford airframes into six-seat airliners, called the Consul, which were much in demand with the new British charter airlines, and sold reasonably well abroad too. G-AJGA is in the colours of Lancashire Aircraft Corporation in this scene at Newcastle; Lancashire was behind the revival of Skyways in the early 1950s.

Second, Airspeed's design for a Douglas DC-3 Dakota replacement, the Type 2 as suggested by the Brabazon Committee, was accepted, albeit alongside a parallel design from Vickers. The Airspeed aircraft, the Ambassador, was to be all-metal and pressurised, with seating for forty passengers, powered by two Bristol Centaurus piston engines; bigger, faster, heavier than the Dakota, but then any formulation for a Dakota replacement was pure guesswork. Someone once said that the title of replacement for the original Douglas DC-3 transcontinental airliner of 1936 could just as well apply to the Boeing 707! The Ambassador was more conservative than the Vickers design – better known as the Viscount, the world's first successful turboprop airliner – and the Ambassador found early favour with BEA, which ordered twenty in 1948.

American aircraft manufacturers were also pursuing the elusive 'DC-3 replacement'; both Convair and the Glenn L. Martin Company built twin-piston engine forty-seat airliners.

The pressurised Convair 240 first flew in March 1947; the first flight of the Ambassador took place four months later. The Convairliner, as the type was generally known, entered service with American Airlines in June 1948. BEA had to wait until March 1952 before it could introduce its Ambassadors into regular service. Aviation writer John Stroud sighed:

'Although a regrettable amount of time will have elapsed between the first flight of the Ambassador and its introduction on the services of British European Airways, its appearance at Europe's airports should do much to enhance the reputation of both British airlines and the British aircraft industry.' But no other airline bought Ambassadors from Airspeed.

The Aviation Photo Company

European airlines either waited for the Viscount, like Aer Lingus and Air France, or bought Convairliners – Sabena, Swissair, Scandinavian Airlines System – or did both, as did KLM and Lufthansa. Airspeed had only contracted to deliver the first five Ambassadors by May 1951, so BEA became resigned to the type's protracted development, but was nevertheless irritated by further delays: 'B.E.A … had looked for the carriage of the bulk of B.E.A.'s International passenger traffic in Elizabethan aircraft during the year 1951,' commented the corporation in its 1951–52 Annual Report, and went on to note somewhat sarcastically: 'In fact, only 1,924 revenue passengers were carried in the Elizabethan, representing 0.3 per cent of the international total of 649,376 passengers.'

There were further complaints after the aircraft entered service in 1952, configured for forty-seven passengers and named Elizabethan in BEA service, the corporation commenting on the early teething problems 'and the delays which stemmed from them, and irritated passengers and airline alike in their early months'. But the Elizabethan had one year's ascendancy as queen of the corporation's fleet until succeeded by the Viscount in 1953, and indeed, the aircraft proved highly popular in service. The Ambassador was short on range, between 450–900 miles depending on load, and so worked best on sectors such as London to Paris, although rather puzzlingly it was used on some of the corporation's longest routes, notably to Cairo in Egypt, routing via Nice, Malta, Tripoli and Benghazi. Its entry into service coincided with the introduction of hot-meal catering on BEA's flights, and the Elizabethan launched a 'Silver Wing' service to Paris reminiscent of the fabled pre-war Imperials service.

G-ALZO was one of the later Ambassadors, delivered to BEA on 25 November 1952 and named *Christopher Marlowe*.

It spent just under six years in the corporation's service before being withdrawn from service in 1958 and stored at Marshalls at Cambridge. Marshalls sold the aircraft on to the Royal Jordanian Air Force (RJAF), installing a large freight door so that the aircraft could be used to fly around Avon jet engines for the fledgling air force's Hawker Hunter jets. It was also used as a VIP transport for the Royal Flight, somewhat fancier than the de Havilland Herons of the RAF Queen's Flight. In 1963 Ambassador RJAF '108' was traded in to Handley Page as part of the air force's order for two new Heralds, and it returned to England and a new career with Dan-Air.

Dan-Air was the second independent to find further use for Ambassadors in the age of the Viscount, following BKS Air Transport, which had introduced former BEA Ambassadors on its Newcastle scheduled services in 1957. Dan-Air bought an initial three in November 1959, followed by another seven over the years, not all of which entered service with the airline; those that did operated from Dan-Air's new base at Gatwick. Dan-Air used the type mainly for charter flying; there was much more ad hoc business available, including one-off flights to European destinations such as those to sports events like motor racing, some military flying, and the occasional rush job, such as rescuing passengers stranded by strike action. One mainstay of the Ambassador operation, however, was the Gatwick–Jersey weekend scheduled service that Dan-Air had started in 1956; and the Ambassadors flew holiday charters, a growing business, to Barcelona, Perpignan and Palma, Munich, Nice and Basel, about as far as the aircraft could reach. One of my Dan-Air colleagues explained to me the finer points of flight operations in those days: 'It was more leisurely, certainly! You'd see the aircraft off in the morning on its way to Palma, and then you knew it wouldn't be back for another nine or so hours, you could go off to the pub …'

Not just the operations were more leisurely. Aircraft utilisation was low, and in any case constrained by crew availability; the Ambassadors never flew much more than 1,000 hours a year. But the capital costs of the aircraft were also low, the engineering was performed in house, and as long as the flights themselves returned a profit, a decent contribution to overheads, it was more important to make the deal than encumber the company with unrealistic fixed costs. As Dan-Air's commercial operations developed, so did the airfields that the Ambassadors visited. More charter flights were flown from regional airports, Manchester and Liverpool initially, and more scheduled services as the network developed. Of course, Dan-Air was only allowed to operate scheduled services over relatively sparse routes – the best trunk routes were reserved for BEA – but the airline gamely did its best, seeing the regularity of these services as a steady source of income over the coming years, and their development as a source of growth. Newcastle to Kristiansand and Stavanger in Norway, Prestwick to the Isle of Man, Gatwick to Ostend; nobody would ever say that Dan-Air had easy pickings. Dan-Air added more Ambassadors to their fleet, but their days as front-line aircraft were over by 1967 when the airline introduced the first Comets on its holiday charter services. They were able to carry twice as many passengers much further, and of course at much higher speeds; gone were the days of leisurely turnarounds and day-long round trips! The remaining Ambassadors, three of them by 1969, did what they did best, flying short sectors across the Channel and the North

Author's Collection

Sea. By the end of 1970 only one Ambassador remained in service, G-ALZO, the most flexible of the Ambassadors because it had a freight door. It continued to see service in 1971, flying the Gatwick to Jersey and Ostend weekend schedules and picking up occasional charter flying; springtime flights to the Dutch bulb fields and weekends in Paris were always popular. Finally, on 26 September, G-ALZO operated the last of its scheduled services from Gatwick, first to Ostend, followed by Jersey. Dan-Air's Social Club took the aircraft for a spin to Reims on 29 September, and that should have been that, except early in October one of the airline's BAC One-Elevens needed an engine change at Zagreb in Yugoslavia. There was no time for sentiment; G-ALZO flew a spare engine down on 2 October, returning the next day and proceeding to Lasham for storage. Dan-Air's engineers had no need to strip it down for spares, it was not in the way, and so this historic aircraft remained at Lasham until it was donated to the Duxford Aviation Society in 1986, which restored it and placed it on display in 2013.

15: VICKERS VISCOUNT 701 G-ALWF

When Britain's airline corporations, aircraft builders and engine manufacturers got together and collaborated, they could produce the goods. Unlike the sorry tale of the Avro Tudor and BOAC, the development of the Vickers Viscount owed as much to BEA and Rolls-Royce as it did to Vickers. The design was an outcome of the Brabazon Type 2 recommendations, ostensibly for the Dakota replacement, which were split between the piston-engine Airspeed Ambassador and the turboprop Viscount. The Ministries accepted the concept of a turbine airliner as being more suitable for short-haul operations than the pure jet, but its execution was something of a moving target; the design could hardly stand still long enough as Rolls-Royce continually upgraded the performance of the Dart engines. The original Vickers design was for a twenty-four-seat, four-engine airliner, powered by four Darts each producing 1,130ehp (equivalent horsepower, an agreed measure of turbine engine output), with around 700 miles range, not much better than the Viking, for which BEA saw the aircraft as a replacement. The sums really did not add up, and the Airspeed design showed more promise at this early stage, so BEA was prevailed upon to order twenty of the Ambassadors. Those were dark days for the Vickers team, even though two prototypes had been ordered; it was difficult to muster the resources to keep on going, but under the leadership of George Edwards the project continued. By the time the prototype Viscount flew in 1948, one year after the Ambassador's first flight, the aircraft had been stretched;

it could now carry thirty-two passengers, and the engines were producing just under 1,380ehp. The balance tilted back in Vickers' favour. The Ambassador experienced design problems that delayed its introduction into service. Rolls-Royce promised yet more power, to more than 1,500ehp, and the Viscount design was stretched further, to carry forty-three passengers in a longer fuselage. BEA's chief executive, Peter Masefield, then became an enthusiast for the project. Not only were the economics of the design beginning to make better sense, the aircraft had undoubted passenger appeal: free of vibration, with large windows for the passengers and the whole enhanced by the reliability of the sturdy Dart engines.

By 1950 the Viscount had turned a corner. The prototype was used by BEA over a period of two weeks in August to launch the first passenger flights between London and Paris, and then for a further eight days on the Edinburgh service during the Edinburgh Festival. BEA ordered twenty of the Series 701 Viscounts, able to carry forty-seven passengers, the same number as the Ambassador, but at 300mph over 60mph faster. G-ALWF was the second production Viscount 701 off the line, flying for the first time on 3 December 1952. Just days earlier, in November, Vickers achieved a notable breakthrough with the sale of fifteen Viscounts to Trans-Canada Air Lines. It was the first significant dollar order for the aircraft, indeed for any British-built aircraft, and one that paved the way for further sales in North America. Just as BEA's early collaboration with Vickers contributed to the Viscount's marketing appeal, the input of the Canadian airline was invaluable in preparing the aircraft for a much wider market than had ever been foreseen. Trans-Canada bought fifty-one Viscounts in total.

Delivered to BEA on 13 February 1953, G-ALWF was used for crew training and route proving, suffering an undercarriage collapse in December that effectively put it out of service for six months.

But after that the aircraft contributed to BEA's increased profitability and maturity of operation. Further improvements came when the Viscounts were re-engined with more powerful Darts, allowing the aircraft to have their seating capacity increased to sixty, G-ALWF being modified in 1958. By this time the larger Viscount 800 series had entered service, so the original Viscounts were deployed on regional and domestic services, and from 1959 on internal German routes to and from Berlin. The

The Aviation Photo Company

The Aviation Photo Company

Ambassadors were retired in 1958: not the Dakotas, however! They remained in service for another four years, until May 1962, outlasting both putative replacements, the Viking and the Ambassador, by a handsome margin. The Viscount 701s, another iteration of the elusive Dakota replacement, followed BEA's Dakotas out of service a mere ten months later, in March 1963.

BEA's surplus aircraft never remained inactive for long, and seven of the Viscounts were sold on to Channel Airways by year's end. Channel excelled at short, cross-Channel routes from its bases at Southend and Portsmouth to Ostend, Rotterdam and the Channel Islands. The airline acquired a taste for Viscounts, using them to develop longer-haul flights to the new charter destinations in Europe as well as on its core route network.

Channel put in more seats as well, up to seventy-one. In due course, in 1965–66, it was the turn of Channel's Viscount 701s to go, all seven of the former BEA aircraft joining the fleet of the Welsh airline, Cambrian Airways. As Cambrian already operated five of the same type, it seemed a neat arrangement; the seating was quickly reduced to sixty-three in Cambrian service! Channel made up the shortfall by buying eleven of the larger Viscount 810 series from the American airline Continental; only minimal repainting was needed, as Continental's livery so closely resembled the existing colours of the Golden Viscounts, and typically for Channel more seats were put in, eighty-two, up from the original fifty-six in Continental configuration.

The Aviation Photo Company

One of the first airline operators to get into the air when the ban on civil flying was lifted on 1 January 1946, Cardiff-based Cambrian had nevertheless struggled to develop its network, even suspending all its services during the winter of 1958–59. But it collaborated with BEA, to the extent that BEA became a minority shareholder in the airline and sold it some Pionairs; this bore further fruit when BEA agreed to transfer to Cambrian its Irish Sea services from Liverpool and the Isle of Man, and some of the Viscount 701s, in 1963, leading to a huge expansion in the Welsh airline's operations; the ex-Channel Viscounts, including G-ALWF, were part of this continuing story.

Cambrian's all-red livery was striking, shown to advantage in this snowy scene. Further expansion followed. Cambrian began competing against British Eagle on the London to Liverpool route, and took up more charter flying commitments, especially on behalf of the noted west of England tour operator Hourmont. But despite BEA's backing, it was still hard for a small airline, however efficient. Britain's licensing authority prevented the independent airlines from competing against the mighty corporations, already endowed with the most profitable trunk routes, but saw nothing odd in allowing the smaller airlines to thrash it out among themselves

The Aviation Photo Company

on much sparser regional routes. So Liverpool to London saw both Cambrian and British Eagle competing against each other, but no one was allowed to compete against BEA on the denser Manchester to London route. Cambrian compounded the problems by splitting its operation; the airline was based in Cardiff, but many flights operated via Bristol, just across the Severn, a very short and uneconomic sector; and most of the flying was now out of Liverpool. Losses in 1967 unnerved the board of Cambrian, which agreed to restructure, selling a majority stake to BEA. The corporation then took the opportunity to place Cambrian with another independent, Newcastle-based BKS, which was also looking for more financial backing, in a new subsidiary, British Air Services.

So the Viscounts were repainted and G-ALWF emerged still wearing a lot of red and still with a dragon on its tail, but with an additional discreet and baffling logo for BAS, a meaningless acronym to most people, but to those in the industry reminiscent

of the late Silver City's parent company, British Aviation Services. When the first jets joined the fleet in 1970 there was a further revision to the livery, with the Cambrian name now followed by 'British Air Services' in smaller type. Finally G-ALWF saw one last application by the signwriter, when British Air Services displaced Cambrian on the fuselage roof.

The decision was taken to withdraw all the early-model Viscount 701s, replaced in turn by the larger Viscount 800 and the One-Eleven jets. G-ALWF flew its last commercial service on Christmas Eve 1971, from Belfast via Bristol, and in May 1972 was transferred, fittingly, to the Viscount Preservation Trust at Liverpool. Longer-term arrangements were made that saw the aircraft moved to the Duxford Aviation Society in 1976, where it is still on view, the oldest turbine-engined airliner in the world; it has been restored to its original BEA colours. Another Viscount, in the colours of French airline Air Inter, is on view at the Midland Air Museum in Coventry.

Chris England

97

16: LOCKHEED CONSTELLATION L-049 G-AMUP

Once the war was over, Lockheed had a head start on its competitors in the rush to sell long-range airliners. Already in 1939 Howard Hughes and TWA were looking for an airliner faster and bigger than the Boeing Stratoliner ordered by Pan American; Lockheed obliged. The Constellation was given a graceful dolphin-shaped fuselage and triple-tail surfaces rather than a single tall fin, to ensure the aircraft could fit in TWA's existing hangars; it was a very attractive plane to look at. The first version, the L-049, cruised at 275mph, carrying around fifty passengers over 2,000 miles; refuelling stops were still required on transatlantic flights. Both Pan American and TWA ordered Constellations in 1940 but America's entry into the war stopped their production temporarily until the United States Army Air Force decided that it too wanted a high-speed transport aircraft, eventually ordering 313 of the military C-69 variant of the Constellation. By the end of the war, fifteen were in service. The Air Force cancelled the rest, preferring to standardise on the Douglas DC-4 Skymaster, but Lockheed decided to complete those already on the assembly line, thus allowing the company to offer early delivery. Advertisements for the Constellation were appearing in British aviation magazines some months before the war in Europe ended. Pan American and TWA started flying them across the Atlantic early in 1946, shaving up to three hours off the flight time of its closest competitor, the Skymaster, and in superior pressurised comfort.

Air-Britain Archive, Peter Berry Collection

BOAC and the government were in a quandary: the airline's transatlantic services were being flown by Liberators – converted bombers – and three Boeing flying boats. It would be some time before British designs deemed suitable for these routes, the Avro Tudor, Bristol Brabazon and the de Havilland jet airliner, entered into service. Pragmatically the government decided to buy Constellations for BOAC, ordering five, which entered service in 1946, and faced down the criticism it received over the outlay in precious dollars. BOAC was a long-standing customer of Lockheed, having sustained many of the strategically important air services in the Middle East and Africa throughout the war thanks to the thirty-seven Lockheed Lodestars the corporation acquired.

Once BOAC had some Constellations, it wanted more. The corporation needed to upgrade services to India and Australia after the latter's respective airlines, Air India and Qantas, introduced Constellations, so five Constellations were bought from the Irish in 1948, who were happy to accept payment

The Aviation Photo Company

in pounds sterling at a handsome premium! When tourist-class services across the Atlantic were introduced – up until then all such flights had been first-class only – BOAC reconfigured its original Constellations with sixty-five seats, up from forty-three, and bought two more Constellations from Pan American for these services at the end of 1952, one of them being G-AMUP.

Constellations took on an even greater role after the two Comet crashes in 1954, as all available aircraft were needed to maintain services following the decision to ground the remaining jets. The corporation decided to improve the quality of its Constellation fleet, for the introduction into service of the Bristol Britannia was still some years away. In a canny move, BOAC arranged to swap its seven early-model L-049 Constellations with later L-749 models from America's Capital Airlines on a one-for-one basis; Capital had bought Vickers Viscounts and no longer needed a large fleet of long-haul aircraft. G-AMUP made the one-way flight to Washington, DC, in March 1955, and was registered N2738A.

As the Viscounts took over Capital's services – the airline bought sixty – so the Constellations were eventually withdrawn, starting in 1958. By 1960 N2738A/G-AMUP was in storage, having flown 30,632 hours over fourteen years.

Even though the first jets were entering service, and BOAC and BEA were flying new turboprop airliners, there was still a place for piston-engine equipment in the fleets of the independent airlines. They needed inexpensive aircraft to sustain their low-overheads requirement, for they were only flown during the short summer season and then usually at weekends; that was their classic *modus operandi* in the late 1950s. Argonauts, Bristol Freighters, Hermes and Vikings made up the bulk of the fleets, but Captain Marian Kozubski, a veteran in the business, thought that Constellations, with their range and capacity, were a good choice and in order to undertake a large programme of charter flying in 1961 for Universal Sky Tours, the precursor to Thomson Holidays, he bought four of them, three from Capital Airlines, for his Falcon Airways.

Kozubski ferried the first, which regained its old registration G-AMUP, to England in January 1961, the next two following shortly afterwards, and the final Constellation, this one bought from TWA, arriving in June. G-AMUP's Capital Airlines red livery was overpainted in black, eighty-two seats were installed and at the end of March the aircraft was dispatched under the command of Captain Kozubski to Georgetown in British Guiana to collect sixty-eight immigrants, its first commercial operation. Kozubski got into trouble when he returned on a more direct course across the Atlantic to Gatwick than originally planned, a breach of safety regulations, and he was subsequently prosecuted by the Ministry. Then there were doubts about the level of equipment aboard; the British authorities had already insisted that improved fire-protection systems be installed before G-AMUP entered regular summer service. In any case, Kozubski and his backers seem to have had a difficult relationship with the authorities, not in itself very unusual, but it all made for a chaotic and ultimately unsuccessful season's operations. For days on end Kozubski did not have any aircraft to fly his charter programmes, and the Constellations still had to be modified; G-AMUP was taken out of service at the end of June for the fire-protection systems to be installed, in the middle of the season, and did not return to service until a month later. One of the former Capital Constellations was never made airworthy, and the third was sold in July to another charter airline, Trans European Airways. The fourth flew on the Austrian register, which the British banned from operating Falcon's charters out of the United Kingdom. Flights were sub-chartered to other airlines, when possible, and Universal Sky Tours transferred much of its flying to another airline, Air Safaris, which was hard pressed to maintain the programme with its fleet of inadequate Hermes airliners.

There followed a war of words between Falcon and the Ministry over the refusal to allow the Austrian aircraft to operate British charter flights. Falcon's joint managing director, Frederick Beezley, claimed that the Director of Aviation Safety even slammed down the telephone receiver after one discussion: 'I think certain officials of the Ministry of Aviation have a personal dislike of Capt Kozubski and myself,' he grumbled. Just as Falcon's operations were beginning to improve and officialdom had relented and allowed Kozubski to use the Austrian Constellation, the Ministry successfully prosecuted him over the earlier Atlantic incident, and then went on to revoke Falcon's Air Operator Certificate on 21 September. It was the end for Falcon, and indeed for Kozubski, as far as his British ambitions were concerned; he went on to fly the Austrian Constellation for two more years before surfacing later in East Africa.

It was not the end for G-AMUP, however. Trans European, having bought its sister ship earlier, now bought G-AMUP in December 1961, carefully repainting it in its blue livery and finally obliterating the dual-purpose eagle/falcon on the nose!

Tony Eastwood Collection

The 1962 summer programme was somewhat skimpy, and Trans European was in trouble soon enough when G-AMUP was impounded by the airport authorities in Tel Aviv in July of that year. Trans European did not long survive that setback, appointing a receiver by the end of the month and ceasing operations by the middle of August.

After a number of debacles, Universal Sky Tours had had enough; Falcon and the Hermes operation of Air Safaris were the last straw. There had to be a better way to guarantee a flying programme, and when all else fails, as it seemed to have done for the tour operator over a number of seasons, it is better to do the job yourself. And that is just what Universal Sky Tours did, setting up a new airline for the summer of 1962 called Euravia, which also flew Constellations but without the fuss and bother of Kozubski's operations. Three Constellations were bought from the Israeli airline, El Al. It was an interim solution and they were cheap to buy but more than adequate for the task ahead. So successful was the first summer's operations that more Constellations were needed for 1963, and Euravia doubled its fleet size by buying Skyways, a storied British airline going back to the earliest post-war years that had now fallen on hard times, and absorbed its three Constellations. Even those were not enough for the 1963 summer season, so both the former Trans European Constellations were added to the fleet in time for the peak summer season, G-AMUP being brought back from its sunny sojourn in Tel Aviv and entering service in August.

The aircraft enjoyed one final year of service, 1964, before joining all its sister aircraft to be laid up at the end of the year, as their replacements, six Bristol Britannias bought from BOAC, began to enter service in time for the summer 1965 season. G-AMUP was scrapped in October, having flown a

The Aviation Photo Company

total of 32,294 hours. During its four years in British charter airline service, G-AMUP had flown 2,292 hours, just under 575 hours a year. By way of contrast, BOAC in its last full year of Constellation operations, 1955, managed around 3,000 hours a year, but then had the advantage of year-round, long-haul flying. British charter airlines might manage four or five flights at the weekend, but only during the summer months, and to Mediterranean destinations; there was little midweek flying. Euravia's successor airline, renamed Britannia Airways, did much to tackle this imbalance in utilisation by encouraging holidaymakers to fly during the week, not just at weekends, and at different times of the year, spreading the summer season over more weeks and developing winter holidays as well.

The Constellation had started as a BOAC flagship in the early days after the war and then saw second-line service with a number of British charter airlines, both as a passenger aircraft and a freighter. Crucially the Constellation allowed BOAC to offer luxury transatlantic service from 1946; just as crucially, it launched Euravia, still with us as TUI. There is an L-749 Constellation in preservation in the United Kingdom, at the Science Museum at Wroughton.

17: DOUGLAS DC-6 G-APSA

Dave Welch

While the British were floundering around at the end of the war, wondering how best to utilise the enormous aircraft manufacturing resources that the nation had built up as part of the war effort, the Americans were pushing ahead with the design of sophisticated airliners, both long and short haul. Lockheed had already flown the beautiful Constellation, and Boeing was quick to develop the Stratocruiser from the B-29 bomber; Douglas had built thousands of Dakotas and hundreds of four-engine Skymasters, and now needed to offer a larger, faster and more comfortable passenger aircraft in order to draw level with Lockheed, the market leader. The outcome was the Douglas DC-6, with a longer fuselage than the Skymaster, pressurised, and powered by four reliable Pratt & Whitney Double Wasps. The first DC-6 flew on 29 June 1946 – there was a military prototype that had taken to the air the previous February, but it was not proceeded with – and production models were delivered to the first customers, American and United, in November 1946. The following year Douglas decided to offer an improved version, with more powerful engines and a 5ft stretch to the fuselage. This was available in two versions: the DC-6A, an all-cargo version with strengthened floor and two large freight doors, able to uplift around 12 tons; and the DC-6B, optimised for passenger work, which could carry up to 102 passengers over 3,000 miles at 315mph. Quite a contrast to Britain's post-war offering, the Avro Tudor, designed to carry thirty-two passengers at a speed of 210mph over a similar distance. Many DC-6As were modified to carry passengers, and as you have probably guessed, DC-6Bs were also converted to carry cargo!

It was not all smooth flying at the beginning. There were two crashes in the early days, one of them fatal and both caused by inflight fires, which led to the type being grounded for four

Tony Eastwood Collection

months. But after that problem was fixed, the aircraft went on to give excellent service, a happy combination of reliability, durability, range, payload and speed, all brought together in an economic package that produced the lowest aircraft costs of that era. These were only surpassed by the greater productivity of the new jets that entered service in the 1960s.

BOAC never flew DC-6s but found an ersatz substitute in the Canadair C-4. When they could, other British airlines did try and buy DC-6s, notably Hunting-Clan, which had two for its African freight services, and Harold Bamberg's Eagle, which operated a total of six between 1958 and 1964. G-APSA was one of the first, entering service in 1959, having been bought almost new from Canadian airline Maritime Central. It is seen here in Nicosia at the end of a trooping flight.

The airline found a willing user in the Ministry, and indeed, it must have been a relief after years of York and Hermes operations for the government to have at its disposal such a reliable and efficient aircraft. It showed: in 1959 one of Eagle's DC-6s flew more than 3,800 hours, the highest annual

The Aviation Photo Company

utilisation ever achieved by a British piston-engine airliner at that time. When the aircraft were not engaged in trooping and other Ministry flights, they were flying holidaymakers to the Mediterranean, or charter passengers across the Atlantic, a growing market. In time G-APSA was repainted in full Eagle colours of red and black, with a large E on the tail.

There was a further change in colour scheme in 1960 when Cunard Steamship acquired a major stake in Eagle, just one of many shipping companies that with the government's encouragement invested in Britain's charter airlines.

The name was changed to Cunard Eagle, and the large E given an elegant tweak; surely the addition of such a prestigious

shareholder meant great things for the future, especially on the North Atlantic, where Cunard was second to none in the passenger market. Indeed, the airline began to acquire turboprop Britannias and was the first independent airline to buy jets, two Boeing 707s intended for a scheduled service between London and New York. But this promising venture was almost immediately vetoed by the British government, and Cunard's ardour suffered a rapid detumescence. The shipping line swiftly swapped partners, adulterously jumping into bed with BOAC, where the two sired a blue-blooded offspring, BOAC-Cunard, which flew BOAC's transatlantic services for the next four years. For Cunard Eagle, meanwhile, which gave up the two jets and a promising network of services in the Caribbean as part of the divorce settlement, there was little time to repent at leisure. Mr Bamberg bought out the Cunard share in 1963, renamed the airline British Eagle, and went on to accumulate a large fleet of Britannias with which he dominated the trooping market for many years.

The DC-6s were still the front-runners during these turbulent times, though with the advent of the Britannias, the end of the Douglas primacy was clearly approaching. Things looked up in 1962 after the government awarded the airline a contract to operate the regular link between London and Adelaide in Australia in support of the Weapons Research Establishment at Woomera. This contract had been operated variously by Freddie Laker's Avro Tudors, RAF Comet 2s, and Dan-Air's Bristol Freighter; once again the government had reason to be grateful to have access to an aircraft that was fit for purpose, the DC-6. In turn, with the conversion of two of British Eagle's newly acquired Britannias for the freight role, thus making them eligible for the Woomera contract, the DC-6s began to leave the fleet. Two of them, including G-APSA, went to Saudi Arabia early in 1964 in exchange for three Skymasters, needed to support British Eagle's charter operations out of Liverpool.

Saudi Arabian Airlines, or Saudair, flew the DC-6s for at least five years. They operated alongside Boeing 707s, Convairliners and Dakotas on domestic routes and occasional international services from Jeddah to Amman, Asmara, Beirut, Cairo and Damascus, as well as flying cargo flights to Frankfurt. In 1971 the Saudi government donated the two DC-6s to Yemen Airways, based in Sana'a, in what had been North Yemen, where they joined the fleet of this fledgling operator. In due course they were replaced in front-line service

The Aviation Photo Company

by Boeing 727 jets, and by 1981 had been withdrawn from service and stored in the open at Sana'a. And there G-APSA might have languished, a sleeping beauty indeed, if a handsome prince had not come to save it. His name was Jeremy Instone, grandson of Sir Samuel Instone, the founder of Instone Air Line, one of the very first airlines to take to the air after the Great War, and later to become part of Imperial Airways in 1924. Sir Samuel died in 1937, but his family took to the air again in 1981, resurrecting the name Instone Air Line. Jeremy Instone takes up the story:

We operated two Bristol 170 Freighters for a number of years as Instone Air Line carrying both freight but mostly horses. We then stopped operating them ourselves and passed them to Air Atlantique/Atlantic to operate on our behalf. Eventually they were sold to Canada. They mostly carried horses for us and freight for Atlantic. We had an hourly rate we charged AA when they carried freight and they would charge us an hourly rate when we carried horses.

We purchased the DC-6 with the intention of carrying horses. It was in fairly bad condition but we didn't realise quite how bad. It was certainly a major factor that it had been on the British register. Preparing for a ferry flight ex Yemen was quite an undertaking and the ferry itself was pretty fraught. One engine blew on take-off and the aircraft returned to Sana'a while we sent another engine. When it happened again to another engine the crew decided to fly on to Djibouti, having tired of the delights of Yemen. The engine was changed with the help of the French Air Force and the aircraft flew on to Athens where it deposited a large amount of fuel on the apron, due to rather tired tanks. The airport authorities weren't very amused so the crew made a quick exit to Southend. I can safely say that if we had known how difficult/expensive the project was going to be we would not have embarked on it!

By the time it entered service small jets were more appropriate for horses, so the aircraft was just used for freight. Atlantic never owned G-APSA. It was always owned by us and AA operated it on a sort of lease arrangement – fly by the hour. Originally we had our name down the side and tail but then as they used it more we allowed them to have just their name/logo. It was mainly used as a back-up for courier company night time ops and by the car companies, moving components between factories. Eventually the aircraft was grounded as it was really too old/expensive to operate and more modern aircraft were taking over. It is still parked at Coventry and was given by us to a company who hoped to restore it to a luxury passenger aircraft. This has not happened as they have not raised the funds.

The Aviation Photo Company

The Instones brought the aircraft back to Southend in April 1987, and after two years of restoration, the aircraft entered service, flying alongside Air Atlantique's DC-6 G-SIXC.

They continued to fly in service for another incredible sixteen years. For the first ten years, 1989 to 1998, the two together flew an average of 577 hours per year, just under fifty hours a month; after that, for the final six years, it was around half that, 266 hours per year. The last commercial flight of G-APSA seems to have been in 23 September 2004 when it carried car parts from Coventry to Zweibrücken; G-SIXC operated its last commercial flight on 25 October, again carrying car components. That was not, however, the end of it. Eighteen months later, both aircraft were in the air again, appearing at air shows during the summer of 2006, and doing some film work. G-SIXC was finally grounded, but G-APSA flew on, and in 2008, forty years after the demise of Harold Bamberg's airline, it was painted in British Eagle colours; it enjoyed an active year, flying around Europe and appearing at a number of air shows.

But it was to prove its last. There were occasional appearances later, but the aircraft was grounded in 2010 due to corrosion problems. Sister G-SIXC was converted into a restaurant at the base at Coventry airport, while G-APSA was eventually bought by the South Wales Aviation Museum and dismantled ahead of a planned move to St Athan in 2020.

Ralf Manteufel

18: BRISTOL BRITANNIA 102 G-ANBA

The Aviation Photo Company

There was widespread recognition after the war that Britain needed to build airliners that could fly across the Atlantic. Imperial Airways had pioneered transatlantic flying boat services, and successor BOAC performed invaluable service with its converted Liberator bombers, helped out by three large Boeing flying boats. But the Americans were already building the next generation of long-range airliners as the war came to an end, and Britain needed to at least catch up with, if not leapfrog, their designs. The Brabazon Committee did try to set out guidelines but somehow mangled the transatlantic designs, even though three of the proposed aircraft were specifically intended for long-haul services. Two of them, the huge Brabazon and the jet-powered Comet, failed to make the grade, even if the Comet had some success in later years in other roles, but the great might-have-been, the Type 3 designed for medium- to long-haul Empire routes, for which the Avro 693 was proposed, never made it out of the design office; instead the government squandered resources on an interim design, the Avro Tudor, whose unhappy tale is related elsewhere in this book. That still left BOAC looking for both medium- and long-range airliners, so after the Tudor had been rejected, and the Avro 693 project cancelled, the corporation issued further specifications to fill these roles.

Bristol had by far the best idea, to build Lockheed Constellations under licence that would have been powered by Bristol's own Centaurus engines. National pride perhaps, ineptitude on the part of the Treasury more probably, caused this idea to be stillborn; there is, of course, irony in BOAC buying Canadian licence-built DC-4s just two years later. Other manufacturers put up proposals but Bristol came up with the next most promising design, the Bristol 175, which over time evolved into a long-range airliner, seating around 100 passengers and powered by Proteus turboprops, also built by Bristol. It was ordered by BOAC late in 1948. Everything about the Britannia, as the 175 came to be known, was complicated. The engines used a reverse-flow intake, with cooling air at one stage moving forward before being decanted aft through various compressors, diffusers, elbows, vanes and pipes; the engine would also have been used on the Saunders-Roe Princess flying boat, hence the design intended to minimise the effect of sea spray. Very few commentators even mention the electrical systems, which powered just about everything else on the Britannia and were a constant source of bafflement and anxiety. The main undercarriage on retraction performed a rearwards somersault before ending upside down, inside the rear inboard engine nacelle. A good-looking craft, the Britannia was fast, quiet, comfortable and – a first for British airliners – it had sufficient range. There were two versions, the original 102 series, referred to by BOAC staff as the 'Baby Brit' – it was never called the 'whispering giant', that was just marketing hype – and the larger, longer-range 300 series, which is discussed in another section.

The Britannia had a prolonged development, and as a consequence missed its slot on the commercial timeline; there was little inclination to buy a new propeller design when faster turbojets were already flying and poised to enter service just one year later. The first flight was in August 1952, but it was to be almost five years before the type entered service with BOAC, in February 1957: Pan American inaugurated the Boeing 707 in October 1958. The Britannia was almost there, had been granted its Certificate of Airworthiness and the first examples handed over to BOAC in December 1955, but during further proving flights a new phenomenon arose when the engines began flaming out in certain atmospheric conditions, and it took many months to work out how to modify them in order to ameliorate if not

entirely resolve this problem. As a tyro salesman with Lloyd International I recall the operations manager advising us that one of our Britannias had suffered a four-engine flame out; at least the modifications ensured that all the engines restarted immediately.

G-ANBA was the first production Britannia 102 off the line, flying in August 1954, and was used intensively for trials after the second prototype Britannia had been lost in a forced landing on the banks of the Severn. G-ANBA was sent to Short Brothers in Belfast for refurbishment in 1957 before entering service with BOAC later that year on routes to South Africa, the Far East and Australasia. The 102 series could carry around ninety passengers and had a practical range of more than 3,000 miles. G-ANBA spent some time flying for BOAC's pool partners, Nigeria Airways and Malayan Airways, before being withdrawn from service in 1962, after five short years, joining its sisters in storage at Cambridge.

BOAC paid £768,000 for each of its Britannia 102s, but failed to depreciate the aircraft realistically, a mistake that would come back to haunt the corporation in 1963 when it had to announce losses and accumulated deficits of more than £64 million, around one third of which was attributable to writing off the Britannia fleets. The corporation was able to claw back some of the losses by selling off these relatively young aircraft, but the figures underline the extent of the shortfall. Euravia, newly renamed Britannia Airways, bought six of the stored Britannia 102s late in 1964 for around £1 million; the arithmetic works out at £167,000 each, £600,000 less than BOAC paid. Britannia had to pay to have the aircraft modified and brought into service, but the deal emphasises one of the few advantages that the British independent airlines enjoyed, namely the ability to buy

The Aviation Photo Company

corporation hand-me-downs at very competitive prices! G-ANBA was delivered to Britannia at Luton in March 1965, converted by Scottish Aviation at Prestwick from its ninety-two-seat configuration to 112 seats, and started flying for Britannia in May, taking over from Euravia's Constellations.

Britannia flew from a number of regional airports as well as Luton. Manchester, Newcastle and Glasgow served important catchment areas and deserved direct connections, something that BEA, for example, failed to understand; the corporation expected most of its regional traffic to be funnelled through Heathrow onto connecting flights. Yet much of the early attraction of inclusive-tour holidays, especially in the Midlands, the north of England and Scotland, lay in their easy and straightforward pattern of operations; direct flights were much less intimidating to passengers who otherwise rarely used airline services. Direct flights saved time for the

passengers, of course, and because of the longer sectors, improved annual utilisation for the airline. The Britannias were long-legged, able to reach the Canaries without a refuelling stop. After the hurly-burly of the early 1960s, Britannia's orderly flight operations with aircraft that were fit for purpose gave the airline, and its tour operators, a commanding presence in the charter and holiday market.

Britannia eventually relieved BOAC of eight of its early Britannias. The remainder went to BKS, which used them on Newcastle scheduled services during the week and inclusive tours at the weekend, and to Freddie Laker, who bought the last two for his eponymous airline. Their final full summer season with Britannia would be in 1969, seven Britannias flying alongside five Boeing 737s, in itself testament to the extraordinary growth that the airline, under the new ownership of the Thomson Group, now enjoyed. G-ANBA was withdrawn from service in November and broken up in June of the following year. The remaining four soldiered on into 1970, useful as a back-up for the jets and also available for ad hoc charter work; the final flight, by G-ANBL, was on 29 December 1970.

The Britannia 102s were in service with Britannia for five years, some for six, the same length of service as BOAC. With BOAC the turboprops introduced new standards of luxury on routes to Africa and the Far East, serving a high-flying elite at prices to match. Britannia's Britannias introduced new levels of comfort and reliability to a more down-to-earth clientele, and at bargain prices. In their different ways, both airlines used the Britannia to fulfil new expectations about the product they offered, albeit at diametrically opposed ends of the market. The Britannia was nothing if not flexible, and the story continues in the section dealing with the larger Britannia 312 series.

19: DE HAVILLAND DH.114 HERON G-ANCI

To me the puzzle about the Heron is why it was not built sooner. Its little sister, the Dove, first flew in 1945. The Heron is a stretched Dove, with twice the number of engines and able to carry twice the number of passengers, up to seventeen. But the Brabazon Committee's slot for the four-engine, fourteen- to eighteen-seat feederliner had been reserved for the Miles Marathon, and if de Havilland had proceeded with a competitive product to the official Brabazon-sanctioned Type 5A feederliner, I suppose government officials would have been shouting 'Not fair!' It is also questionable whether a market existed for such a relatively small airliner. Captain Fresson, a shrewd airline operator in the Highlands of Scotland, thought it did. He pointed out that the Dakota was good for longer routes but too expensive for the shorter-haul stages; what he wanted was a 'monoplane reproduction of the pre-war DH.86 four-engined biplane, seating fourteen to sixteen passengers, with variable-pitch air screws and de-icing equipment'. That is what the Heron offered, sturdily underpinned by a fixed undercarriage.

It first flew in 1950, five years after the Dove, and entered service in Norway in 1952. BEA bought three to replace de Havilland Rapides on Scottish island and ambulance services. The pioneer British operator was Jersey Airlines, which used the aircraft on its Gatwick–Jersey and Jersey–Paris services from May 1953. Squadron Leader West of *Aeronautics* was impressed: 'Although this aircraft is small, I found that I had ample room when I was seated – and I require a lot of space.

I was also very much impressed with the square-type windows which are a great improvement on the earlier types.' The cabin was only 5ft 8in high, but the large windows made it airy, and the squadron leader has a point; the seats were singles on either side of the aisle, so there was room to spread out.

G-ANCI was bought new by Dragon Airways for services out of Liverpool and Newcastle. You would expect an airline with a name like Dragon to have Welsh connections, and that is indeed where it started, flying joyrides from an airstrip near the Butlin's holiday camp at Pwllheli, but by the time G-ANCI was delivered in June 1955 the airline had moved to Liverpool, and later that year transferred itself to

The Aviation Photo Company

Newcastle in order to fly a network of services on behalf of Hunting-Clan. Hunting-Clan had used its Viscounts and Vikings to fly a northern network from Newcastle to London, Manchester and Glasgow and also to a number of points in Europe but realised quickly that it was not going to work, so the Viscounts were leased out, the routes cut back and Dragon's Herons used instead. *Flight* magazine noted in October 1955: 'On the Newcastle–London route, Herons of Dragon Airways will be used in place of Vikings, since the capacity of the smaller aircraft is regarded as adequate for the traffic offering (passengers carried on the route last winter averaged 11 per aircraft).' Then Hunting-Clan had another idea, and together with two local shipping lines, bought out Dragon Airways and transferred all northern network operations to it. But that did not work out either, and in January 1957 Dragon suspended all its Newcastle services.

Help was on the way, however. If Hunting-Clan could not make a successful fist of it, Silver City, with much more experience of short-haul operations, thought it could. Silver City's parent company, British Aviation Services (BAS), had gone on a buying spree, having already bought Manx Airlines and Lancashire Aircraft Corporation; Dragon Airways was next on the list. BAS also controlled Silver City and Air Kruise, both at Lydd Ferryfield, and flying boat operator Aquila. All the northern airlines were grouped together into its northern division under the Silver City name, but retained their separate bases, Ronaldsway on the Isle of Man, Blackpool and Newcastle.

Silver City retained two of Dragon's Herons, but not G-ANCI. It was sold to Lord Calthorpe, an aspiring entrepreneur and pilot, who quickly found work for it flying on behalf of Blackbushe-based Dan-Air Services, with whom it spent the summer of 1957 flying to the Channel Islands.

The Aviation Photo Company

Unusually for Dan-Air, the cheat line is not red; it retained the previous blue but the lettering was in black shaded with red. After that lease had run its course, G-ANCI was transferred to Cambrian early in 1958 to boost this Welsh airline's capacity, and repainted in the airline's red colours. Cambrian was on a roll, alas short-lived, flying two Dakotas and now four Herons to the Channel Islands from Bristol, Cardiff and Liverpool, and more ambitiously to Belfast, Manchester and Paris from Bristol and Cardiff.

But by 1958 fewer Britons were spending their holidays in the Channel Islands and more of them were flying abroad on international inclusive tours. Cambrian's loadings suffered, especially to the Channel Islands; instead of around 40,000 passengers per year, Cambrian managed just under 10,000 in 1958. Drastic measures were called for and in October 1958 all services were suspended, the Herons grounded and

The Aviation Photo Company

then disposed of. The Dakotas were retained and used on the quickly reinstated Manchester services that had shown the most promise. And indeed, under Wing Commander Elwin's pragmatic leadership, Cambrian soon pulled itself out of the shadows and with considerable help and investment from BEA went on to flourish as a respected low-cost contributor to the airline industry. What happened to Cambrian can be read in the section on the Vickers Viscount.

Lord Calthorpe had to take back G-ANCI, and this time he became more actively involved in its future, leasing the aircraft to a new Leeds-based airline, North-South Airlines, and occasionally piloting the aircraft himself. North-South started by flying from Leeds to points on the south coast, which included Sandown on the Isle of Wight, then suspended the services during the winter of 1959–60. G-ANCI undertook some limited charter flying before resuming its

Bournemouth, Exeter and Sandown weekend services for the summer of 1960. Revenue and utilisation were bolstered by midweek charter flying from Manchester.

North-South made few livery changes to the Cambrian scheme, and it is always good to see a Union flag. Lord Calthorpe was meanwhile becoming more proactive in the management of his aircraft and rechristened his own company Mercury Airlines; originally it had been named somewhat injudiciously Overseas Air Transport, just as Overseas Aviation and its Canadairs were grabbing the headlines in a not altogether flattering manner. He took back G-ANCI and from 1961 flew it on scheduled services from Manchester to Exeter and the Isle of Wight.

Meanwhile, its former operator, North-South, was trying unsuccessfully to recover from a bad 1961 season, which had not been helped by the withdrawal of Lord Calthorpe's two

The Aviation Photo Company

Ron Roberts

Herons, and early in 1962 put up the shutters. Mercury now took over some of North-South's routes out of Leeds, and over the next three summers developed a network out of Manchester, as well as continuing to link the Isle of Wight and Exeter with Liverpool and Leeds. A respectable charter programme was also undertaken, including flights for the Atomic Energy Authority and the Ministry of Defence, and some inclusive-tour flights to Ostend.

All the more surprising, then, that suddenly, at the end of the 1964 season, Lord Calthorpe announced he was closing the airline. The catalyst for this drastic action was the return of a Labour government following the election on 15 October. Despite Mr Wilson's new administration only having a majority of four, Lord Calthorpe's backers had major concerns about the policies and consequences of a socialist government, and in truth the independents could expect even less favourable treatment

in the immediate future, an apparently daunting prospect after thirteen years of Tory ambivalence and broken promises. The closure was tidily done. British Midland and Dan-Air were awarded many of Mercury's routes, and British Midland also took over Mercury's handling unit at Manchester, and its traffic manager, Michael Bishop, later to be the airline's driving force and charismatic leader. With hindsight, Mercury's closure seems uncalled for, but that is easy enough to say when it is not your own money at stake. No other airline at the time closed down for such overtly political reasons, and the Labour government gave the independents an easier time than was expected; there was no forced nationalisation, existing institutions were respected and the new government's level of competence was no more or less than that of the Conservatives.

Lord Calthorpe regained control of the two Herons and a Dakota. G-ANCI was leased to South Coast Air Services, based at Shoreham, during the summer of 1965, before being bought by Executive Air Transport, an air-taxi operator and engineering company based at Coventry. It was leased to an Israeli airline, Avitour, for a year, returning early in 1967 before setting off for a stint with a small Belgian airline, during which time it flew commuter services on behalf of Sabena; it carried Sabena 'Common Market Commuter' titling as it flew between Brussels, Eindhoven and Rotterdam five days a week.

When it returned to the United Kingdom at the end of 1968 it was bought by Keegan Aviation, which advertised it for sale: 'It is well equipped with airline radio aids, has 15 passenger seats, plus two crew, has ample hours available for immediate use in public transport category. A first class aeroplane.' The asking price was £17,500. It quickly found a buyer in Channel Airways, and 'Mike' Keegan delivered the aircraft himself to Southend on 14 November 1968.

Channel Airways, a spunky airline that was prepared to have a go at anything, had recently inaugurated a so-called 'bus-stop' service, starting from Southend, then via Luton, East Midlands, Leeds, Teesside, Newcastle and Edinburgh to finish at Aberdeen. The idea was to take the flights for as few or as many sectors as the passenger wished; travelling all the way was exhausting, with average sectors of only 65 miles and ten-minute turnarounds at stops en route. There were a number of feeder services, from Norwich and Ipswich to Southend, another serving East Midlands and Liverpool. Herons were needed for these feeder services, and G-ANCI

was the first of four to enter service, seen below in the hangar looking very smart after a repaint into Channel's gold and black livery.

G-ANCI remained in service for a year and then its Certificate of Airworthiness expired in November 1969. It was withdrawn from service, and later scrapped; so was the 'bus-stop' service at the end of 1969. Channel's later history is recounted in the section on the Hawker Siddeley Trident.

Channel Airways most likely did not pay the full asking price for G-ANCI, but it indicates how well the second-hand value of these useful airliners held up. The initial

The Aviation Photo Company

purchase price, fifteen years earlier, was around £40,000, too high for most people, although corporate customers and air forces were ready buyers, just as they had been for the Dove. That high price was a problem for the Heron; a second-hand Dakota, which carried more passengers and freight, could be bought for between £15,000 and £20,000. And despite Captain Fresson's reasoning, the Dakota did not in fact cost much more to operate; the margin was surprisingly narrow. Later Herons had retractable undercarriages, which added 20 miles an hour to the original cruising speed of 165mph; some operators re-engined their aircraft with American Ly-

coming engines, which further enhanced the performance. Two prototypes and 148 production aircraft were built, the last in 1964.

Four Herons are preserved in the UK, one displayed dramatically on a plinth outside the old terminal building at Croydon, representing the aircraft that flew the last passenger service out of Croydon on 30 September 1959. Two others are at Newark and at the de Havilland Aircraft Museum at Salisbury Hall; both were formerly BEA ambulance aircraft used in Scotland. The fourth, preserved Heron G-AORG, is flown out of Jersey in Jersey Airlines colours.

20: DOUGLAS DC-7C G-AOIE

Douglas did not really want to build the DC-7, the ultimate stretch of the original DC-4 design but was persuaded to do so by long-standing customer American Airlines. Even then, Douglas only thought it would build a small number for this airline. In fact the company built 338, an impressive total for the last of the piston-engine line as the jet era approached. The DC-7 had powerful but troublesome Wright Turbo-Compound piston engines, a longer fuselage than the DC-6 and bigger wings, so was able to carry more fuel. As with the DC-6, Douglas tweaked the design so that the final version, the DC-7C, evocatively named the Seven Seas, could carry its payload of passengers non-stop across the Atlantic both eastbound and westbound, a saving of several

hours; it could even fly eastbound non-stop from San Francisco to London, and across the North Pole from Scandinavia to Japan and California. DC-7Cs entered service with Pan American during 1956 and required a competitive response from European airlines in particular; its performance was superior to the Super Constellation, and Alitalia, KLM, Sabena, Swissair, Scandinavian Airlines System and TAI in France all bought the type. So did BOAC.

BOAC should not have had to buy DC-7Cs at all as it already had the Bristol Britannia on order, the first of which ought to have entered service in 1955. But fate ordained otherwise, and in any case the first series of Britannia was not regarded as a transatlantic aircraft. The year 1954 came and went, with no sign of the Britannia being anywhere near ready, and so early in 1955 Sir Miles Thomas, BOAC's chairman, floated the idea of buying DC-7Cs as a stopgap until the long-range Britannia, the 300 series, which had been ordered in 1953, could join the fleet, optimistically forecast for October 1956. The 300-series Britannia would do everything that the DC-7C did, flying more or less the same number of passengers at much the same speed over similar distances but could carry a bigger payload and, in charter configuration, about thirty more passengers.

When BOAC announced its order for ten DC-7Cs at a cost of £10.6 million, *Flight* magazine commented: 'The Britannia promises to be more than a match for its rival, and so far as delivery dates are concerned there is little to choose between them.' If only. The first DC-7C for BOAC, fitted out for sixty first-class passengers, was delivered at the end of October 1956 and began flying the New York service in January 1957, exactly one year before the Britannia entered service on the London to New York run. All the DC-7Cs had been delivered by April 1957, and took over the twenty weekly New York flights, including the first-class Monarch services.

They had a short reign: first Britannias and then jet Comets and Boeing 707s took over, and by the end of 1961 the DC-7Cs had been withdrawn. Two were converted into freighters. G-AOIE, the fifth, was laid up for more than two years, an indication how sudden and pervasive the jet transformation had been; it also meant that BOAC was still paying standing charges and amortising the DC-7C fleet when no revenue was coming in. The only likely takers were the charter airlines, and indeed the bulk of BOAC's fleet was sold on via an American broker to Saturn, an American supple-

Tony Eastwood Collection

mental, in 1963 and 1964, for less than £150,000 each: later BOAC had to write off £4.6 million of the 'residual' value of the DC-7Cs. G-AOIE went to a new British independent, Caledonian Airways, that had started commercial flying in November 1961 using a DC-7C leased from Belgian state airline Sabena, just as anxious to be rid of its DC-7Cs as BOAC but commercially somewhat more nimble. Caledonian used five of Sabena's aircraft over the course of time, two of which were lost in accidents, and eventually the penny dropped for BOAC, which made G-AOIE available in April 1964: 'Obviously, as Caledonian were going to get the aircraft anyway it seemed better that they should get them from BOAC,' noted *Flight* magazine. 'Now common sense has prevailed and BOAC have agreed to a lease purchase deal agreement with Caledonian.'

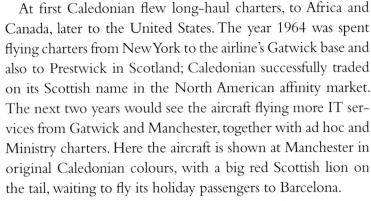

R.A. Scholefield

The Aviation Photo Company

At first Caledonian flew long-haul charters, to Africa and Canada, later to the United States. The year 1964 was spent flying charters from New York to the airline's Gatwick base and also to Prestwick in Scotland; Caledonian successfully traded on its Scottish name in the North American affinity market. The next two years would see the aircraft flying more IT services from Gatwick and Manchester, together with ad hoc and Ministry charters. Here the aircraft is shown at Manchester in original Caledonian colours, with a big red Scottish lion on the tail, waiting to fly its holiday passengers to Barcelona.

In 1965 the first of Caledonian's Britannias began to enter service, three acquired on lease-purchase from BOAC; the corporation was not going to make the same mistake again! G-AOIE was repainted in the new blue and gold livery and stayed in service for another two years. By the end of 1966 G-AOIE was idle, only flying very occasionally, until her delivery flight to Brussels in April 1967 following her sale to a Dutch airline.

The aircraft's swansong was with Schreiner Airways, which took on the aircraft in 1967 for a final season's inclusive-tour flying, before Schreiner itself decided to pull out of the business in October that year.

After that, the aircraft's history is convoluted. It was stored in Holland before being bought in 1969 by aviation entrepreneur Bill Armstrong, the founder of Autair, and it was registered in the name of Autair Limited, the British parent company of a number of helicopter operations worldwide. Armstrong had previously owned Rhodesian Air Services, which subsequently became Air Trans-Africa, based in Salisbury, Rhodesia in which he continued to have an interest; this airline operated DC-7 freighters in the late 1960s. The aircraft reappeared on the British register as G-AOIE in November 1969, but whatever the plans were, they did not come to fruition. The aircraft was ferried from Holland to Shannon, in Ireland, in 1970, its last flight, and was later used by the fire department there, before being transferred to the DC-7 Aero Museum at Waterford in 1982; the picture shows it in the process of being dismantled for transportation. When the Waterford venture closed, the aircraft was stored and eventually scrapped, although the nose section was saved and transferred to the Cavan and Leitrim Railway at Dromod, where it now nestles between old railcars, the nose section of a Boeing 707, and a Great Northern Railway Gardner-engined bus.

Fergal Goodman

21: BRISTOL BRITANNIA 312 G-AOVF

Britannias are mentioned throughout this book in different sections, an indication of the importance of Britain's long-range airliner project in the scheme of things. Before the war Imperial Airways had tried to pioneer long-distance routes, and when peace returned the need to match the performance and range of American airliners was realised, if not always fully understood. BOAC eventually whittled down their requirements to the Medium Range and Long Range Empire proposals, and the Bristol Britannia emerged as the aircraft that most closely met both specifications, thanks in part to the development potential of Bristol's own Proteus turboprop, which allowed the design to evolve from a forty-four-seat piston-engine design to one that that could carry more than twice as many passengers 50mph faster, with much greater range, superior payload and in turbine comfort. The longer-range 300 series benefited from a fuselage extension, extra fuel tanks in the wing, beefed up landing gear and uprated Bristol Proteus engines, and they proved to be excellent load carriers, especially as freighters, able to carry 16½ tons in the voluminous cabin over 4,000 miles. BOAC as well as other airlines were interested; El Al Israel Airlines and Canadian Pacific placed small orders, and valiant attempts were made to sell the aircraft in the American market. I am sure that the Britannia would have sold even better if Douglas had not put up a formidable competitor in the DC-7C, which could do almost everything that the Britannia could do and was available earlier. BOAC settled on eighteen of the 312 series, the first of which entered service at the end of December 1957, just three days before El Al's inaugural Britannia flight.

Maybe it was the Sabra spirit and national pride, but El Al's Britannia operations just thrived; the airline seemed able to derive maximum benefit from the aircraft's undoubted capabilities and, helped by smart route planning, consistently flew non-stop sectors across the Atlantic from London and Paris at a time when many airlines still had to stop and refuel en route, usually at Canada's Goose Bay or Gander. Despite BOAC's experience with long-haul flying, having bought DC-7Cs as insurance against the late delivery of the Britannias, the corporation struggled at first with its Britannia 312 operations. During the first year of operations fewer than three-quarters of westbound flights across the Atlantic were non-stop and, even worse, half of them were late. BOAC had to devote much time and effort to debugging the aircraft, despite its previous experience with the smaller 'Baby Brit' 102 series Britannia; to the corporation's frustration the bigger Britannia was still virtually under development. BOAC's comments in later years are telling: 'Too much effort was concentrated [by Bristol] on Bristol's own stuff, the airframe and the engines'.
'Approximately a third of the total equipment of the Britannia was electrical, the majority supplied by subcontractors,' explained *Flight* magazine in an article dated 31 January 1963. 'Not to mince words, some of it was "simply not good enough" … It was possible to pick out other components which caused Bristol and BOAC to enter into a series of very expensive development programmes *after* the aircraft was in scheduled service.'

All eighteen Britannias were delivered to BOAC over the period of fifteen months, starting in September 1957 and with the final delivery in January 1959. G-AOVF joined up in January 1958. Utilisation was low at first, around three and a half to four and a half hours per day over the first year, picking up as the year wore on.

However, BOAC persevered with the type; for an interim period of two years Britannias were the flagships of the fleet, which included flying the prestigious all first-class London to New York services, until displaced, first by Comet 4s and then in 1960 by Boeing 707s. Britannias continued flying to North America, serving other points including San Francisco and Chicago, and to New York indirectly via Manchester and Prestwick in Scotland; most flying to Bermuda and the Caribbean remained with the Britannias, and they were used by BOAC's pool partners and 'associated airlines'. G-AOVF inaugurated BOAC's round the world service in August 1959, flying to Tokyo via North America and the Pacific; in Tokyo it met the Comet, which had flown eastabout from London to Tokyo. By this time the Britannias were flying almost eight hours a day; they carried ninety-one passengers in a mixed first/tourist configuration. BOAC even managed to wangle a discount on air fares for turboprop equipment, and Britannias were used on the short-lived 'Skycoach' low-fare services to Africa, the Caribbean and Far East. By 1962 and '63, the Britannias were only flying six hours a day; Britannias could still be used on cabotage and other routes that did not see

The Aviation Photo Company

much competition, but those were getting fewer and fewer. The decision was taken to withdraw them, and G-AOVF flew its last BOAC revenue service in January 1964. It did not remain idle for long.

There were two significant British independent airlines in the 1960s, British United (BUA) and British Eagle; and there were also a number of smaller specialised operators. Both BUA and British Eagle acquired large fleets of Britannias that they used on a variety of services. BUA flew Britannias on trooping flights to British garrisons in Africa, to the Middle and Far East as well as on low-fare flights to Central and East Africa; two were converted into freighters for the Africargo service. BUA's Britannias began to be replaced by jet equipment in the mid-1960s. But the true enthusiast for Britannias was Harold Bamberg's British Eagle. He acquired, through lease-purchase, thirteen of BOAC's Britannia 312s (the others went to Caledonian and Lloyd International), as well as eight other Britannias. Some were converted into freighters, some were used on the restricted-frequency scheduled services from Belfast, Edinburgh and Glasgow to London Heathrow, others flew inclusive-tour passengers on their holidays, or special group charters across the Atlantic. But most of them performed the company's contract services, flying for the government and its defence ministry, carrying British forces and their families to Africa, Singapore, Malaya and Hong Kong, hauling personnel and equipment to Australia's Woomera rocket range and bringing British immigrants to Australia on behalf of Qantas. At its peak, the airline had more than fifty flights a month to Australia and the Far East. G-AOVF joined the fleet in March 1964 and was given the name *Friendship*. Here the aircraft is seen during a turnaround at Singapore's Paya Lebar airport.

The Aviation Photo Company

As the long-term government contracts drew to a close in 1968, British Eagle decided to convert G-AOVF into a freighter, and the aircraft was dispatched to its engineering centre in Liverpool in February, returning six months later as a series 312F. It did not see much more service with British Eagle, which found it difficult to readjust after the loss of much of its contract flying and was continually thwarted by officialdom in its efforts to develop elsewhere. The airline went out of business in November 1968 and its aircraft were parked up; there was a sudden glut of Britannias on the second-hand market. Despite its freight door, G-AOVF languished at Heathrow for more than a year, having been repossessed by BOAC, still its registered owner. I cannot help thinking that the last thing BOAC wanted was to have all its old Britannias back! But they all found new homes eventually; many of them were passed on to Monarch Airlines, a charter airline based at Luton that had been formed by two of Harold Bamberg's former colleagues.

The Aviation Photo Company

The Aviation Photo Company

No reader should be deprived of the splendours of the Monarch livery! Britannia G-AOVT is now on display at Duxford.

Two of the former Eagle Britannias, including G-AOVF, went to Donaldson International, a new charter airline based at Gatwick but with a stylish, Scottish persona. Donaldson flew ad hoc charters from Gatwick, and holiday charters from Glasgow; but the winter months were lean. That changed in 1970 when Donaldson bought G-AOVF and began using it on freight charters. In the winter Donaldson flew the aircraft on regular freight services to Hong Kong, a strong 'two-way' market; as well as manufactured goods, bales of clothing materials were sourced from Britain and the Continent and sent to Hong Kong, where they were then made up and returned as fashion items. During the summer of 1971 G-AOVF went back into passenger configuration and was used for the Glasgow holiday programme, its last summer of flying passengers, before resuming freight operations the following winter.

The Britannia continued flying cargo into the middle of 1972, by which time Donaldson had acquired a fleet of Boeing 707s, some of them expensively converted with freight doors. G-AOVF was parked at Coventry but soon found another user, a relatively new cargo airline based at Gatwick known as International Aviation Services or IAS for short.

IAS was the brainchild of aviation veteran Alan Stocks, who had previously managed two Kenya-based charter airlines, both of which flew Britannias. By 1972 he was starting to fly on his account and G-AOVF was the second Britannia to join his cargo airline. Interestingly, his expertise, and that of his partner Robin Grant, in the African market marked a pivot away from the Far East. With its poor infrastructure, long distances and increasing demand for Western goods, Africa was a developing destination for cargo airlines. It was difficult and

The Aviation Photo Company

time-consuming to transport goods by sea, rail and road to Central and East Africa; much better to fly them there direct, with the added bonus that time-sensitive return cargos, flowers, fruit and fresh vegetables, were now available. As for Nigeria, with its new-found oil wealth, the country's main port was clogged for many years; flying cargo in meant avoiding the bottlenecks. A second major market was in the oil-rich Gulf States, where there was increasing demand for European luxury goods; cargo flights from Britain almost always picked up additional business at Dutch, German and Italian airports.

G-AOVF spent three years with IAS, flying alongside a Canadair CL-44 and Douglas DC-8 jets, and IAS leased in extra capacity for the peaks. In December 1976 IAS offered the Britannia for sale, and eventually it passed to Invicta.

The Aviation Photo Company

Invicta appears elsewhere, under the heading for the Douglas DC-4 Skymaster. As an airline it metamorphosed continuously during its two decades under the direction of its founders, the Kennards, based at the Kent airport of Manston. At first it was a short-haul airline, ferrying holidaymakers across the Channel, but then merged with British Midland Airways – both companies by then were owned by the same shareholders – an arrangement that suited neither airline. After the divorce Invicta resumed operations in 1969 as a cargo airline, but then bought some former Air Canada Vickers Vanguards, so went back into passenger charters, later acquiring two Boeings. By this time the company had backing from the European Ferries Group; however, the passenger business did not prosper and the airline increasingly relied on cargo charters and contract flying for other airlines. Operations were terminated abruptly in 1975 when European Ferries withdrew its support, but that was not the end of it. Early in 1976 the Kennards resurrected the name and operations of Invicta, leasing two Britannias from IAS Cargo, one of them G-AOVF. In November 1978 Invicta bought the aircraft and it appeared in Invicta colours.

The aircraft continued in service for another two years, flying livestock between England and Italy, before it got further lift under its wings when it was sold in 1981 to a company in Zaire, International Air Center Airlines (IAC), and placed on the country's register as 9Q-CAZ. There were a number of Britannias in Zaire at this stage hauling goods and supplies, even the occasional passenger, around this vast country, which has little in the way of infrastructure or roads; the last Britannia only left Zaire in 1997! What should have been a three-year operation was cut short, however, and by June 1981 the aircraft was back at Manston, Invicta having

also given up the ghost by this time. There the aircraft remained until February 1983 when it was ferried to Southend following its sale to a New Zealand company, which then fell through. Its last flight was on 31 May 1984 to RAF Cosford after it was sold to the Cosford Aerospace Museum, G-AOVF clearly still in fine fettle!

Now the aircraft is in the care of the Royal Air Force Museum and has been repainted in RAF colours even though it never flew with the service. I cannot help thinking that if the military connection is so important then this aircraft should be in the colours of British Eagle, with whom it carried so many of Her Majesty's forces and their families on government trooping flights.

Other Britannias are preserved at the Duxford Aviation Society, the XM496 Preservation Society at Kemble, and the Britannia Aircraft Preservation Trust at Liverpool.

Ken Elliot

Eighty-five Britannias were built, around two-thirds for BOAC and the RAF. There is a coda to this story. When the Canadians were looking for a long-range aircraft to replace its maritime reconnaissance and transport aircraft, they chose the Britannia as the basis for two licence-built variants, the piston-engine Canadair Argus, and the Canadair CL-44 freighter with Rolls-Royce Tyne engines, more recognisably a lengthened Britannia and fitted with an innovative swing tail that allowed easy access for loading. Two British cargo airlines flew CL-44s, Transmeridian Air-Cargo (the latest iteration of Keegan's airline) and Tradewinds.

After Keegan sold Transmeridian, the airline merged with IAS Cargo to form British Cargo Airlines in 1979, a short-lived venture that only lasted eight months before it collapsed. The British government had a laissez-faire attitude towards the independent airlines, nowhere more evident than in its casual neglect of the cargo charter airlines, which began to see intense competition in the 1970s and '80s from new African and East European airlines that gained access to the market by cutting rates drastically; it also did not help that Britain's manufacturing industry was in decline and exporting less and less.

Air-Britain Archive

22: DAN-AIR AND ITS COMETS

The de Havilland Comet's tale has a sad beginning that dashed Britain's hopes of leading the world in new airliner technology but quite a cheerful ending as the airliner usefully carried millions of British holidaymakers to their resorts in the sun.

The jet airliner project was a leap into the unknown, the Comet flying higher and faster than any previous airliner, and de Havilland tested the aircraft to destruction before it entered service, or so the company thought. After the aircraft entered service with BOAC on 2 May 1952 orders began to come in, including one from Pan American. But there were accidents, a lot of them. Some were attributable to imperfect take-off techniques, cured by adding a drooped leading edge. But three others in quick succession involved the disintegration of the aircraft in the sky. After the third, on 8 April 1954, the aircraft's airworthiness certificate was withdrawn and the aircraft design re-evaluated. The wreckage of one of the aircraft, G-ALYP 'Yoke Peter', was recovered from the sea by the Royal Navy and painstakingly reassembled at the Royal Aircraft Establishment (RAE) at Farnborough; at the same time the RAE pressure tested the fuselage of another Comet, G-ALYU, in a water tank. Yoke Peter was found to have suffered metal fatigue at the corner of the Automatic Direction Finder (ADF) aperture, leading to violent decompression; Yoke Uncle's fuselage then failed, also at the corner of a square window, after about 3,000 pressurised 'flights', much earlier than de Havilland had expected. The problems of metal fatigue were anticipated but clearly not understood, for which de Havilland cannot be criticised; but it is significant that there was a catastrophic failure when the RAE tested the whole fuselage, whereas de Havilland tested only parts of the fuselage. The Court of Inquiry commented: 'The test sections of the cabin differed from the cabin as fitted to the aircraft in several respects … [T]he windows of special interest in this Inquiry were rather near the bulkhead, so that the stresses to the skin around them might have been appreciably different from those in similar places in the complete cabin.'

The RAE came out of the debacle with its reputation enhanced, and the Royal Navy's contribution was magnificent. Had another manufacturer built the Comet, for example Vickers, might the story have ended differently? The One-Eleven, built by Vickers' successor British Aircraft Corporation, also had its share of problems when it flew into the unknown, in its case deep stall associated with the high T-tail design, so maybe the implication is false. Much more robust was BOAC's unstinting support for the Comet; the corporation never seemed to waver, ordering nineteen of the developed Comet 4 in 1957, which entered service in 1958,

The Aviation Photo Company

some two years after the Russian Tupolev Tu-104. BOAC even wanted to order a larger derivative, the DH.118 or Comet 5, but was obliged to order the Vickers VC10 instead.

G-APDB was the second production aircraft, delivered on 30 September 1958. Two days later it positioned to New York and on 4 October launched BOAC's transatlantic service, flying eastbound from New York to London with five fare-paying passengers, twenty-three free-riders and sixteen staff members. Indicative of the times, the Comets had to be stood down one week later due to strike action, G-APDB only resuming the transatlantic service in mid-November, by which time Pan American had introduced the mighty Boeing 707 on its transatlantic services. BOAC brought its own Boeing 707s into service in May 1960. Comets were used on many other routes, however, to South America, East Africa, Singapore, Hong Kong, Tokyo, Johannesburg and Sydney, and remained in service until 1965; five of the Comets, including G-APDB, were then sold to Malaysian Airways for £150,000 apiece.

The Aviation Photo Company

With a new registration, 9M-AOB, it helped launch Silver Kris Jet Services from Singapore and Kuala Lumpur to Bangkok, Hong Kong and Jesselton. Later renamed Malaysia-Singapore Airlines, the airline was a regional carrier, finding its feet in the world of international aviation. After the arrival of Boeing 707s, the Comets flew to other destinations including Djakarta, Manila and Phnom Penh, before being replaced in turn by Boeing 737s. It was time for the Comet 4s to come home, and in 1969 they did, to a new owner, Dan-Air in London.

BEA was an unexpected beneficiary of the Comet. The aircraft was designed for 'Empire' routes but then BEA found itself on the back foot after miscalculating future aircraft requirements. BEA had thought the future lay in ever larger turboprops, and had ordered the Vickers Vanguard, whereas actually European passengers wanted to travel by

jet, so almost every other European airline bought French-built Caravelles. Hence the corporation was glad to be able to acquire Comets, suitably adapted, to meet the competition. The fuselage was stretched by 38in, the wings cropped and the pinion tanks deleted. BEA ordered the type in April 1958, and the first of eighteen Comet 4Bs entered service in April 1960, just one year after the Caravelle first flew for Air France: not a bad recovery. Four of BEA's Comets were registered to Olympic Airways and flew with the Greek airline under a somewhat opaque 'consortium' arrangement. G-APYD was one of these aircraft, seen here in Olympic colours and with Greek registration SX-DAL, but with a BEA sticker by the door; there was a pool agreement between the two airlines that allowed them to operate on behalf of each other as necessary.

And the arrangement clearly worked; the Comet was not returned to BEA until the end of 1969. By then BEA was beginning to dispose of its Comets; nine of them went to its new charter subsidiary, BEA Airtours, and BEA soon found new homes for the others.

One of the most engaging entrepreneurs in British civil aviation was Squadron Leader Jack Jones, who was prepared to try anything at least once! His airline, Channel Airways, operated short-haul flights from its base at Southend, scheduled and charter, gradually moving further afield until the destinations outran the range of his fleet. When he signed a major three-year deal with Lyons Tours, he needed to boost capacity and bought five Comets from BEA for service in 1970; G-APYD was one of them. Seating capacity was upped from 86 to 109, and heavy-duty batteries installed, but otherwise the aircraft was left unchanged, including the paint scheme.

Channel's jet fleet could not operate out of Southend satisfactorily, so it was moved to Stansted, which has a much longer runway, but that led to a split operation. The airline found it difficult to sustain its jet operations as aircraft had to be maintained by an outside contractor, spares were in short supply and the Comet fleet was in a constant state of operational chaos, leading to flight delays and expensive sub-charters in order to protect the Lyons programme; it brought down Channel in the end. I joined another Stansted-based airline in 1971 and well recall the scenes in the terminal with long lines of disconsolate Channel passengers going nowhere; as it happened my own airline was not much better, and both subsequently collapsed in 1972, cursed by Stansted blight! There was nothing wrong with the Comets as such, they just needed looking after. And there was really only one airline that could do that: Dan-Air.

The Aviation Photo Company

There was one further development of the Comet, at least in its civilian role, one that had the range of the Comet 4 and the capacity of the Comet 4B, and this became the Comet 4C. It was not used by either of Britain's state corporations but enjoyed modest sales abroad and was also ordered by another British state-owned airline, the Royal Air Force's Transport Command.

Five entered service with 216 Squadron in 1962 as the Comet C.4 and stayed in service for thirteen years, elegantly flying members of the Royal Family, diplomats and other VIPs around the world as well as performing medevac flights. When the end came, they were sold to Dan-Air for £25,000 apiece, an excellent deal: low mileage, one careful owner!

Dan-Air bought forty-nine of the seventy-six Comets 4, 4B and 4C that were built; fifteen others had previously been written off in crashes or as a result of heavy landings.

The Aviation Photo Company

It is difficult to overestimate the importance of the Comet to Dan-Air's commercial stature. While other charter airlines were chugging along in the holiday charter market with turboprop Viscounts and Britannias, Dan-Air simply overtook them by going jet as early as 1966. With its own maintenance facility the aircraft were kept flying with becoming regularity; utilisation was never very high, but then it did not need to be as the aircraft carried few overheads, and the crewing establishment was low. At least two Comets were kept on standby to allow back-up for non-operational aircraft. The Comets were ideal for regional charter flying, and also for shifting large numbers of passengers when the need arose, such as cruise ship change-overs. As the years went by, the quality of the Comets improved; Comet 4s were displaced by Comet 4Bs and Comet 4Cs. The Comets were joined by more modern aircraft, BAC One-Elevens

and Boeing 727s, but even after the fuel crisis of 1973 they still held their own, although they burned twice as much fuel as a One-Eleven and needed a three-man flight crew. Between them, Britannia and Dan-Air dominated inclusive-tour flying in the 1970s, Britannia flying expensive, modern Boeing 737s intensively, Dan-Air relying on its huge fleet of assorted aircraft to meet varying levels of demand with extra capacity available whenever it was needed, for example when another British charter airline went bust! British Eagle, Court Line, Laker: Dan-Air had the spare capacity to pick up the pieces when these airlines failed, and very often the residual business as well.

G-APDB came back on to the British register in June 1970 and was reseated for 109 passengers; it flew until early 1974. It is now preserved at Duxford, although not in Dan-Air colours.

The Aviation Photo Company

The Aviation Photo Company

The Aviation Photo Company

G-APYD may have been plagued with technical problems when flying for Channel but enjoyed a better relationship with Dan-Air, staying in service for another seven years before its final journey to the Science Museum's establishment at Wroughton in October 1979. There the conservators had to cope with the product of an unexpected intruder, a queen bee having gained access and started making honey! The interior had to be scrubbed out. The aircraft is shown at Gatwick in a revised livery, with solid red tail. Dan-Air took some pride in the appearance of its aircraft, one of the many benefits of having its own engineering establishment. Dan-Air's aircraft were hand-painted, the sign-writer having devised the distinctive logotype, which he applied freehand as he walked down the side of the fuselage on a trestle.

The last Dan-Air Comet illustrated, G-BDIX, was formerly XR399 with the Royal Air Force.

It wears an 'unofficial' livery with revised lettering and a modified cheatline, but still in red and black; it has also gained a grey polyurethane coating on the lower fuselage. Inside the seats were covered with whatever material was available! It could make for some strange combinations, but eventually an interior designer imposed some order. When travelling on a Comet, one had to be careful to protect one's head; the entrance doors were quite small. More unexpectedly, condensation tended to freeze inside the aircraft at altitude, which then rapidly melted on descent, allowing some very cold drops of water to rain down on unsuspecting passengers' heads. G-BDIX went to the National Museum of Flight at East Fortune in Scotland in 1983, where it resides currently outside Hangar 1.

23: BOEING 707-420 G-ARWD

In any comparative study of civil aviation it is disheartening to see just how often the British managed to get it wrong, and the Americans got it right. Never was this truer than in the history of jet transports. Britain should have gained a significant lead with the Comet but lost it. Boeing, already building jet bombers, effortlessly overtook de Havilland, as did another great American manufacturer, Douglas. Both Boeing and Douglas went on to build long-range jets that proved capable of significant development during their lives. De Havilland could have improved and enlarged the Comet too but was denied the opportunity by the British government, which preferred to support the VC10 proposed by Vickers as part of a larger restructuring of the aircraft manufacturing industry.

Boeing designed its jet airliner in parallel with the KC-135 tanker-transport, but widened the fuselage by 4in to allow six-abreast seating. The wings were much more sharply swept than the Comet's, at 35 degrees rather than 20, allowing the Boeing a cruising speed of 600mph, 100mph faster than its British rival. The engines were in pods, hung from the wing. Being a larger aircraft than the Comet, the Boeing 707, as it came to be known, had greater range, although early models did not have non-stop transatlantic capability. Later models, the -320 and -420 variants, were 8ft longer, could carry up to 189 passengers and were designed for intercontinental operations with a range of 3,800 miles.

As orders for these more advanced Boeing 707s began to flow, BOAC was anxious not to be left behind and persuaded the government to allow it to order fifteen Boeing 707s with Rolls-Royce engines in October 1956. At the time, the corporation still had large, unfulfilled orders for Britannias and the Comet 4, and was about to be badgered into buying even larger numbers of VC10s, so the order for Boeings was labelled a 'stopgap', one of those misleading euphemisms so beloved of government ministers: the Boeings outlasted the Britannias and Comets and flew alongside the VC10s until the early 1980s. The Boeing 707 with Rolls-Royce engines, which was sold to a number of other airlines, was an elegant albeit partial solution to the perennial problem of buying British. The Boeings entered service in May 1960, just a few days before the government passed into law a bill that seemed to threaten BOAC's protected status.

Britain's two state-owned corporations, BOAC and BEA, enjoyed a privileged position as the nation's two flag carriers, which meant they had had first choice of any international and domestic air routes, and both had consequently built up sizeable networks in their respective spheres. Other British airlines were barred from operating these scheduled routes, a consequence of the restrictive bilateral agreements between most countries prevalent at the time, but the smaller independent airlines soon adapted to being locked out of these markets and found other ways of making a living. Holiday charters to the new Mediterranean resorts, weekend flying to the Channel Islands and Isle of Man and contract flying for the government kept many of them in business; but now they

Author's Collection

wanted access to some of the routes they had been denied in the past. Early in 1960 the government proposed a deal that sounded better than it was. It removed the corporations' automatic monopoly and allowed independent airlines to apply for scheduled routes. What nobody realised at the time was that the government had no intention of allowing other British airlines to compete with the corporations on existing international routes! Yes, if they could find any, independents could apply to fly on new routes, but after decades of development there were not many of those around: BOAC and BEA had been given the best ones.

There was one route, however, that was available and promised good returns, and that was between London and New York. The Americans already fielded two airlines on this route, Pan American and TWA, and there was in theory no reason why the British should not do the same. At the time, a number of shipping companies had invested in the

smaller British independent airlines, and Cunard, famous for its transatlantic liners the *Queen Elizabeth* and *Queen Mary*, was looking around for an aviation partner. The shipping line would have liked a tie-up with BOAC, but linking a private company to a state-owned corporation did not seem feasible at the time. Instead Cunard bought Eagle, Harold Bamberg's energetic long-haul airline, which had already established itself in Bermuda and the Caribbean, and now flew between Bermuda and New York. With Cunard's market reach and name awareness, and Eagle's aviation know-how, the newly renamed Cunard Eagle was set to challenge BOAC on the London to New York route, and speedily posted an application, which to general consternation was granted in 1961. Cunard ordered two Boeing 707s, almost identical to those bought by BOAC, a move that was seen as premature when later that year the government, under extreme pressure from BOAC, overturned the decision and denied Cunard Eagle the London to New York route after all! Cunard was now in the unhappy position of having two expensive aircraft and no business for them. Nevertheless, Cunard Eagle accepted the first Boeing 707, registered G-ARWD, in February 1962. The aircraft is seen in a Boeing publicity photograph sporting its British registration.

The airline tried to rescue something from the wreckage of its failed business plan and placed the aircraft on the Bermuda register in order to operate a more limited route network based on the island, with links to New York, Miami, London, the Bahamas and Jamaica. The aircraft made its debut in London in May 1962 to launch a new service from London to Bermuda and Miami, the latter a promising destination in its own right and a hub for South American services.

All of which made BOAC sit up and take notice: maybe Cunard, a politically powerful organisation, might be able to retrieve even more from the wreckage, including a second attempt at the London to New York route. Objections to a public–private venture were overruled, and BOAC found a willing seller in Cunard. Just a month after the launch of Cunard Eagle's London–Bermuda–Miami service, BOAC and Cunard announced the establishment of a joint venture, BOAC-Cunard, to which Cunard contributed the two Boeings together with the promising Bermuda and Bahamas operations, in exchange for 30 per cent ownership. Cunard Eagle's jet operations and transatlantic ambitions were effectively wiped out, leaving the airline fielding a small fleet of Britannia turboprops and Douglas DC-6s; gratifyingly, the airline bounced back just a year later when Bamberg bought the residual operator, renamed it British Eagle and set it on course for another few years of glory.

Martin Harrison

BOAC lost no time in repainting the Cunard Eagle Boeing in its colours and put it back on the British register as G-ARWD. For good measure the corporation absorbed the Bermuda and Bahamas networks into its own operations.

The aircraft should have been painted in BOAC-Cunard colours, as that was the company to which the aircraft was assigned. It did not, however, suit BOAC to acknowledge the existence of this joint venture so obviously; what if the Americans granted a permit to BOAC-Cunard alongside the existing BOAC permit, and then the joint venture's ownership reverted to Cunard, say? In any case, as was obvious at the time, BOAC-Cunard was just a paper company; the actual operations were performed by BOAC. For two years BOAC squirmed before finally agreeing a solution with the Americans that allowed BOAC-Cunard to market its services provided the public was made aware that the aircraft were operated by BOAC. Finally, G-ARWD could be repainted in BOAC-Cunard colours, shown overleaf at Berlin's Tempelhof airport in May 1966.

Copyright R.N. Smith Collection Image

Jonathan Walton

Just a few months later it was all over anyway. The Labour government disapproved of the partial denationalisation of one of its state corporations and applied pressure on BOAC, which then bought out the Cunard shareholding in October 1966; Cunard made a handsome profit on the deal. So it was back to the paint shop again for G-ARWD, to emerge in the final version of the BOAC livery with the big, blobby blue nose.

Even though the corporation had a full inventory of VC10s, it continued buying later-model Boeing 707-320Cs, and kept the original fleet of Rolls-Royce 707s in service until 1973, their useful life extended by the delayed introduction into BOAC service of the Boeing 747. The aircraft were in excellent condition, flying more than eleven hours a day, their reliable engines now extended to 9,000 hours between major checks, and with possibly another 15,000 to 30,000 flying hours feasible, suggesting a further six to ten years of service. With the introduction of the Boeing 747 and Super VC10, however, the 707s were no longer needed for front-line service and they began to be sold out of the fleet, although they did not have to go very far.

BOAC's sister corporation, BEA, faced tough competition from Britain's charter airlines, which were developing demand for low-cost flights within Europe tied into inclusive-tour package deals. BEA responded to these market pressures in various ways, the most enterprising of which was to establish its own charter airline, BEA Airtours, which started flying ex-BEA Comets in 1970 to European holiday destinations. The Comets had a limited shelf life, however, and BEA Airtours looked around for a suitable replacement for its Tango flights, choosing second-hand Boeing 707s, which it wanted to buy from American Airlines. That did not go down well with the powers on high! Instead BEA Airtours was 'persuaded' to take over the BOAC Rolls-Royce 707s, acquiring its first two early in 1972. G-ARWD joined in January 1973 and is seen at Gatwick later in the year, looking very spruce newly painted in its modified BEA livery.

At first, the Boeings flew European services but they had the range to fly further afield, and began operating charters to North America and the Far East; Airtours was one of the first companies to fly to Florida.

When the two corporations merged in 1973 the new name British Airways was introduced in a piecemeal fashion. After BEA Airtours was renamed British Airtours, G-ARWD was repainted in a version of the new British Airways livery in 1975.

Although a low-key airline, British Airtours was a force to be reckoned with in the charter market; its size and backing gave it a presence in most areas of charter activity. British Airways had its own in-house tour operators, and the flexibility to use its scheduled services as well as its subsidiary's charter flights, so an astonishing variety of destinations could be offered. As airlines dropped out of the transatlantic market, British Airtours continued flying advance booking charters, in competition with Laker and Dan-Air. When charter airlines began leasing their aircraft and crews to foreign flag carriers, British Airtours was busy there too, leasing its Boeings to Syrian Arab Airlines and helping launch Air Mauritius. G-ARWD spent two years flying for the latter from 1979.

When the lease ended, it was time for G-ARWD to be retired, and the 707 was traded into Boeing in May 1981 as part of a deal for nine Boeing 737s that started to enter

The Aviation Photo Company

The Aviation Photo Company

service with British Airtours in 1981. The airline remained an important player in the field for another fifteen years, taking over surplus TriStars, DC-10s and Boeing 757s from its parent company; its name was changed to Caledonian in 1987, after British Airways, now privatised, bought British Caledonian Airways. Through a number of ownership changes and mergers, Caledonian evolved into the now defunct Thomas Cook Airlines, owned by German tour operator Neckermann.

The Aviation Photo Company

24: VICKERS VISCOUNT 831 G-APND

J. Exton Collection, via J.S. Davidson

This section is about the 800-series Viscount, which followed on from the earlier 700 series. It is also about three significant airlines in Britain's aviation history, all of which used Viscount G-APND: Airwork, British United Airways and British Midland Airways.

Even as BEA was introducing the first of its new Viscounts early in 1953, the early series 701, it already wanted to order a larger version, with a 13ft longer fuselage and more powerful Rolls-Royce Darts, able to carry eighty-six passengers. But then the corporation had second thoughts and decided to go for something not quite so big: a recurring motif in BEA's history. The stretched Viscount that was finally ordered in 1954 was only 3ft 10in longer on the outside but by moving back the bulkhead, the new 800 series managed a cabin longer by 9ft 3in; it had uprated Darts and could seat seventy-one passengers, but its range was down to around 700 miles; earlier 700-series Viscounts managed 990 miles. Later versions of the 800 series had beefed up structures and greater range, but BEA, which bought twenty-four Viscount 802s and nineteen Viscount 806s to add to its fleet of twenty-seven of the smaller sixty-seat 700 series, was prepared to accept the penalty as most of its sectors were below 500 miles.

BEA was pleased to have the new aircraft, commenting: 'The cruising speed has been increased from 310 to 360mph and the interior of the aircraft has been designed for mixed class operations.' Despite their lack of range, the Viscounts travelled around, even as far as Bahrain and Kuwait in the Persian Gulf. Not coincidentally, the corporation with its all-Viscount front-line fleet, had its best year ever in 1959, making its biggest ever profit, more than £2 million.

Airwork ordered Viscounts in 1954 but when plans for their introduction were thwarted by the Treasury and the Civil Aviation Minister's bureaucrats, the airline did not accept delivery and sold the aircraft on to the Cuban airline Cubana. Airwork was the most important British independent airline of the 1950s; it had significant multi-million-pound trooping contracts to the Far East and was an early operator of low-fare safari services to East, Central and West Africa, also known as Colonial Coach Class. The trouble was that the African services had to be flown by older and smaller aircraft than the regular services operated by BOAC, so Airwork used twenty-seven-seat Vickers Vikings, which took three days to get down there and another three days to get back. Airwork flew the Handley Page Hermes on its trooping contracts but was not allowed

to use these relatively modern aircraft on low-fare services to Africa.

Airwork was a wide-ranging organisation with interests in many spheres of aviation activity. Its history went back to before the war when it had developed Heston Airport in north London for private flying. By the 1950s it had achieved an impressive global presence as well, helping to establish a number of airlines worldwide: Egypt, India, East Africa, Germany, New Zealand and the Sudan. It pioneered crop-spraying with helicopters and provided oil-exploration support flying in Iran, Iraq, Kuwait and Ecuador. Other activities included extensive contract work for the armed services, maintenance and flying training principally, both in the United Kingdom and Middle East. And now Airwork was busy adding to its portfolio of British airlines. Transair, a feisty newspaper carrier that had branched out into trooping and inclusive-tour flying, was taken over in August 1956. The next to succumb was Freddie Laker and his organisations at Southend, the airlines Channel Air Bridge and Air Charter, and Aviation Traders, the maintenance group; they became part of Airwork early in 1958. Then in November 1958 Airwork took over Morton Air Services, a third-level operator of Doves and Herons that had recently migrated from Croydon to join Transair at Gatwick. Curiously, all these airlines continued to operate completely independently. Air Charter bought Britannias, Transair was the first independent to introduce Viscounts, while Mortons bought Dakotas; they all just went their own sweet way.

The Safari services to Africa were shared between Airwork and friendly rival Hunting-Clan. The latter had also got into difficulties with its Viscount orders but gamely went ahead and accepted delivery, flying them out of Newcastle for a while before leasing them to Middle East Airlines in Beirut. The situation changed quite abruptly late in 1957 when, after some horse-trading with the Ministry and BOAC, both airlines were allowed to introduce Viscounts on their respective Safari services. Hunting-Clan had just got back its Lebanese Viscounts, and so was able to take immediate advantage of the concession, lending one of its Viscounts briefly to Airwork to allow the latter to start up Viscount services as well, as Airwork scrabbled around to find its own Viscounts. Both airlines placed orders for new 800-series Viscounts, and Airwork managed to procure two Viscounts from BOAC early in 1958.

A year later Airwork the airline was in poor shape. Its long-term Hermes trooping contract to Singapore ended in mid-1959; the new contract had been awarded to Hunting-Clan, which had just bought some brand-new Britannias. Airwork still had its Safari services, but those now needed Viscounts. The airline put up its entire fleet of piston-engine aircraft for sale and simply dismissed all the flying crew. The Viscounts, including those on order, were transferred to Transair, although still flown in Airwork colours. G-APND, one of the last Viscounts built, was delivered to Transair in February 1959 and was soon joined by sister ship G-APNE. Hunting-Clan's Viscounts were delivered during the same period. Cynically, Airwork's dismissed pilots were invited to apply for Viscount positions at Transair but with loss of all seniority.

G-APND was a series-831 Viscount, almost the final iteration of the Viscount design. The Rolls-Royce Darts delivered a third more power at take-off than those originally fitted to early model Viscounts. Range with a full load of sixty-two passengers was now 1,275 miles: still not enough. Airwork's Viscounts sometimes had slipper tanks on the forward edge

The Aviation Photo Company

of the wings that added another 400 miles. The Viscount was not ideal for the long hauls down to Africa, but the airlines were capacity-restricted, so the obvious choice of aircraft, the Britannia, would have to wait.

G-APND did its duty in Africa for two years, sometimes standing in for the Sudan Airways 'Blue Nile' Viscount, but mostly flying for its parent, which itself was about to become part of an extended family (later known as the Air Holdings Group). Under government pressure, and as part of a so-called new deal for civil aviation in Britain, enshrined in the passing of the 1960 Civil Aviation (Licensing) Act, Airwork merged with Hunting-Clan to form British United Airways (BUA). In the next few years more airlines would join them; Silver City and Manx in January 1962, Jersey Airlines four months later. They may all have flown as British United but there were still many different operating companies wriggling under the surface!

As part of the deal with the government, Safari services to East and Central Africa were revamped and rebranded Skycoach, with a complex revenue-sharing and operating pattern involving not just BUA but BOAC, Central African Airways, East African and South African Airways. For a time G-APND even carried East African markings. But Skycoach was short lived; BUA introduced Britannia services in October 1961 and charged normal IATA fares from then on.

However, G-APND still staged round West Africa on a two-day journey to Accra, and Viscounts flew many of the longer-distance routes from Gatwick: to Gibraltar, Malaga, Barcelona, Palma, usually on a weekly basis; and more frequently to Rotterdam, and Paris via Le Touquet, the Silver Arrow service. Trooping flights to Germany accounted for

thirty flights a week, usually flown with Viscounts, of which there were eleven in the fleet. When the jet BAC One-Elevens started arriving in 1965, they took over the front-line international routes from Gatwick; the Viscounts continued flying regional services to the north of France, the Channel Islands, Dublin, Dusseldorf and Amsterdam, many of them part of the former Silver City and Jersey networks. G-APND was sent off to Jordan for three months but returned in early 1967 and continued in service for another two years, long enough to receive British United's new colours; they look splendid on the ten-year-old Viscount in Chris England's photograph taken at Exeter. Here's a hint on how to tell a Viscount 800 series from a Viscount 700: rectangular doors had replaced the earlier oval doors.

Chris England

Dietrich Eggert

When British United elected to go to an all-jet fleet, the Viscounts were sold off. G-APND went to British Midland Airways (BMA) in January 1969, one of five Viscounts to join the airline that year. Originally a small regional carrier flying Dakotas and Argonauts, British Midland Airways had graduated to turboprops by the mid-1960s, acquiring its first Viscounts, also from British United, in 1967. The airline was expanding its network of both international and domestic services from its base at East Midlands Airport, which served the industrial triangle of Derby, Nottingham and Leicester. British Midland flew to Amsterdam, Belfast, Dublin, Dusseldorf and Glasgow during the week, and to the Channel Islands at weekends. G-APND is depicted at Dusseldorf in June 1969.

Looking for more opportunity, British Midland ordered BAC One-Elevens for holiday charter flying out of East Midlands, Luton and Manchester. More adventurously, the airline tried its hand at operating long-haul affinity group charters out of Stansted with two Boeing 707s.

The airline got an unexpected break in 1970 when it was able to take over the Teesside to London Heathrow scheduled services, its first appearance at Britain's premier airport; the airline went on in later years to assemble a formidable array of services out of Heathrow, both domestic and international, a strategy that ensured its survival through the following decades until its acquisition by British Airways in 2012. British Caledonian stayed glued to Gatwick; it got taken over by British Airways in 1987.

The early 1970s were not easy times for any of the airlines. Affinity group flights to America suffered extreme enforcement measures from both UK and American authorities

Jonathan Walton

taking some Heralds in part exchange, signalling a change of course as the airline decided to concentrate on developing scheduled services.

G-APND received BMA's new livery in 1972, shown to advantage at Manchester; the Viscount flew its last flight for British Midland on 28 September 1973, before sale to Arkia, Israel's domestic airline.

The Viscounts began to be replaced by Douglas DC-9s, an unusual type on the British register, which served the airline for the next twenty years.

When the end came in 2012 the airline had cycled through Boeing 737s and Fokker F100s to Airbuses and Embraer jets. British Airways paid £172 million for British Midland, and acquired more than twenty Airbuses and, more significantly, fifty-six slot pairs at Heathrow.

G-APND eventually came back to Britain in 1989, albeit in bits, for spares recovery. Former British Air Ferries Viscount G-APIM is preserved at Brooklands.

and lost money. British Midland pulled out and deployed its Boeing 707s elsewhere; the airline took to leasing them out to other operators, and its first customer was Sudan Airways, which needed them for its 'Blue Nile' services. Inclusive-tour flying became intensely competitive as airlines such as Court Line fought for market share, so British Midland decided to give that a miss too, selling the One-Elevens in Brazil and

The Aviation Photo Company

25: VICKERS VANGUARD G-APEP

Vickers built just forty-four Vanguards in total, so why write about them? Vickers had been the most successful British airliner manufacturer since the war, building more than 1,000 Viscounts and Vikings (including military variants) and its next project, the Vanguard, a development of the successful Viscount formula, but bigger, faster and with better economics, was a logical engineering choice, driven in part by the quest for lower operating costs. Vickers and BEA were already talking about a successor to the Viscount early in 1953 just as the corporation was taking delivery of its first Viscounts, and by 1956 the design had evolved into a large turboprop airliner, powered by Rolls-Royce Tyne engines, capable of carrying up to 132 passengers over short to medium distances, and 4 tons of freight in the lower holds of the double-bubble fuselage.

Vickers agonised whether the engines should be jets but concluded that over such short distances jets gave no advantages in travel time, and the turboprop was thriftier. Powered by logic, the decision and the design were flawless, but were overtaken by the rapid improvement in pure-jet economics, as well as the emotional and marketing appeal of the new jets such as the French-built Caravelle, ordered by no fewer than eleven European national airlines; BEA had to respond by changing strategy, ordering the de Havilland Trident, and buying Comets as a stopgap. The Vanguard not only had competition from first-generation jets; the American manufacturer Lockheed built the similar four-turboprop Electra, which entered service early in 1959, beating the Vanguard

into the air by two years and scooping up any possible orders from US airlines. Only BEA and Trans-Canada Air Lines, loyal and grateful Vickers clients, ordered Vanguards. It was a disappointing sequel to the amazing success story that was the Viscount; that's why it is worth writing about.

Here is another interesting reason. The Vanguard was developed in parallel with the Bristol Britannia, a similar turboprop design albeit with greater range and thus more flexible than the Vanguard. BOAC's Britannia 312 series first flew in July 1957 and entered service at the end of the year. The Vanguard was ordered by BEA in July 1956 as the Britannia was in full development mode; the Vanguard first took to the air in January 1959 and should have entered service in mid-July 1960, but problems with the Tyne engines delayed entry into service, and BEA's scheduled operations did not start until March 1961. I find it interesting that Peter Masefield, chief executive of BEA at the time the corporation instigated design studies of the Vanguard, subsequently became chairman of Bristol, put there by a government exasperated by the manufacturer's inability to effectively develop and produce the Britannia. One of the many questions I never got around to asking Masefield was whether he ever tried to sell the Britannia to his former employer BEA!

BEA ordered twenty Vanguards, and so did Trans-Canada Air Lines. Trans-Canada's had more powerful engines and a greater payload, so BEA changed its mind and converted fourteen of its orders to a similar specification to the Trans-Canada version; the other six were too far down the

Tony Eastwood Collection

manufacturing process to be converted. Trans-Canada ordered three more, which, together with the manufacturer's prototype, made up the total production.

G-APEP was a series-953 version, with the more powerful engines and greater payload. Named *Superb*, it was delivered to BEA in December 1961. The Vanguard never really got a break with BEA, shoved aside by the Comets that BEA had had to buy in a hurry when the corporation realised that it had miscalculated future passenger requirements; these had already been delivered to BEA by the time the Vanguards entered service. The Vanguards operated to Paris, to tourist destinations in Spain, Italy and Austria, the low-fare 'colonial' routes to Malta and Gibraltar (then the gateway to the Costa

del Sol) and domestic trunk routes. Most of the flights were in an all-economy 132-seat configuration, but some of the domestic services offered first-class seating in a comfy cabin with purple décor at the back of the aircraft. Utilisation was low, just over six hours a day, which meant each aircraft was sitting on the ground for eighteen hours a day not earning its keep. Fares were low on the routes that the Vanguard typically flew; even though it had the lowest seat-mile costs in the fleet it was a struggle to make money with the big Vanguard, as typically only two-thirds of the seats were occupied! The type was saddled with the overheads of the domestic operations, although many passengers would have been connecting to international services at BEA's Heathrow hub. To the irritation of BEA, independent airlines then began operating limited jet services on some domestic trunk routes, so BEA had to respond with jets, too. The chairman of BEA complained in 1969:

Last year our London–Edinburgh route lost £197,000 – we had hoped that this would have broken even but we suffered from the many strikes by Edinburgh airport personnel which reduced our revenue. This was with an all-Vanguard operation. On London–Glasgow the loss with a mixed Trident/Vanguard service was £566,000. In the main this was attributable to the high cost/low yield of the Trident operation.

What to do about the Vanguard, which was clearly not paying its way? After losing £6 million flying the passenger Vanguards, BEA decided to give it a second chance. The corporation had a small fleet of all-cargo planes, the Armstrong Whitworth Argosy, but these were over-specialised, expensive to operate and too small to cope with the growth in freight traffic; whereas the Vanguard, with its capacious fuselage as well as underbelly cargo holds, could be converted into a decent freighter, capable of carrying 18 tons. The fact that the Argosies were some five years younger than the Vanguards did not dissuade BEA from withdrawing the Argosy fleet and undertaking the conversion of nine Vanguards, renamed Merchantman in its new role.

The Aviation Photo Company

Barry Friend

Powered by four Rolls-Royce Dart engines, the Argosy could load and unload cargo at each end of its fuselage, but as the picture of G-ASXN makes clear, that fuselage was rather short. The Merchantman carried 5 tons more payload than the Argosy, flew some 130mph faster and benefited too from the speedy loading capability now possible by using loaders and pallets, so the type quickly displaced the Argosies, which had all gone by the end of 1970. G-APEP was converted early in 1971.

BEA built its new Cargocentre for the fleet at Heathrow, which suffered from teething troubles and industrial unrest; then BEA had to face up to the painful task of amalgamating its functions with those of BOAC after the two corporations merged their operations in 1973 and rebranded under the name British Airways. European cargo operations were a disappointment, however, not helped by Britain's relative industrial decline: 'The European cargo market has dropped

sharply,' British Airways stated in its 1975–76 annual report 'and today we carry about half the tonnage shipped in 1971.' British Airways responded by using the aircraft on cargo charter services as well as its scheduled freighter routes, with the

The Aviation Photo Company

aircraft travelling further afield, sometimes to the Middle East in connection with the oil boom, even to the United States.

BEA Cargo had become British Airways Cargo, and the image of G-APEP landing shows it in the new livery; it also illustrates the large freight door in the forward fuselage and the blanked off windows of the freighter conversion. But now the Merchantman was the 'specialised' freighter, just as the Argosy had been ten years previously, and it too was about to be displaced by the more flexible new aircraft that British Airways was introducing, in this case the wide-bodied Lockheed TriStar, which could carry in its belly holds almost as much cargo as the Merchantman. British Airways explained it in its annual report for 1976–77: 'Cargo earns British Airways about one eighth of its total revenue, but is responsible for only about half that proportion of costs. A high proportion of all air cargo is carried in the holds of passenger aircraft.' The Merchantman began to be withdrawn from service in 1975 and the last flight was performed in December 1979. The remaining five aircraft were bought by a British independent, Air Bridge Carriers, a cargo airline that also flew Argosies and was part of the storied Hunting Group, a name familiar to airline enthusiasts from its activities in the early post-war years.

G-APEP was transferred on 12 November 1979 and then laid up in open storage at Castle Donington for two years before re-entering service in July 1982. The glory days of regular long-haul freight flights to the Middle and Far East were over, but there was business to be had nearer home, delivering newspapers, hauling car parts between factories in Britain and Europe and developing the rapidly expanding market for distributing small parcels, packages and documents, no longer a monopoly of the Royal Mail and European postal services. The Vanguards, to which name the type

The Aviation Photo Company

reverted, filled in gaps in other airlines' fleets; at various times Austrian, KLM and Swissair used the Vanguards. Much of this work involved night flying, and not a lot of that! Air Bridge Carriers did not need to fly the aircraft intensively, they just needed to be available at critical times. Vanguard utilisation was low, 500 to 600 hours a year per unit; the airline averaged between 1,500 and 2,000 hours for the combined fleet throughout the 1980s, which ran at between four and five aircraft, Vanguards and later Lockheed Electras. The hours increased in the 1990s, however, with the fleet achieving more than 8,000 hours by the mid-1990s, but G-APEP's contribution remained modest.

G-APEP makes an impressive sight in the air, still carrying its original BEA name *Superb*. It was converted to carry race horses and flew the British and German contingents down to Barcelona for the 1992 Olympic Games. The airline's name changed late in 1992, to Hunting Cargo Airlines, so G-APEP received a new handle even if the stripes stayed the same. The Vanguard flew mostly for DHL, outlasting its sister ships by some margin, so that by January 1995 G-APEP was the last remaining Vanguard flying, during the week connecting regional airports in Britain at night with the main DHL hub at Brussels, and at weekends carrying newspapers from Liverpool to Belfast. The end came on 30 September 1996 when G-APEP flew its last commercial flight, from Belfast to Coventry. The aircraft was donated by Huntings to the Brooklands Museum, and was skilfully positioned on to its extremely short runway on 17 October, returning to its birthplace: a fitting conclusion to a long career of almost thirty-five years in which the aircraft flew a total of 44,019 hours.

The Aviation Photo Company

26: AVRO 748 G-ATMJ

Or is it an HS 748? Or worse still, a BAe 748? In fact G-ATMJ is all three types, the changes of name reflecting the consolidations that took place in Britain's aircraft manufacturing industry over the decades: from Avro, to Hawker Siddeley and finally British Aerospace. The design for a sturdy twin-engine turboprop, hunting for the elusive Dakota replacement trophy, signalled Avro's return in 1959 to the civil marketplace ten years after the fiasco of the Avro Tudor had played itself out. In parallel, the Indian government was looking for a medium-sized transport for its military, so contracted to build the type under licence. Somewhat larger than the Dakota, the 748 could carry up to fifty-two passengers or around 5 tons of cargo over 900 miles and operate from semi-prepared strips under 4,000ft long. It was powered by the Rolls-Royce Dart, and as the engine was developed, so was the 748. It faced competition from the Fokker F27 Friendship, which had several years' start on it, the Handley Page Herald, and turbine conversions of the American Convairliners; nevertheless it sold reasonably well, 380, over a thirty-year production run and proved durable in service. With its short undercarriage it really could tackle rough, unprepared airfields; on one occasion a Hawker Siddeley salesman memorably said that the airstrip the 748 had used was so unprepared 'it wasn't even awake!' Air forces liked the aircraft, many being used for government and VIP transport; the RAF flew a number for the Queen's Flight. It had the narrowest fuselage of the

Barry Friend

twin turboprops, and always felt cramped in its two-by-two seat layout. Astonishingly, Channel Airways, based in Southend, wanting to squeeze the very last penny from its revenue, literally did that with its 748s; they were operated in a three-by-two configuration, without armrests, seating up to sixty-two passengers.

Those name changes: Avro – the name derives from its founder Alliott Verdon Roe – was better known for its bombers, Lancasters, Lincolns and Vulcans, but had a respectable pedigree as a builder of transports; the York, the Lancastrian, even the much smaller Anson-derived Nineteen – the last two illustrated here – all played their roles in the development of Britain's civil aviation after the Second World War.

The Manchester-based manufacturer had been part of the Hawker Siddeley Group since 1936 but retained its name, as did the other constituent parts of the group that included Hawker, famous for the Hunter jet fighter, and Gloster, the latter being merged with Armstrong Whitworth, builder of the Argosy freighter, in 1961. Two years later, Whitworth Gloster and Avro were consolidated to form Avro Whitworth within the Hawker Siddeley combine, by which time de Havilland had also joined the group. The decision was taken to rebrand all aircraft types with the Hawker Siddeley name: the de Havilland Trident became the Hawker Siddeley Trident, for example, and the Avro 748 was renamed the Hawker Siddeley 748, or more familiarly the HS 748, or just 748! There was a further name change in 1977 when the British government nationalised the aircraft manufacturing industry, bringing together Hawker Siddeley, the British Aircraft Corporation and Scottish Aviation; the HS 748 became somewhat unconvincingly the British Aerospace 748, or BAe 748.

The 748 entered service with Aerolineas Argentinas early in 1962, one of the small number of operators that used the first version of the 748, for Avro was already planning to enhance the type's performance, installing more powerful Dart 7 engines and beefing up the structure to increase payload and range. By October 1962 this Series 2 version had been certificated. Two of this type were ordered by Autair, a helicopter operator that had branched out and acquired Dakotas, which it used on charter services. Encouraged by the British government to develop scheduled services over unserved routes, Autair enthusiastically applied to operate services out of its Luton base to Blackpool, Dundee, Hull and Teesside, and bought Ambassadors and later Heralds to fly them.

The Aviation Photo Company

The Aviation Photo Company

The two 748s, G-ATMI and G-ATMJ, delivered in 1966, were occasionally used on scheduled services and their introduction into service coincided with a new name for the airline, Autair International, and an attractive two-tone blue livery. However, they spent most of their time flying inclusive-tour charters before being made to earn their keep working for other airlines. G-ATMI went to join the Caribbean airline

LIAT, flying for it during the winter months and returning to Europe during the summer. G-ATMJ spent 1968 flying for Jamaica Air Service (1967), joining its de Havilland Herons on domestic services, before returning for another long engagement in 1969, this time with the Azores airline SATA.

Making money on scheduled services was hard work, especially when pioneering new routes, and Autair increasingly turned to the holiday charter market; it bought One-Eleven jets and developed a close relationship with tour operator Clarksons. Not even switching the scheduled services to Heathrow, which the airline did in 1969, could save them and so they were all withdrawn at the end of the year. The Heralds were sold off, but Autair retained the 748s, which were readily marketable. G-ATMJ returned from its sojourn in the Azores in mid-1970 to spend a year flying for British Air Ferries throughout most of 1971.

British Air Ferries was best known for its cross-Channel vehicle ferry but had built up a considerable business carrying passengers on the relatively short hop across the Channel from Southend to Ostend and Rotterdam, and the two

Autair 748s were leased in to boost the passenger services. Except the airline was no longer called Autair: in a dramatic change of livery and business, in 1970 Autair had become Court Line, flying a large fleet of BAC One-Elevens on holiday charter flights, tastefully painted in pastel hues. Court Line had hotel and other interests in the Caribbean, and had bought a controlling interest in LIAT, Leeward Islands Air Transport, already a 748 operator, based in Antigua. LIAT used some of the Court Line One-Elevens during the winter months, and when G-ATMJ was returned off-lease from BAF, it was painted all over pink and sent off to join LIAT for the winter months, with the Antigua registration VP-LAJ. It was back in Europe, however, by April of the following year, 1972, and still in pink, was leased for six months to a French airline, Rousseau Aviation, which retained the Antigua registration. Rousseau already operated 748s on domestic services from Nantes and its base in Dinard in north-western France, collaborating with the French domestic airline Air Inter. Despite the renowned intellectualism of the French, the airline was named after its founder, not the philosopher!

The Aviation Photo Company

Barry Friend

Sister ship G-ATMI had a similar career, flying in turn for LIAT, SATA and British Air Ferries; at the end of 1971 it was sold to LIAT. By the end of 1972 VP-LAJ was out of the fleet too, sold to Britain's Civil Aviation Authority (CAA) and back with its old registration G-ATMJ.

Britain's aviation ministry had always had a civil aviation flying unit (CAFU), ever since the first Ministry of Civil Aviation had been established in 1944. After the Civil Aviation Authority was formed in 1972, the CAFU, based at Stansted, was transferred to it. The aircraft provided flight inspection services, calibrated radar and ground approach equipment and checked out operating crews, using a fleet of Hunting Percival Princes, de Havilland Doves, Chipmunks and 748s, painted in a distinctive black and red livery. The CAFU also operated flights for the British government, using civil-registered Hawker Siddeley 125 business jets, and the former Court Line 748 was mainly used in a transport role, flying educational trips for school children and providing a much-needed air link for parliamentarians between London and Strasbourg in France, the inaccessible home of the European Parliament.

There was really not enough work for the aircraft, and by early 1975 G-ATMJ began operating flights for Dan-Air out of Gatwick, which needed extra summer weekend capacity for its Jersey and Bern (Switzerland) scheduled services but was in the process of deploying most of its 748 fleet to Aberdeen in support of its oil support operation there. Eyebrows were raised at the commercial operation of this aircraft on behalf of a British airline, but no home-based operator had the temerity to raise an objection before the regulatory body, which, of course, was the Civil Aviation Authority!

The CAA markings were painted out, and a very small 'Dan-Air Services' sticker, just visible, was applied to the rear

Barry Friend

The Aviation Photo Company

passenger door. Fortunately, Dan-Air's colours were also red and black, so G-ATMJ did not look out of place.

The arrangement continued for some years, before the CAA sold G-ATMJ to Dan-Air in July 1978, which converted the aircraft to Series 2A standard, with more powerful Dart 7 Mark 532 engines, and sent the aircraft up to join its sister 748s in Aberdeen, among them, the ex-Autair 748 G-ATMI, which Dan-Air had bought in 1975.

Charlie Stewart's atmospheric photograph shows G-ATMJ in Aberdeen, with a green Morris Minor support van from Dan-Air Engineering, and a Bristow Helicopters Sikorsky S-61 in the background. The 748s flew oil-rig workers from Aberdeen to Sumburgh in the Shetland Isles, where connections were made with helicopters to transfer the passengers out to the rigs in the North Sea. The 748s were well suited for operations into and out of Sumburgh's restricted 09/27 runway. The livery, still showing the compass rose on the tail, was the final iteration of the red and black colours traditionally used by Dan-Air. By 1982, however, the demand for these flights was beginning to diminish as North Sea activity switched from exploration to production; other business opportunities were called for, and help came from an unlikely source.

After years of losses on the Scottish Highlands and Islands routes, it finally dawned on British Airways that the payload-restricted Viscount was too large and too uneconomic for many of these services. The corporation had bought two 748s in 1975, but only in 1982 did it decide to withdraw all the Viscounts and acquire more 748s, which it needed in a hurry. Three 748s were leased from Dan-Air, G-ATMJ being registered to British Airways in June 1982; it stayed with British Airways for seven years.

Charlie Stewart

Jonathan Walton

Charlie Stewart

Arno Landewers

After British Airways was privatised, a dingy blue and grey livery was introduced, and G-ATMJ had another repaint. British Airways operated a sizeable fleet of 748s, modernising the inventory over the years. Late in 1989 G-ATMJ was handed back to Dan-Air and repainted in that airline's latest red and blue livery.

Unlike the previous photographs, this one was not shot in Aberdeen but at Berlin's Tegel Airport in 1990. Dan-Air had a long connection with Berlin, flying the bulk of the German city's inclusive-tour charter flights for two decades; limited scheduled services were begun in the 1980s, to Amsterdam and later to Saarbrücken, in West Germany, using 748s. G-ATMJ's pristine appearance, after twenty-five years, is a tribute to Dan-Air's engineers. The aircraft did not last long in this role. Bad things were beginning to happen to Dan-Air: intense competition on

the Gatwick scheduled services from new airlines such as Air Europe; the erosion of its tour operator client base; and the reunification of Germany, which removed the airline's privileged status in West Berlin in 1990. Dan-Air was forced to close down its Berlin operations in 1991, and G-ATMJ was flown to Manchester and into storage. By the middle of the following year six of Dan-Air's remaining 748s, including the two ex-Autair aircraft, had been sold to Janes Aviation, and a few months later Dan-Air was sold to British Airways: the end of Dan-Air but not of G-ATMJ.

Janes specialised in flying for the Royal Mail, and the interior of G-ATMJ was stripped out to allow it to fly night mail services all over the country and to Ireland. That, and the carriage of newspapers, constituted the bulk of the airline's business for some years; later the airline would also fly for courier and express parcels services including Lynx, DHL and Securicor, and even try its hand at passenger scheduled services. In 1993 the name of the airline was changed to Emerald Airways, and G-ATMJ got a new colour scheme.

Seen here at Bournemouth towards the end of its career, in 2006, G-ATMJ's certificate of airworthiness expired in September of that year, a few months after Emerald had itself ceased operations. The aircraft was subsequently broken up.

In 2020 two HS 748s were still in service with Canada's Air North flying in the Yukon, and the Indian Air Force continues to operate the type. In Britain, G-BEJD is currently being restored in Dan-Air colours by the Speke Aerodrome Heritage Group at Liverpool.

Howard J. Curtis

27: HANDLEY PAGE HERALD G-APWJ

I never flew in a Herald even though they were always buzzing around the airports I used to frequent in the 1980s – Gatwick, Jersey, Manchester and Stansted – usually painted in the RAF-style stealth livery of Air UK. And for all that there seemed to be a lot of them, that was not the case; only fifty were built. Handley Page initiated the design for a medium-size, high-wing, short-haul airliner after it had taken on the responsibility for building the Miles Marathon in 1948; the Herald resembled an enlarged Marathon, powered by four Alvis Leonides Major piston engines. Looking over their shoulders, Handley Page's designers could see that turbine engines, the Rolls-Royce Dart in particular, were the trending technology, but at the time the Dart did not have sufficient power and its reliability was an unknown issue; that of course changed after the Vickers Viscount entered service. The first Herald flew in 1955, painted in the colours of Australia's Queensland Airlines.

The Aviation Photo Company

Like the Marathon, the Herald had stunning short-airfield performance; it still remains the largest airliner ever to have landed on Alderney's tiny airfield. Even though Handley Page garnered some interest, firm orders for the original type never materialised and the company found increasing customer resistance to a new piston engine airliner. Meanwhile, the Dutch firm Fokker had successfully launched the very similar F27 Friendship, which was powered by two Rolls-Royce Darts. This had taken to the air in 1955, only three months after the first flight of the Herald, and looked promising; Fokker was gaining orders and had access to the American market

through a licensing deal with Maryland-based Fairchild. It was time for Handley Page to rethink the Herald and do what, with hindsight, seems the obvious thing; re-engine the Herald with two Rolls-Royce Darts, by now delivering 2,100ehp (equivalent horsepower), half as much again as those fitted to the early Viscounts. Indeed, with further design tweaking, the Dart Herald with two engines could do almost as much as the original Viscount 700 series, carrying up to fifty-six passengers over 500 miles and at much the same speed. The only trouble was that the Dart Herald had lost the sales impetus to the Dutch aircraft. To help things along, the British government agreed to buy three Dart Heralds in 1959, which were then lent to BEA, but by then Fokker and Fairchild between them had already sold 135 aircraft; cruelly, Queensland Airlines' new owner Ansett bought F27s instead of Dart Heralds. The next big order for Heralds came in 1960 from Jersey Airlines, which wanted six of a slightly longer version, the 200 series. G-APWJ was part of this order.

There had been a Jersey Airways before the war, but it had gradually been taken over by the railway companies, and then forced to 'relocate' to England during the German occupation of the Channel Islands. Quick work saw a resumption of air services soon after the German surrender in May 1945, but despite local opposition, the airline, by now renamed Channel Islands Airways, was swallowed up at nationalisation in 1947. It became an important station in the British European Airways network; the corporation did not neglect the Channel Islands but imposed its rigid overhead structure and controls so that what had previously been a profitable operation became just another loss-making BEA domestic service. There still seemed to be room for a bit of local entrepreneurship, however; a charter airline, Jersey Airlines, began flying de Havilland Rapides early in 1949 and when restrictions on scheduled services were lifted the airline was able to build up a modest network based on Jersey and Guernsey, flying to the south coast, Gatwick, Manchester and nearby airports in France. When the airline outgrew the eight-seat Rapides, it bought seventeen-seat de Havilland Herons. As business developed, Herons were supplemented by thirty-two-seat Dakotas. Then the airline took the plunge and ordered fifty-seat Heralds, which began to be delivered in 1962.

The Heralds were an excellent choice. The sectors Jersey Airlines flew tended to be short but intensive, requiring ten landings per aircraft per day during the peak summer months; with its high wing and large double doors at the rear, ground handling was efficient and the Herald allowed fifteen-minute turnarounds en route. Passengers got a nice view from the windows, and the Herald had the widest fuselage of that generation of twin-turboprops. G-APWJ joined the airline in June 1963, except that the operator had changed its name, a leitmotif for this particular aircraft: it was registered to Transair but painted in the colours of British United Airways, or to be totally accurate, British United (Channel Islands) Airways. This is what had happened. Early in 1960 the government changed the rules for British airlines, hinting heavily that it would like to see some consolidation among the independents, so the two largest, Hunting-Clan and Airwork (which already owned Transair, Air Charter, Channel Air Bridge and feeder airline Mortons), merged to form British United Airways (BUA). When the independents realised that the government's new rules, far from offering new opportunities, were little more than window dressing, other smaller airlines began to rethink their long-term futures and began knocking on the door of British United and its dynamic managing director, Freddie Laker. First to succumb, early in 1962, was the Silver City Group, which included Manx Airlines as well as the car ferry operation, the latter soon to be merged with Laker's Channel Air Bridge. A few months later, Jersey Airlines was taken over, and its operations combined with newly acquired Manx. Now there was British United (CI) Airways and British United (Manx) Airways; to keep it simple, the aircraft were just painted in the new BUA colours.

The Aviation Photo Company

Barry Friend

More Heralds were bought. G-APWJ got to fly further afield, to Blackpool, Manchester and the Isle of Man. A new colour scheme was introduced in 1966–67; G-APWJ looks fine in Barry Friend's photograph taken at Southampton, showing the aqua-and-sandstone stripes and bold lettering. More changes were about to happen. British and Commonwealth Shipping, a major shareholder in BUA, decided to buy out the other shareholders and take control of the airline and some of its appendages, including the Channel Islands, Manx and Morton subsidiaries; the latter were all hived off into a new airline, British United Island Airways (BUIA), in November 1968. Livery changes were minimal: you had to be in the know to understand what BUIA meant!

Seen here at Gatwick, the Dakotas in the background were also repainted in the BUIA colours as they had been previously operated by Mortons. But soon enough a further repaint was called for. Again, G-APWJ did not change hands; it did

The Aviation Photo Company

157

not even change parents! But circumstances dictated a change of name. The government realised that the present rules and regulations were just not working and commissioned a very detailed study into the future of British civil aviation in 1967. It took two years to come out, and when it did, the Edwards Report was robust: it thought there should be a strong independent airline operating alongside the state-owned corporations, and the whole lot should be regulated by a professional and independent aviation authority. The report also recommended that BOAC and BEA should come under a national holdings board. The Civil Aviation Authority was successfully established, bringing together both economic and safety regulation of the airline industry. Unexpectedly the notion of the national holdings board quickly led to the merger of the two corporations; soon BEA and BOAC found themselves joined as one, renamed British Airways in 1973. The competing independent airline, the 'second force', was created in 1970 by amalgamating British United Airways with a vigorous long-haul charter airline, Caledonian, which flew modern Boeing 707s. The merger of BUA and Caledonian was a buyout of the former by the latter, so British and Commonwealth lost control of the airline, but the shipping company chose to retain BUIA; only now it had to change its name again! The new airline was dubbed BIA, or British Island Airways, and given a completely different paint scheme, using a deep orange as the main colour, illustrated in Dietrich Eggert's powerful image of the aircraft at Gatwick.

Again, you had to be in the know to understand what BIA stood for. The route network remained much the same, focussed on the Isle of Man, Blackpool, the south coast and the Channel Islands, although the airline lost the Gatwick–Jersey service, which was retained by the merged

Dietrich Eggert

Caledonian/BUA. However, the airline picked up flying contracts with British Caledonian, as the latter had been renamed, including the Silver Arrow rail/air/rail service between London and Paris via Gatwick and Le Touquet. Passenger numbers bumped along at around 500,000 a year during the 1970s. Attempts were made to broaden the network, flying more regional services to Holland and Belgium, for example; however, the work remained seasonal and low fare. An ambitious attempt to get a number of routes out of Gatwick failed, but the airline did break out of its niche in 1978 when it acquired BAC One-Eleven jets for inclusive-tour charters, and took over six Heralds and the Southend-based scheduled service network of British Air Ferries, to Ostend, Rotterdam, Basel and Dusseldorf. In 1979 more than 900,000 passengers were carried, although that would prove to be the last year of G-APWJ flying for BIA. By this time the aircraft had acquired another new paint scheme, one that was more enlightening.

The Aviation Photo Company

British and Commonwealth was buying other airlines as the decade came to an end, first Air Anglia with its strong east coast operations, many of them connecting with Amsterdam, and then Air Westward, a new start-up in the West Country. The temptation to merge all the airlines was irresistible, and sure enough, in January 1980, they were all merged into a new entity, Air UK. It was time for the paint brushes again, and for G-APWJ to get a new makeover. The aircraft wore these colours for another five years and was the last Herald to fly with Air UK: twenty-two years of service flying more or less the same routes with more or less the same parents but under so many different names. G-APWJ flew its last official service on 29 June 1985, from Jersey to Southampton, but then had to be hurriedly pressed into further service to stand in for an unserviceable Fokker F27 at Leeds. In July the Herald was then donated to the Duxford Aviation Society, in whose care it has been ever since.

BIA, and its successor, had a similar relationship to the Herald as did Dan-Air to the Comet; half of all the Heralds built flew with BIA at one time or another! Other large fleets were flown by British Air Ferries and Channel Express, the latter only withdrawing its last Herald in April 1999. Ironically, both Air UK and Channel Express replaced their Heralds with Fokker F27s; indeed Air UK went on to expand its Dutch connections, first by buying more Fokker products, and later when the airline was bought out by Dutch airline KLM and merged into its operations. By that time Handley Page, the manufacturer, had long departed the scene, brought down by the unsuccessful debut of the Jetstream, another aircraft that was launched with the wrong engines. The Jetstream was salvaged, however, and given new engines, but not before Handley Page had passed into history early in 1970.

Tony Eastwood Collection

28: AVIATION TRADERS CARVAIR G-APNH

If there was one thing Freddie Laker was not afraid of – and the evidence is that there were not many things he did fear – it was cutting off the noses of aircraft to make them perform better. He got an early start with the Avro Tudor when he converted some early airframes into Super Trader 4B freighters, which involved lengthening the nose by 6ft. The photograph of G-AGRG page 33 clearly shows the new, unpainted nose section. He then followed Silver City by introducing the Mark 32 version of the Bristol Freighter, which had a longer nose than earlier marks, on his Channel Air Bridge service. G-AMLP was converted to Mark 32 standard by Laker's engineering company Aviation Traders (ATEL); it could carry three cars and sixteen passengers.

The Aviation Photo Company

But his most ambitious rhinosectomy involved the DC-4 Skymaster. There was no obvious replacement for the Bristol Freighters on cross-Channel work, and by the end of the 1950s they were beginning to wear out and becoming costly to operate. In addition, competition from sea ferries was growing sharper as new shipping lines challenged both the traditional British Railways services and Silver City's short air crossing. This affected Laker's operation less as his flights out of Southend, on the northern banks of the Thames estuary, only faced off against the overnight ferry service between Harwich and the Hook of Holland. Sectors out of Southend were longer than those from Lydd Ferryfield in Kent, utilisation of the aircraft higher and the need for frantic twenty-minute turnarounds less acute. Moreover, Channel Air Bridge reckoned that rather than compete head-on with the Channel ferries, the company could outflank them by operating further inland into Europe, where ships could not follow! It was somewhat removed from the original Silver City concept of extremely short air passages, which maximised the number of cars that could be carried, but then Laker was not someone who readily accepted conventional economic theories.

Already a satisfied Douglas DC-4 user, Laker proposed rebuilding the Skymaster with a new nose section, relocating the cockpit above the fuselage and providing a large door that allowed unimpeded access to the interior. Skymasters were readily available on the second-hand market and, being

Robin A. Walker

P.G. Ryle via Steve Ryle

somewhat elderly, relatively inexpensive. The modified DC-4, called the Carvair, could carry five cars and twenty-two passengers as a car ferry; ex-military C-54s worked better as they weighed 2 tons less than the post-war DC-4. Cars were loaded by a scissor lift, although at least one company later built a ramp. The first Carvair, converted from a Skymaster already in the fleet, flew on 21 June 1961, wearing Channel Air Bridge colours but with parent company's British United markings on the tail; the name changed to British United Air Ferries after Silver City joined the group in 1962, and during that year two more Carvairs were added. Three more Carvairs joined the fleet in 1963 and another two in 1964. G-APNH was converted in 1965; a further two Carvairs were delivered, one in 1966 and the last in 1969, making eleven for the home side. Another ten were sold to other airline customers. G-APNH, like most British Skymasters, was an ex-military C-54 and had joined the fleet of Air Charter in March 1960, having previously flown with Independent, an inglorious British charter airline that was closed down late in 1959 and the subject of further comment in the chapter about Skymaster G-APID.

The aircraft was sold to a Dutch company, Euravia, but never entered service, instead joining Air Charter in March 1960. Air Charter London markings were applied briefly before the aircraft transitioned to its new corporate owner.

Laker's four Skymasters flew out of Southend on cross-Channel Coach-Air and Rail-Air routes to Calais, Ostend and Rotterdam; all four were transformed into Carvairs. It took two years to rebuild G-APNH; it entered service early in 1965, painted in full British United Air Ferries (BUAF) colours – a misnomer, as only British United titles appeared on the fuselage – by which time the aircraft was twenty years old, flying

Tony Eastwood Collection

Author's Collection

on BUAF's newly minted 'deep penetration' routes to Basel, Geneva and Strasbourg.

These routes were not altogether a success, even if James Bond's adversary Goldfinger did use the service to smuggle gold into Switzerland. G-APNH had a more adventurous life than the other BUAF Carvairs, having been equipped with extra tankage, so could undertake cargo charter flights further afield. These included a two-month sales trip for Aviation Traders to Australia and New Zealand, followed by a stint on the Dar-es-Salaam to Lusaka oil lift late in 1965; the oil embargo that followed the unilateral declaration of independence by Rhodesia affected Zambia as it had previously imported its supply from Rhodesia using the Mozambique Beira pipeline, so at some expense the British government undertook to fly in oil in 44-gallon drums from Dar for a period of months.

The vehicle ferry began losing serious money in 1966 and by early 1967 it was in crisis; flying cars simply did not bring in enough revenue, just one tenth of a comparable passenger load. And fewer people were taking their cars abroad by air. In 1962 BUAF had carried 135,000 cars: by 1966 that figure was down to 90,000. Laker had been sacked as managing

director of British United in August 1965 and was no longer around to defend his old bailiwick. The new managing director axed all the deep-penetration routes, leaving the Carvairs flying the more traditional routes out of Southend to Rotterdam, Calais and Ostend. And at the end of 1967, the car ferry was established as a separate company with a new name, British Air Ferries, and a new livery.

There were other changes. The new airline moved out of its grandiose London office to more suitable quarters at Southend Airport. Passenger services were enhanced using turboprops such as the Viscount and HS 748. The company paid more attention to freight, which paid better than ferrying cars. Channel Air Bridge had carried around 10,000 tonnes a year, so 25,000 tonnes in 1968 was a creditable increase. The divorce from British United became final in 1968 when many of the airline components of British United passed to ownership under the British and Commonwealth shipping group; not British Air Ferries, however. It remained as part of the rump with some curious bedfellows, including a cargo airline in New Zealand, Aviation Traders Engineering at Southend, some tour operators and a franchise to try and sell the Lockheed TriStar.

Not all turnaround efforts succeed, but BAF persisted. The airline realised that the short sea crossing from Lydd was no longer viable, and at the end of October 1970 closed down its historic Lydd–Le Touquet route and withdrew the last of the Bristol Freighters. It was the passing of an era, although other airlines continued to operate passenger services from Lydd. In 1971 just 19,680 cars flew across the Channel, but passenger numbers remained steady at around 275,000 a year. And things were about to look up; late in 1971 the airline was bought by T.D. 'Mike' Keegan, a storied entrepreneur with a string of aviation enterprises to his credit. The owner of a freight airline, Transmeridian Air Cargo, he wanted to develop 'deep-penetration' routes to Switzerland using Canadair CL-44 turboprops, and in order to acquire the licences, it was simpler just to buy BAF, which already held them.

G-APNH was not part of the deal, however. On 18 March 1971, while landing in a crosswind at Le Touquet, the nose-wheel collapsed, severely damaging the nose of the aircraft, although not the eleven passengers and seven crew members. There was some consideration given to rebuilding it with a new nose, but in the end the engines and other parts were salvaged and the fuselage broken up in situ.

BAF's Carvairs flew their last car ferry services on New Year's Day 1977. Keegan had enthusiastically reinstated the Basel route and, indeed, I used the service on one occasion, enjoying the silver service in the spacious passenger cabin, but from 1977 he switched the remaining Carvairs over to cargo operations, stripping off the paint to maximise payload. He retained BAF for another six years, until 1983, transforming it into a successful wet-lease operation with a large fleet of immaculately maintained Heralds and Viscounts.

29: VICKERS SUPER VC10 G-ASGC

After the Comet's abrupt withdrawal from service in April 1953, there were plenty of British aircraft manufacturers ready to take up the challenge of jet travel, not least de Havilland itself, which persevered and went on to build the Comet 4. Three other aircraft builders were keen to submit proposals for a new jetliner, all of them piggybacking on the designs for their jet bombers that were to become the V Force: the Avro Vulcan, the Handley Page Victor and the

Vickers Valiant. Vickers, riding on the success of its newly launched Viscount, had the most realistic concept, using the wings of the Valiant with Rolls-Royce Conway engines embedded in the root as in the Comet, designed to carry around 120 passengers over 4,000 miles. The project, later known as the VC7, was ordered in tiny numbers for the RAF, and aroused interest in Vickers stalwart Trans-Canada Air Lines; in BOAC, not so much. The corporation was keener on the stretched de Havilland DH.118, or Conway Comet, but failed to get government support; its chairman, Sir Miles Thomas, resigned in a huff in May 1956, and shortly after the Ministry of Supply cancelled the VC7 project. The Conway Comet never left the drawing board. The VC7, with its large wing, would have had good airfield performance, necessary for its RAF role, and of interest to BOAC, which needed, or thought it needed, an aircraft that it could use on its African and Far Eastern routes with good 'hot and high' capabilities.

Vickers now turned to another proposal, this from BEA, for a jet replacement of the Viscount and worked on designs for the so-called Vanjet, which would have had a double-bubble fuselage and three rear-mounted engines; Vickers hoped to be able to meet both corporations' requirements but then decided to concentrate on the BOAC proposal, abandoning the Vanguard fuselage and going for four engines. Vickers was impressed by the performance of the rear-engine configuration, which allowed an uncluttered wing with more scope for lift devices and a lower landing speed, and led to a reduction in cabin noise, albeit with a penalty in aircraft weight; there had to be massive steel beams to carry the Rolls-Royce Conways. As the design evolved, so did BOAC's requirements; the impressive airfield performance suited the demands of its route structure, and in any case, the government, which had allowed BOAC to buy Boeing 707s on the understanding that any future orders would be for British-built aircraft, did not want the manufacturer to come up with a clone of the American Boeing and Douglas designs. Under BOAC's new chairman Sir Gerald d'Erlanger and its chief executive Basil Smallpeice the corporation was coaxed in early 1958

into ordering thirty-five of the new jets, now called the VC10. The order included not just units intended for the Far East and African routes but for the North Atlantic market as well, BOAC having persuaded itself that the relatively small 135-seat VC10 would be as economical to operate as the larger 174-seat Boeing 707. It was to be the start of a long and stressful relationship.

Vickers then admitted it had done its sums wrong and would need an order for at least forty-five aircraft for it to continue with the contract, and offered a larger version, the 189-seat Super VC10, more suitable for transatlantic routes. BOAC took the bait, and in 1960 ordered ten more aircraft, Super VC10s, to the satisfaction of the Minister of Aviation: 'There is no doubt that your decision will be most helpful to the aircraft industry.'

Later that year, BOAC changed its tune and began admitting that it too had done its sums wrong, and that the VC10 would cost more to operate than the Boeing 707. It now wanted a smaller Super VC10, with up to 163 seats, but in greater numbers, ordering thirty of the revised Super VC10s, and downsizing the standard VC10 order to fifteen, later further reduced to twelve, making forty-two in all.

D'Erlanger resigned in 1960, and the new chairman, Sir Matthew Slattery, did all the sums again and was not happy with the outcome, telling the Minister that flying a fleet of VC10s rather than having an all-Boeing fleet would cost the corporation around £11 million a year more; all this against a background of BOAC's mounting deficits. These became overwhelming, leading the Minister to fire both Slattery and Smallpeice late in 1963, and to appoint a new chairman, Sir Giles Guthrie, to sort out the mess. Guthrie more or less immediately gave the government a fright by

The Aviation Photo Company

The Aviation Photo Company

telling it, just as the first VC10 was entering service with BOAC in April 1964, that the corporation had ordered far too many aircraft and he now wanted to cancel all the Super VC10s and buy six turbofan Boeing 707-320Cs instead. The Minister was appalled: 'The prospects of the aircraft would be ruined. The industrial dislocation … would be very serious. Several thousand people would lose their jobs.' Guthrie was reined in, but he had made his point: it was the last time the government interfered with BOAC's fleet plans. The Super VC10 order was reduced to seventeen, and of course BOAC went on to order many more 707-320Cs.

The Super VC10 was introduced on the London to New York route in April 1965. G-ASGC was delivered in March 1965 to BOAC, before being transferred a year later to BOAC-Cunard. Outside the BOAC maintenance facility at Heathrow, its colours reflect the short-lived association between the corporation and Cunard Steamship.

Just a few months later BOAC-Cunard was dissolved and the aircraft was repainted in full BOAC livery. Note the addition of the exterior emergency exit markings, a requirement that began to be introduced from 1966.

BOAC, renamed British Airways in 1973, continued to deploy the Super VC10s alongside the Boeing 707s, flying them to Mexico City, Africa, the Middle East and Gulf, Pakistan and India. By the end of 1976, the standard VC10s had been withdrawn and the Corporation began to withdraw its Super VC10s from service in 1979; immediately prior to their retirement some were used on European routes for a time. G-ASGC's last commercial flight was from Amsterdam to London on 22 October 1979, after which it was stored at Heathrow. By March 1980 all the Super VC10s had been withdrawn. G-ASGC is now displayed at Duxford in BOAC-Cunard colours, and there are a number of other VC10s preserved around the country.

Duxford Aviation Society

In commercial service, time was called on the VC10s because of new noise regulations, but the sturdy airframe was good for many more years and indeed the Royal Air Force did not retire its final VC10 until 2013, fifty-one years after the type's first flight. Fifty-four VC10s were built in total, so the minimum build that Vickers required was surpassed! Apart from the RAF and BOAC, it sold in penny numbers. Boeing responded by introducing the Boeing 720B, a shortened and lighter version of the 707, seating up to 149 passengers and with four Pratt and Whitney JT3D turbofans, with impressive 'hot-rod' performance. This comment from Air-India, quoted in *Flight* magazine, sums up the dilemma for airlines in choosing between the VC10 and 720B: 'Noting that the 720B has an excellent airfield performance, which is what Air-India are looking for … if all other technical and financial matters were equal the rear-engined passenger appeal of the VC10 could well in itself justify the purchase of this type. Air-India are, he says, seriously interested in the VC10, not least for its passenger appeal.' But Air-India never bought VC10s and Boeing went on to sell the 720B to Ethiopian and Pakistan, airlines that were potential customers for the VC10, highlighting the difficulties that Vickers, by now part of British Aircraft Corporation, faced in marketing and selling it. However attractive the aircraft, all the other requirements, including financing, engineering and spares support, have to be slotted in as well. BOAC's figures consistently show that even the Super VC10 was more expensive to fly than the Conway-powered Boeing 707, both by flying hour and

per capacity-ton-mile. Much is made of the VC10's superior passenger appeal and higher load factors that it attracted, but the extra revenue earned should surely have contributed to higher profits, not just compensated the airline for the type's higher operating costs: that is just running to catch up.

Still, by the end, British Airways noted approvingly in 1977 that 'the best long-haul type for fatigue-cracks and repairs is the Super VC10, whose maintenance cost in British Airways service is very much lower than that of the 707, and is to some extent offsetting its higher operating cost.'

30: BRITISH AIRCRAFT CORPORATION ONE-ELEVEN G-AVGP

When I was a teenager, the One-Eleven, Britain's first short-haul jet, was always in the news and raising our hopes; it was even sold off the drawing board in 1963 to American Airlines, the very same airline that had launched the Douglas DC-3. The idea for the aircraft came originally from Luton's Hunting Aircraft, better known for its Pembroke light transports and Provost trainers, which in 1956 set about designing a small jet airliner that would carry up to forty-eight passengers at speeds of 450mph over 1,000 miles and could replace Convairliners as well as Viscounts. The design faced competition, from France's Caravelle which first flew in 1955, and to a lesser extent from the de Havilland Comet, which although designed for medium-range Empire routes, was actually a bit short on range,

so it was developed into a stopgap jet airliner for BEA's European services. After Hunting became part of the British Aircraft Corporation (BAC) in 1960, its projected H.107 airliner was assessed favourably against the in-house design from Vickers (a scaled-down VC10) and the Vickers/BAC team decided to beef up the Hunting design, widening the fuselage so that it could take five-abreast seating, substituting Rolls-Royce Speys for the planned Bristol-Siddeley Orpheus jets and adding two more seat rows so that it could carry sixty-nine passengers; it would now cruise at 540mph over 1,200 miles. By early 1961 BAC had decided to go ahead with this proposal, now renamed the BAC.111 – better known as the One-Eleven – and secured its launch order, for ten aircraft from British United Airways, which wanted the jets as a straight Viscount replacement; the first entered service in April 1965. In order to secure the American Airlines order, the One-Eleven was upgraded to carry a higher payload over a greater range within the same fuselage dimensions; an additional central tank was fitted, together with more powerful Speys and a strengthened undercarriage. The enhanced series were known variously as the 300 and 400 series, more or less identical, but the 400 series had a restricted maximum take-off weight in order to comply with the then US legal limit imposed on two-crew-member operations. When this was lifted, the gross weight of the aircraft was increased to match that of the 300 series. In practice most of these upgraded One-Elevens were sold as 400 series.

An early buyer of the 400 series was Southend's Channel Airways, which ordered four in 1966. G-AVGP was the first to be delivered, configured with eighty-nine seats, in June 1967. Channel flew Viscounts out of Southend on inclusive-tour charters, scheduled services to the Channel Islands and a high-frequency service to Ostend. The One-Eleven appeared on all these services, causing some dismay at Southend because of its noise levels; also the runway was rather short, which restricted the operations of the jet. In 1968 Channel decided to switch its jet operations to Stansted, having taken delivery of two more One-Elevens and two Tridents. Intended for the holiday charter market, both aircraft types had unique seating configurations, the One-Elevens squeezing in ninety-nine passengers, the Tridents 139. Channel's purchase arrangements were flexible; the airline only took delivery of two Tridents, one of which spent a lot of time parked up at Stansted without its engines, and although a total of six One-Elevens was ordered, only three were delivered.

The Aviation Photo Company

After the second One-Eleven was accepted by Channel in 1968, G-AVGP was returned to the manufacturer. It was never converted to ninety-nine seats, which would have required cutting additional emergency exits above the wing. Instead BAC, with a buoyant order book, was content to have an almost new aircraft on its books for immediate delivery to new or potential customers. An anticipated deal with Dominicana did not result in a contract, but instead the aircraft was leased to Autair International in Luton in time for the 1969 summer season.

Autair, originally a helicopter operator, had tentatively entered the inclusive-tour market as early as 1961, flying Dakotas, and had progressed through Vikings, Ambassadors, Heralds and HS 748s, branching out into scheduled services and being acquired by the Court Line shipping group along the way. Autair's operations changed dramatically in

1968 as a result of buying One-Elevens and signing major contracts with the ambitious and energetic tour company Clarksons. In 1969, the year G-AVGP joined Autair, the airline flew 566,000 passengers, more than three times as many as in 1967. So successful was the holiday charter operation that Autair decided to abandon its skimpy scheduled service network altogether in October 1969 and to concentrate wholly on the inclusive-tour business, ordering a brand-new fleet of planes and changing the airline's name to Court Line. Three of the One-Elevens were immediately disposed of, all of them, including G-AVGP, going to Cambrian in 1970; a fourth Autair One-Eleven joined Cambrian a year later.

Cambrian, by now a subsidiary of British European Airways (BEA) and part of its British Air Services group, had solid credentials as a low-cost regional carrier, flying from Bristol, Cardiff and Liverpool, a difficult network of very short routes – Bristol to Cardiff is 26 miles – which it operated with aplomb and praiseworthy efficiency. The airline had previously flown charter programmes for Hourmont, a major regional tour operator, which had since switched its business to Court Line. So Cambrian formed its own in-house tour operator, Cambrian Air Holidays, and the One-Elevens flew holiday charters, building up business in a cut-throat market, as well as scheduled services, mainly from Liverpool to Glasgow and Heathrow.

The Aviation Photo Company

Ralf Manteufel

Both Cambrian and its partner Northeast had emerged from a period of losses, and following some pruning of staff and routes, had regained a measure of profitability as they introduced new jets. The Cambrian fleet was given a makeover late in 1971, sporting a new livery with a bright orange-red roof, but this was short-lived.

A mere two years later the government decided that all the state-owned airlines – BOAC, BEA, BEA Airtours, BKS and Cambrian – should be amalgamated under the British Airways name, so it was all change again for Cambrian, the fifth time in ten years that its aircraft had changed livery.

Dietrich Eggert

Cambrian, Northeast, and two former BEA divisions, Channel Islands and Scottish, were brought together as British Airways Regional Division (BARD). Aircraft were repainted in the new British Airways style; the aircraft is seen here at Palma in Majorca in April 1978.

But results for BARD were disappointing; losses were made in 1974 and 1975. Then the small regional airlines got sucked up in the feuding between the former BOAC and BEA divisions – 'To some extent the Divisions became inward looking and defensive particularly towards the Headquarters organisation,' the chairman complained in the 1977 report – so that year it was all change again; no more divisions based on the former airlines, instead a Commercial Operations Department with geographical subdivisions based on routes. What had been BARD now fell largely under Domestic Services, UK and Ireland Division. At least the aircraft did not have to be repainted, but it represented a further distancing from the former subtle

variations in regional preferences and marketing. G-AVGP spent its time flying out of Manchester and Birmingham on European services, but the corporation still struggled with its domestic operations. In 1979 British Airways decided to withdraw most of its remaining Viscounts and abandon twenty-six of the regional services, affecting among others Bristol, Cardiff and the Isle of Man; it had already handed over to British Midland Airways all its Liverpool services, bedrock of the old Cambrian, in 1978. The late 1970s were a difficult time for British Airways, but in 1981 the government appointed Sir John King as the corporation's new chairman and he set about reconstituting the airline and preparing it for 'privatisation', which he successfully accomplished in early 1987.

G-AVGP saw some further livery changes. In 1980 the 'airways' was dropped from the logo. More significantly, new colours were introduced in 1984, which brought back the 'airways' in a sombre blue and grey scheme.

Dietrich Eggert

Dietrich Eggert

Tony McGhee

The aircraft had been modified with hushkits, which brought down the noise level a little. At the end of 1988 the remaining five One-Elevens were withdrawn, replaced by One-Elevens brought into the fleet following the takeover of British Caledonian. G-AVGP's last flight was, appropriately enough, flying from Manchester to Birmingham on 31 October 1988. It then flew to Bournemouth for storage. And that might have been that.

Except that there were wheels within wheels, and they kept on turning! In 1986 British Airways had invested in a regional airline, Brymon, which flew out of Plymouth and London City Airport. At the same time British Airways began to collaborate with a newcomer at Birmingham, Birmingham Executive, which had been flying small Jetstreams since 1983, and which in 1988 began operating some of British Airways Birmingham routes. Birmingham Executive was bought out

The Aviation Photo Company

The Aviation Photo Company

by British Airways in partnership with Maersk Air, a Danish company owned by the huge A.P. Møller shipping group, and renamed Birmingham European; Maersk also acquired a stake in the holding company of Brymon. British Airways contributed its five One-Elevens, transferring them to Maersk for £10 million. G-AVGP was soon back at work in April 1990, in a shiny new livery, laid out with seventy-four seats at a generous 33in pitch, and flying to Ireland and other European destinations.

That arrangement lasted about two years, before the two partner airlines, Maersk and British Airways, decided to merge the two subsidiaries, Brymon and Birmingham European, into the new Brymon European Airways. The story unfolds in the photographs!

During all these manoeuvres G-AVGP continued flying out of Birmingham. British Airways, however, was experimenting with its approach to operations out of regional airports; collaborating with small regional airlines was one possible solution. As in the early days with Cambrian, low-cost, regionally based airlines offered an escape from the overheads of the intercontinental giant that was British Airways, and as a shareholder, BA still benefited. And yet, it was not quite what the airline was looking for; it wanted the British Airways brand out there, and to this end had already begun franchising its operation to a number of smaller airlines. CityFlyer at Gatwick was the first, followed by Loganair in Scotland. Now Maersk and British Airways decided to reset their partnership in 1993. Brymon European was split up

The Aviation Photo Company

into its original constituent airlines, the Brymon operation reverting to British Airways and Maersk taking over what was formerly Birmingham European. Both airlines then became franchisees of British Airways, so G-AVGP continued flying out of Birmingham, over the same routes, but now back in British Airways colours!

You have to look carefully, but there is a small 'Operated by Maersk Air' painted near the nose. The franchise arrangements gave British Airways great exposure as more airlines signed up; I recall seeing British Airways check-in desks at almost every airport in the British Isles in the 1990s. Franchisees paid British Airways to use its marketing and reservations systems,

which gave them access to a global network, and British Airways also benefited from the interline revenue that was generated. Franchising did mean that the British Airways brand was in the hands of other operators, something that the airline was not always comfortable with. In the case of Maersk, the Danish airline put much effort into its operation, eventually replacing the One-Elevens with Boeing 737s and operating more than half of British Airways' routes out of Birmingham.

Not just time caught up with G-AVGP. Increasingly stringent noise regulations made its continued operation within Europe impossible, and after thirty years on the British register, the aircraft was struck off in December 1996, having flown 47,708 hours. Even that was not the end of it. The One-Eleven was sold on for further use in South Africa, joining a newly established carrier, Nationwide, and continuing in service until 2003. The aircraft was broken up in 2005.

More than thirty-five years of service speaks to the One-Eleven's integrity, strength and reliability. Maybe the aircraft was overbuilt, but it was tough, at home in the most difficult operating conditions, and sold worldwide, doing well in the USA, Central and South America. Later it became popular as a business jet; there were more than fifteen registered in Saudi Arabia. The aircraft had a certain friendly chubbiness, it was well built and well thought out. Two airstairs, an auxiliary power unit, single-point refuelling and waist-high baggage loading compartments meant the aircraft was self-supporting and allowed quick turnaround times on scheduled services. For charter airlines the One-Eleven made good economic sense. Able to carry eighty-nine passengers over reasonable distances, it was the right size for many of the smaller holiday destinations, in Italy and Greece, and did well from regional airports, an important market for charter airlines. More than half the holiday market came from outside London and the South-East, and tour operators recognised that it was more attractive to sell direct flights from local airports than to expect holidaymakers to connect through London's congested airports. I write further about the One-Eleven in the section that deals with the stretched 500 series, which carried up to 119 passengers.

Appropriately BAC's hard-worked development One-Eleven, G-ASYD, was donated to Brooklands Museum, an excellent choice for preservation.

31: HAWKER SIDDELEY TRIDENT G-AVYB

Whatever else it may have done, the Trident did not satisfy the Goldilocks principle: it was never the right size. That was largely the fault of the launch customer, British European Airways (BEA), shared to a certain extent by the manufacturer, de Havilland. Also there was a problem with the porridge: the government insisted on adding some unwanted ingredients.

The success of the French Sud Caravelle, a short-haul airliner with two Rolls-Royce Avons mounted on the rear fuselage, which Air France had ordered in February 1956, took BEA by surprise. The corporation had expected to continue using aircraft powered by efficient turboprops for the foreseeable future, and indeed ordered the Vickers Vanguard in July 1956, but was mindful that almost every European airline would in due course order the sleek French jet. So in July 1956 BEA issued a specification for a jet aircraft with 'more than two engines' able to carry between eighty and 100 passengers up to 1,000 miles. De Havilland, Avro, Vickers and Bristol all came up with proposals, of which the DH.121 and Bristol 200 attracted the most favour. BEA preferred the DH.121; the government wanted the Bristol 200. BEA then added to the mix by downsizing its specification, saying it needed to carry at most eighty passengers over very short sectors. De Havilland was persuaded to go along with BEA's demands, designing a smaller aircraft powered by three Rolls-Royce Speys, and optimised for high speed, 600mph, rather than airfield performance. The manufacturer has been criticised for agreeing to the downgrading of the specification, which rendered the airliner unsellable in world markets, but in fairness, the customer is always right, and de Havilland may well have felt that if it did not comply then Bristol, with its '200' project, might. The government succeeded in stirring the pot further by persuading the various aircraft manufacturers to band together to form larger groupings. So de Havilland agreed to come under the wing of the Hawker Siddeley group; ironically, Hawkers had been collaborating with Bristol on the rival design. The DH.121 was renamed the Hawker Siddeley Trident, the name alluding to its three-engine layout and triplicated control systems. A pioneer in automatic landing development with BEA, the type entered service with the corporation in February 1964. Designed for passenger use only, I always thought the BEA Tridents had an attractive configuration, which included two 'club' compartments with seats that faced each other across tables.

Hawker Siddeley tried to do the best it could to make the aircraft more appealing to other buyers, upscaling the type from its lowly BEA format. Airfield performance was improved by making the wing bigger and installing leading-edge slats. More powerful Speys were used, extra

tankage put in and, by rearranging the cabin, passenger accommodation was increased from eighty-eight all-tourist to 126. Hawker Siddeley managed to sell thirteen of this version, the Trident 1E; one of the purchasers was English regional and charter carrier Channel Airways, based at Southend. Channel startled the industry by announcing an order for five of the Tridents, specially modified to carry 139 passengers. I was always amused by the optimistic way that this version was referred to as the 1E-140! To achieve this increase, Channel installed seven-across seating in the forward cabin, three on one side of the aisle, four on the other. It was a tight squeeze. With so many passengers, range suffered, around 1,000 miles, on a par with BEA's Tridents.

G-AVYB entered service in May 1968, and is seen at Gatwick, not an airport frequented much by the airline as its jets flew out of Stansted. The airline only accepted two of the Tridents; they were too large to use on scheduled

The Aviation Photo Company

services and Channel was a latecomer to the Mediterranean inclusive-tour market. Channel did perform some charter flying, including regional services to destinations such as Palma in Majorca, but the airline was never a serious player until 1969 when it signed a major agreement with Lyons Tours to perform all its charter flying for three years, 1970–72. But instead of using the Tridents the airline bought five Comets from BEA, trying in vain to trade in the Tridents to the corporation. So the Tridents flew less and less, although G-AVYB had a reprieve in 1971 when it was used by Hawker Siddeley for a demonstration tour of South America, followed by a contract for some charter flying out of West Berlin. Sister ship G-AVYE gallantly surrendered its engines and various other parts to keep G-AVYB in the air, and at the end of 1971 Channel was able to sell the two aircraft to BEA for use by BKS, now known as Northeast. Northeast adjusted the seating down to 123, and as well as being used on its trunk services out of Newcastle and London Heathrow, G-AVYB flew inclusive tour charters for Airways Holidays at the weekends.

BEA did see the error of its ways, or as aviation historian Derek King has put it, 'with exquisite hindsight, BEA then realised they needed a longer-range version of the Trident' and BEA subsequently ordered enhanced Tridents: the 2E, able to carry ninety-seven passengers over 2,200 miles; and the Trident 3B, which had a longer fuselage, seating up to 146 passengers, and a booster engine, the RB 162, which helped the airliner get off the ground a bit quicker and was useful in hot-and-high conditions. The corporation ended up with seventy-two Tridents in its fleet, withdrawing the last of them when new noise regulations came into effect on 31 December 1985.

Steve Aubury

Charlie Stewart

When Northeast was folded into the new regional division of British Airways in 1976, G-AVYB made the move too, flying its last Northeast flight from Heathrow to Newcastle on 31 March 1976. The aircraft was subsequently repainted in British Airways colours.

The aircraft is listed as withdrawn from use and scrapped at Heathrow on 19 May 1981. Duxford has a beautifully preserved Trident 2, and there is a Trident 3B stored at the Science Museum facility at Wroughton. There are also Tridents on display at Manchester Airport and the North-East Land, Sea and Air Museum.

32: BRITISH AIRCRAFT CORPORATION ONE-ELEVEN 500 G-AWWZ

The One-Eleven had two competitors, the Douglas DC-9 and the Boeing 737. The One-Eleven was first on the runway, in August 1963, but some momentum was lost after the crash of the prototype in October of that year, and the DC-9 followed the One-Eleven into the air in February 1965, narrowing the gap to eighteen months. From the beginning Douglas marketed a bigger version of the DC-9, able to carry 115 passengers, powered by Pratt and Whitney JT8D engines of 14,000lb thrust, which first flew in August 1966. Last at the gate was the Boeing 737, which did not take to the air until April 1967; it was different from the other two, having a wider fuselage that could seat passengers six-abreast, and the engines, also Pratt and Whitney JT8Ds, were hung from the wings rather than attached to the rear fuselage. Boeing almost immediately marketed a lengthened version, the Boeing 737-200, able to carry up to 119 (later 130) passengers, which became the standard version; it entered service in April 1968.

The Rolls-Royce Spey, which powered the One-Eleven, simply did not have the puff of the more powerful JT8D; stretched versions of the One-Eleven suffered a penalty in weight and range. Even so, early in 1967 BEA was prevailed on to order the longer One-Eleven, the first of the so-called 500 series, optimised for its short-haul routes. The corporation took some persuading but a sweetener from the government of £25 million, which also covered an order for the bigger Trident 3, helped. The One-Eleven 500 was lengthened by 13ft 6in and in BEA service carried ninety-seven passengers. Subsequent 500-series aircraft had slightly more powerful engines, with 12,500lb thrust, and could carry 109 passengers in charter configuration over 1,500 miles, good for most European and Mediterranean destinations. British United ordered five, later increased to eight, in March 1968, followed a few days later by Caledonian, a Gatwick-based charter airline, which ordered three. Caledonian had a fleet of turboprop Britannias, an aircraft flexible enough to fly across the Atlantic but equally happy going down to Palma in Majorca. When the time came to replace the propeller aircraft, Caledonian had to split its orders: for long-range charters it bought Boeing 707s; for the inclusive-tour market, One-Eleven 500s.

Both the Boeings and the One-Elevens transformed Caledonian radically and significantly. The 707s, superior long-range 320Cs with cargo doors and a 38-ton payload, allowed Caledonian to dominate the growing market for cheap fare charters

Air-Britain Archive

across the Atlantic; additionally the airline was able to pick up major contracts from the British Ministry of Defence and the Australian airline Qantas, the latter for migrant flights. Even more dramatic was the arrival in April 1969 of the One-Elevens, accompanied by some handsome inclusive-tour contracts, which saw passenger carryings literally soar. In 1968–69 Caledonian carried 83,259 IT passengers. A year later, the figure was 345,315; that is an increase of over 400 per cent. The airline benefited from the exponential growth in the inclusive-tour market during that era, but the point is, it benefited.

G-AWWZ was the third One-Eleven delivered, here at Gatwick with one of Caledonian's Boeing 707s. All three of them arrived in time for the 1969 summer holiday season, and a fourth was quickly ordered. If things had not turned

out differently, Caledonian would surely have flourished in the 1970s, adapting to the change in transatlantic charter rules so that it would have garnered a large share of the advance booking charter market, and increasing its volume of inclusive-tour traffic, probably following Britannia Airways with the early purchase of Boeing 737s from a manufacturer with which it already had close ties, to upgrade the quality and scope of its fleet.

But it was not to be. The publication of a far-reaching review of British aviation in 1969, the Edwards Report, proposed the setting up of a Second Force airline, allegedly to counter the dominance of the state-controlled corporations, BOAC and BEA, themselves to be made even more substantial through their own merger to form British Airways. The Second Force would be drawn from the only two airlines that the Edwards Committee could think of:, British United and Caledonian. Truth to tell, there were not many airlines left after the depredations that the British government had inflicted on them during the previous two decades. British United had the know-how to operate scheduled services, and some engineering heft; Caledonian was praised for the 'vigour of its management'. British United operated long-haul services to South America and Africa, and so seemed an obvious choice as a second flag carrier on one of the few routes open to a second British airline, London to New York, a route on which Caledonian already operated charter services.

Attaining the right flight level for the merger was beset with turbulence, bolts from the blue and thunderstorms, but in the end the tie-up was rescued by a change of government in June 1970, when the Tories under Ted Heath unexpectedly won a snap election called by Prime Minister

Harold Wilson. The Labour administration had added to the vagaries of climate by blowing hot and cold on the concept of the Second Force, but the Tories were quite clear in which direction the wind was blowing and sanctioned the takeover of British United by Caledonian. On 30 November 1970 the merged airlines became Caledonian/BUA, although the name was changed less than a year later to British Caledonian Airways. G-AWWZ faithfully reflects these changes.

The Aviation Photo Company

The Aviation Photo Company

The Aviation Photo Company

The merger involved a change of course for both airlines. Caledonian was a pure charter airline. British United had been heading towards greater charter participation under its outgoing managing director, Alan Bristow; hence the order for One-Eleven 500s. It was just as well that British United and Caledonian ordered more or less identical One-Eleven 500 aircraft! Now the goal was to increase scheduled-service flying and all effort was refocused on that task. It did not happen immediately, but British Caledonian turned its back on charter services. In 1970 the two airlines flew just over 1.5 million charter passengers; in addition British United carried 630,000 on scheduled services. Four years later, the ratio was almost exactly reversed. In 1974 British Caledonian, or BCal as it was familiarly known, carried around 1.3 million scheduled service passengers; charter carryings were down to 600,000 people. It was time for some of the charter One-Elevens to move on.

British Caledonian retained the former BUA units, but in 1975 began disposing of the Caledonian aircraft. G-AWWZ was leased to a British charter airline, Monarch, which eventually bought the aircraft outright. Monarch was a significant Britannia operator, as Caledonian had been, and faced a similar dilemma as to how to replace this flexible machine. It tried to span the gap by buying Boeing 720Bs, a smaller version of the 707.

The Aviation Photo Company

But the 720B with four turbofans was not ideal, especially after the price of fuel ran away after the 1973 Arab–Israeli War, jumping fourfold from $3 a barrel to $12. Following the collapse of Court Line in 1974, charter airlines needed additional capacity to take up the slack. Monarch took over two ex-Court Line One-Elevens for the summer 1975 season and added G-AWWZ at the end of the year, reconfiguring the aircraft to 119 seats, the new standard for charter airlines. Monarch bought the aircraft early in 1977, and for the next few years G-AWWZ flew a typical inclusive-tour. The statistics suggest utilisation was a leisurely seven to nine hours a day, around 3,000 hours a year, but in reality the aircraft would have flown 2,000 of those hours intensively during the peak summer months, from May to September, with four sectors of up to three hours' duration each day, and then some night flying as well. When the time came to replace the Boeing

720Bs and the One-Elevens, Monarch went with a Boeing mix, ordering the 737 in 1980 and the larger 757 in 1981. G-AWWZ was sold out of the fleet at the end of the 1985 summer season and passed on to British Island Airways, a new airline with an old name.

The name British Island Airways was derived from British United Island Airways (BUIA), an assortment of regional airlines brought together under the ownership of British and Commonwealth (B & C), owner of British United Airways. When British United was sold off to Caledonian in 1970, BUIA was retained by B & C, which gave it a new name, British Island Airways, and an attractive orange livery. A regional airline at first, BIA later flew charters, using One-Elevens bought from Gulf Air, and which entered service early in 1979. Not an easy relationship, regional scheduled services and inclusive-tour flying; they do not have much in common, although they can complement each other. When B & C went to the next stage, acquiring two more regional airlines, Air Anglia and Air Westward, it decided to change the combined airlines' names to Air UK, and then in short order, agreed to sell off the charter division and its aircraft to the managing director, Peter Villa.

Villa started operations in April 1982, and did well; growing the business, making money and adding planes. In 1986 he raised capital by selling 15 per cent of the shares on the Unlisted Securities Market. G-AWWZ was one of two One-Elevens acquired from Monarch, and together with two more One-Eleven 500 series bought in 1984, took over much of the inclusive-tour flying, later to be displaced in turn by expensive McDonnell Douglas MD-82s, which the airline purchased at the wrong time just as Britain's Thatcher-era economic boom was ending. Suddenly the airline was announcing huge losses in 1988 and 1989, unsustainable for a poorly capitalised undertaking, and the airline went into receivership early in 1990.

G-AWWZ, a mere twenty-one years old, still had some life left in it. Solidly built, the main problems facing One-Elevens by this stage were not structural but impending noise restrictions. One-Elevens, even with hush kits, were noisy. Still, new regulations, referred to as Stage 3, would not start biting until 1992, and nimble airlines, such as Dan-Air, could use the type in the meantime, and that is what happened. Dan-Air had a large fleet of 500-series One-Elevens and an expanding scheduled-service network as it took advantage of the liberalising trends within Europe. G-AWWZ entered service with Dan-Air in April 1990.

With a different registration, however. As the aircraft had previously been with an airline now in receivership, Dan-Air

The Aviation Photo Company

knew from experience that some creditors might have a claim against the company, even a lien on the aircraft. Better to change the registration so that the aircraft did not turn up on airport 'wanted' lists! But even with its new marks, the airline only lasted one summer season with Dan-Air. The same forces that acted against British Island Airways now came to haunt Dan-Air, which suffered significant losses financially that year, and had to call in a company doctor in October; faced with a severe diminution of charter business, he redoubled efforts to establish the airline as a significant scheduled service carrier out of Gatwick. G-BSYN was let go as the airline tried to standardise its fleet, but even that was not the end of the story.

Instead, the aircraft went to Ireland and to a by now familiar name, Ryanair, with whom it was registered EI-CCW. At this stage of its development, Ryanair primarily operated low-cost services from airports in Ireland, Cork, Dublin, Galway,

Knock and Waterford, to Luton and three other UK airports. It was somewhat constrained in what it could do; it could not yet operate domestically within Britain. That had to wait for the passing of the so-called Third Package on 1 January 1993, which allowed any European airline to fly between anywhere in Europe, and from 1997 for those airlines to operate domestically within any European country. EI-CCW spent three years going backwards and forwards between Ireland and Britain, but by 1994 the airline wanted to standardise on the Boeing 737 and the One-Eleven was returned to the lessor in April. It briefly took up its old registration, G-AWWZ, and was transferred to British World Airways for onward sale to the South African airline Nationwide Air Charter, being deleted from the British register for the last time in November 1994. As ZS-NMS it spent another six years in South Africa, some of it flying as a code share for the Belgian airline Sabena, before being withdrawn in 2000 and scrapped in 2005.

There are two former BEA One-Eleven 500s in Britain, one preserved at Duxford and the other on display at East Fortune in Scotland.

The Aviation Photo Company

33: BOEING 737-200 G-BMOR

The Boeing 737 was Boeing's response to the demand for a short-haul jet, one that could operate economically on stages up to three hours. It followed the BAC One-Eleven and Douglas DC-9 into the market in early 1965, the twin-engine jet first flying in April 1967, two years after the One-Eleven had entered service. The 737 had a wider fuselage than the other two, to the same dimensions as the Boeing 727, and could carry 100 passengers six abreast; and instead of engines mounted on the rear fuselage, the Pratt and Whitney JT8Ds were mounted under the wing. Sales were slow at the start, but over time the design has proved long-lived, and stunningly successful. More than 10,000 have been built; more than 560 have passed through the British register.

Author's Collection

The German airline Lufthansa was the first to order the Boeing 737, which caused heartbreak for BAC, which had hoped to sell it the One-Eleven. Lufthansa's early variant was quickly superseded by an improved version with a 6ft extension to the fuselage that allowed up to 130 passengers to be carried, and with greater range, more than 2,000 miles. British charter airline Britannia was the trend-setter, in 1966 ordering three of the new Boeing 737-200s for Mediterranean holiday flights, the first European airline to commit to this enhanced type.

Delivered in 1968, G-AVRL the first of the Britannia 737s, is seen at Luton in the company of the aircraft they would all soon replace, the Bristol Britannia, appropriately G-ANBA,

written about elsewhere in this book. Both aircraft carried 117 passengers, a commercial and operational convenience, but the seating capacity of the 737-200 was later increased to 130. Other British airlines followed Britannia's lead, none more so than British Airways, which became a dedicated 737 user in 1978. New start-up charter airline Air Europe ordered three for delivery in 1979. G-BMOR was the second to be delivered, on 4 May 1979, just a few minutes before the airline's inaugural flight. Its registration letters reflect the initials of the airline's chairman, Martin O'Regan, who with Errol Cossey, both of them formerly with Dan-Air, had established the airline with backing from Harry Goodman's Intasun Holidays.

With its fresh 'wide-look' interior and jaunty livery, Air Europe's brand-new aircraft promised a holiday flight that would be different from the norm, and invariably delivered above expectations. Credit to Britannia where it is due; the airline had turned away from buying cheaper if well-used second-hand aircraft for its flights, seeking to balance the higher cost of new aircraft by flying them more efficiently. Air Europe followed a similar route but offered enhanced cabin service that was much appreciated by its passengers.

By the time I joined Air Europe, in 1982, there were seven 737 aircraft in the fleet. Air Europe cleverly augmented its summer capacity by leasing in two aircraft from Air Florida, an airline whose requirements were diametrically different from Air Europe's – the main holiday season in Florida is during the winter months. In turn Air Europe sent two aircraft to Florida during the lean European winter months. The fleet ratio then became nine in the summer to five in winter, reflecting demand more closely, and an efficient way to utilise what were expensive aircraft. In 1982 Air Europe's aircraft were flying 12.8 hours a day over short- to medium-length sectors, the highest level of utilisation of any British airline, beating even British Caledonian's long-haul DC-10. Britannia's 737s came in at ten hours a day. However, there were some clouds in the sky.

First, although the 737 was a successful charter aircraft, new developments on the horizon were even more promising, especially the larger Boeing 757, which carried 100 more passengers than the 737, and over greater distances. Already rival charter airline Monarch had ordered the type, and Air Europe was quick to follow, in 1983 taking on two aircraft diverted from a British Airways order that had had to be trimmed back under government direction. Boeing

The Aviation Photo Company

737s were more suited to the rapidly deregulating market in the USA, where demand was strong for smaller aircraft able to offer point-to-point flights rather than through a 'hub'. And the dollar was weak, so British 737s could be sold very profitably in America. Finally, BA was anxious to pursue its fruitful cooperation with Harry Goodman and his companies, offering him attractive charter deals on his holiday business. Did Goodman really need his own airline? He was tempted to liquidate Air Europe, although in the end he compromised, doing a deal with British Airtours, the BA charter subsidiary, in which he sold some of the Air Europe 737s and laid off a number of staff. As a sweetener, British Airtours leased three Boeing 737s, including G-BMOR from April 1983.

The Aviation Photo Company

Roger Richards

G-BMOR spent a year with British Airtours, then returned to Air Europe for the 1984/85 season before being transferred in May 1985 to Guinness Peat, an Irish financing group, which placed the aircraft with a low-cost airline in America, Air California (AirCal).

Of course, the aircraft had to be repainted before it could join AirCal, and is seen in Roger Richards' picture somewhere in between, still flying anonymously for Air Europe, just prior to it acquiring an Irish registration and full AirCal titles. In 1987 AirCal was taken over by American Airlines and for a while the aircraft wore American titles with its

AirCal livery, but the lease was ended early in 1988, and the aircraft was then placed with a British airline, Air UK Leisure, and put back on the British register, regaining its former marks G-BMOR on 31 March 1988.

The aircraft, one of two taken on for the summer season of 1988, was needed to help launch this new charter airline based at London's Stansted Airport. Although it bore the name of a well-established and indeed historic airline, Air UK, whose roots went back to the very start of Britain's post-war civil aviation (see the story of the Handley Page Herald), Air UK was the minority shareholder, the other two shareholders being Viking, a charter broker, and the Bricom Group, successor to British and Commonwealth. The aircraft's stay was temporary as the airline had already ordered the Boeing 737-400, an enlarged and re-engined iteration of the 737, the first of which was delivered to the airline in October 1988. G-BMOR stayed with the airline for longer than planned as there were issues with the CFM engines when the first 737-400s were delivered, leading to a temporary grounding of the type, but by August 1989 the aircraft was off the British register again, this time never to return.

The Aviation Photo Company

It went to France and eventually Nigeria, where its AOC expired in 2008.

Air UK Leisure expanded in the 1990s, acquiring a total of seven Boeing 737-400s. Viking rebranded itself as Unijet and established in parallel a long-haul charter airline, Leisure International, which flew Boeing 767-300s. But Air UK's and Leisure's interests had begun to diverge by this stage; Air UK was in the process of being absorbed by Dutch airline KLM, which had little interest in charter operations. Air UK Leisure was bought out by Unijet in 1996 and continued flying under the Leisure International name until it was taken over by First Choice, parent of Air 2000, in 1998 and absorbed into the latter's operations. Air UK Leisure survived longer than Air Europe; the latter reorientated itself as a scheduled airline and then flamed out during the economic downturn of 1991 brought on by the first Gulf War.

Leisure International had begun replacing its Boeing 737-400s with Airbus A320s, showing how the European manufacturer had successfully intruded on what had been Boeing's turf. After the 737-200, the US manufacturer built what are now referred to as Classic 737s, of which the 737-400 was the most ambitious, with a longer fuselage and able to carry 172 passengers, but with disappointing range characteristics. It was fine for operations out of Gatwick, less so on longer sectors from regional airports such as Glasgow. Boeing's answer was to redesign the wing and in 1993 launch the next series of Boeing 737s, the New Generation, which could fly more than 3,000 miles; the fuselage of the -800 and -900 variants was further extended, increasing the passenger capacity to 220.

34: DOUGLAS DC-10 G-GSKY

With the obvious exception of the Dakota, Douglas did not make its mark on British civil aviation in the way that its quality products deserved. Partly this was because of the post-war difficulties in buying modern airliners with US dollars; but even when these restrictions eased, Douglas products failed to gain significant orders. The last Douglas airliner bought by British Airways' predecessor BOAC was the Douglas DC-7C, and that was in the mid-1950s. The

DC-8, which looked much like the Boeing 707, attracted no new orders at all, and only a very small number were ever placed on the British register; and the DC-9, a short-haul jet of similar configuration and size to the BAC One-Eleven, did not enjoy much success in Britain either. The wide-bodied DC-10, subject of this section, and which flew head-to-head with the Lockheed L-1011 TriStar, failed to receive an endorsement from the nation's flag carrier British Airways; but then the TriStar, which was bought by British Airways, had Rolls-Royce RB.211 engines whereas the DC-10 relied on American powerplants, the General Electric CF6, and Pratt and Whitney JT9D.

Both the DC-10 and Tristar were designed to fill a gap below Boeing's jumbo jet 747 and were at first just intended for the American transcontinental market. Both aircraft had virtually identical configurations, with single engines under the wings and a third at the rear. The TriStar had a graceful s-duct to the engine buried in the fuselage; Douglas just mounted the third engine on top of the fuselage, with the tailplane and fin above it. The DC-10 could load 380 passengers, the TriStar up to 400, but they usually carried around 250 people in two classes, over 3,500 miles. From the outset Douglas offered a true intercontinental version as well, with more powerful engines, bigger wingspan, higher take-off weights and beefed-up undercarriage, able to carry its passenger payload over 5,000 miles. US carriers tended to order the original DC-10-10 version, which entered service in August 1971; foreign airlines went for the intercontinental DC-10-30, which began flying across the Atlantic with Swissair in December 1972.

Freddie Laker, enraged by the enforcement activities of the British authorities on his cheap transatlantic group charter flights, thought there had to be a better way to carry low-fare passengers to America: 'The government's policy doesn't mean the rest of us have to let our brains stagnate.' In 1971 he proposed what he called a Skytrain service: 'It is to be quite unlike the conventional air services. It is to be more like a railway service. Passengers are not to reserve their seats in advance. They are to go to the airport, buy their tickets, and board the aircraft – all in one sequence – just as passengers go to a railway station, buy their tickets and join a train.' To give his project some heft, and serendipitously avail himself of an attractive offer from Douglas, he ordered three DC-10-10s, part of a cancelled order from a Japanese airline, that were delivered the following year, 1972.

The decision on Skytrain was not delivered so promptly; it would be another five years of hard struggle before both British and American governments finally caved and allowed Laker to launch his service from London to New York. In the meantime, after the first aircraft had been delivered in 1972 and before the eventual launch of Skytrain in September 1977, Laker had some large and expensive aeroplanes with seats to fill.

He was helped by Britain's new airline regulator, the Civil Aviation Authority, which proposed a simplification of charter rules but at the opposite end of Laker's scale; rather than passengers just turning up on the day, charter passengers would have to book three months in advance. It just about worked, and over the years the advance booking period was progressively reduced; by 1978 it was down to twenty-one days. The DC-10s were pressed into service on European IT flights as well as group charters to the USA and Canada; Canada never had to adjust to Skytrain and its transatlantic charter business was huge, almost as large as that of the United States.

When Skytrain started out, it was beautifully simple, and cheap: £59 one-way, around half the scheduled service fare. Passengers could buy tickets six hours in advance, payment in cash, at one location in London, at Victoria Station, and another in New York, at a site in Queens. If a passenger could not get on a flight, he or she could wait for the next day's service. Passengers could check on availability, as one correspondent noted:

The Aviation Photo Company

'There are 190 seats left at 3 P.M. and there are no lines. Please bring your luggage and passport with you when you come to purchase your ticket.' That was the word on a recent weekday afternoon from the recorded message that tells callers about seat availability on Freddie Laker's nightly 11 o'clock 'Skytrain' to London.

Problems arose when too many passengers wanted to return at the end of the summer season; queuing passengers, in shantytowns covered with plastic sheeting to keep off the rain, waited patiently outside Victoria Station, sometimes for days. After a time Skytrain was revamped so that it became more like a regular scheduled service with passengers able to book in advance but in so doing lost its elegant simplicity. It was no longer down to a simple cash register; now there had to be reservation systems, and advertising, and sales staff, and commissions, and booking clerks. Los Angeles was added to the network one year later, a disappointing route to start with; the DC-10-10s did not have enough range for a non-stop flight, so the aircraft had to refuel on the eastern seaboard. This was turned to some advantage when flights from Los Angeles and New York were combined during the lean winter months. Laker ordered long-range DC-10-30s to allow him to fly to Los Angeles direct; he really wanted them for the London to Hong Kong route, but that he was never allowed to operate. They were also useful for the Miami routes that he started in 1980. He bought a further DC-10-10 in 1977 and two more were ordered for 1979, the sixth and final aircraft being G-GSKY, which was delivered in March 1979, eighteen months after the launch of Skytrain.

G-GSKY was configured like the earlier aircraft with 345 seats and galleys below the main cabin – cabin crew and catering carts went up and down in lifts – but had two extra features: it had a personalised registration, just then coming into fashion – its sister ship G-GFAL bore Laker's initials; and it had extra tankage, which increased the type's flexibility on the critical London to New York sector. Its arrival coincided with the start of a run of bad luck for Laker. The DC-10 type was already somewhat battle-scarred, following two crashes in the early 1970s that were caused by the failure of a cargo door that blew out, causing decompression and loss of control. The fault was rectified, but then on 25 May 1979 there was a devastating accident involving an American Airlines DC-10-10 at Chicago; the starboard engine and pylon separated from

the wing shortly after take-off, causing the aircraft to flip over and crash with the loss of all on board. All DC-10s were grounded from 6 June for around six weeks while the cause of the crash was investigated; incorrect maintenance procedures were eventually blamed for the accident. Both British DC-10 operators, Laker and British Caledonian, were severely penalised by the grounding order. For Laker's Skytrain the results were stark. In June 1978 the airline had carried 28,000 passengers on the New York Skytrain service; a year later, during the grounding, only 2,789 in that month. Skytrain recovered somewhat; in June 1980 Laker carried more than 40,000 passengers on the New York route. But for American passengers at least, the DC-10 never quite overcame the shadow cast on its reputation and it may have impacted Skytrain sales in the United States.

There were more headwinds that Laker began to encounter in his ambitious plans for a global network as he unsuccessfully bid to introduce the Skytrain formula to Europe, Hong Kong and Australia. Only the United States approved Skytrain, and none of the major carriers competing on the prime North Atlantic routes liked that; it forced them to dilute their fare income by offering similar low fares to Skytrain. By 1981 its competitors were beginning to catch up and Skytrain's share declined sharply: in June 1981 Laker's New York service carried only 20,000 passengers, half the level of the previous year.

And there were other problems. In 1981 the first of a fleet of Airbus A300s was delivered to Laker. These 284-seat wide-bodied aircraft were intended for the European Skytrain routes, but as Laker had been denied them, other uses had to be found for the expensive aircraft. He hoped to take a larger slice of the holiday market, but truth to tell

Laker was not a significant player in this field, and most of the large British tour operators contracted their charter flying with their own in-house airlines, so were unlikely to use Laker's Airbuses to any great extent. Laker struggled. He took delivery of three Airbuses, which carried 550,000 charter passengers in 1981 at an average utilisation of eight hours a day, not nearly enough. Most British charter airlines would expect to get at least twelve to fourteen hours from their new jets.

The Laker magic evaporated, leaving him with huge debt. In the old days he would have done a canny deal on aircraft but he could not dispose of the Airbuses, and the DC-10s were committed to transatlantic flying even though load factors on Skytrain were so sad. Everything began to go wrong as passenger numbers plummeted and the banks became more demanding: even British Rail contributed by going on strike periodically and suspending the Gatwick rail link. After some frantic months of negotiations the airline closed down on 5 February 1982.

Laker's long-term rival British Caledonian picked up many of Laker's leavings, including the Los Angeles route and two of the DC-10s, one of them G-GSKY. Strictly speaking this story should end here, but G-GSKY went on to a new life, albeit with the new registration G-BJZE. The registration had to be changed because otherwise airport authorities, air traffic control organisations, government bodies, hotel owners, bus companies and others with unpaid bills to the Laker group of companies had the tiresome habit of putting liens on ex-Laker aircraft. So on 31 March 1982 the aircraft was re-registered and transferred to British Caledonian.

It looked just like any other DC-10 in the British Caledonian fleet, but flew charters exclusively in a joint venture

The Aviation Photo Company

with the Rank Organisation, which had recently invested in a number of tour operators, including Blue Sky, formerly owned by British Caledonian. In 1982 the airline carried 387,000 passengers, and did well in the ensuing years, adding long-haul charter flying to its operations. Indeed, along with British Airtours the two were the only charter airlines able to fly across the Atlantic in the early to mid-1980s; British Caledonian picked up advance booking charter business and holiday flying to Miami. Still, the airline was uncomfortable with its role as charter carrier, which it regarded as downmarket, so the aircraft was repainted to identify less with British Caledonian. At first it was 'British Caledonian Charter' but eventually the more anonymous BCA Charter was adopted briefly. It still looked like a British Caledonian aircraft!

Finally British Caledonian's management got the message and in 1985 rebranded the airline Cal Air, adding a third

DC-10-10, also from ex-Laker stock. By the following year the airline was carrying more than 1 million passengers a year, a significant player in the charter team, and one that had a true long-haul capability.

The next difficulty arose in 1988, when British Airways bought out British Caledonian and took over its aircraft and services. British Airways already owned a charter airline, British Airtours, which flew TriStars and Boeing 737s, and in any case, Cal Air was part owned by the Rank Organisation. The solution was for Rank to buy out the British Caledonian holding, but it had to give the airline a new name, Novair. The lion disappeared from the tail, although it reappeared in

The Aviation Photo Company

The Aviation Photo Company

different guise when British Airways in turn renamed British Airtours as Caledonian, reintroducing the lion in a blue and yellow livery.

Novair bought two Boeing 737-400s to fly alongside the three DC-10s and they were delivered in 1989. Unfortunately the Boeings were grounded for four weeks during the summer following two in-flight fan-blade failures just as the summer season was starting, which required expensive sub-charters. Worse, the British economy was tanking and the holiday charter market with it. There was also more competition as new airlines spread their wings, and technological changes allowed twin-engine aircraft to fly across the Atlantic. Novair's DC-10s were joined by Boeing 767s and 757s in the quest for market share on the Florida holiday routes. Even though Novair had two more aircraft in 1989 than 1988, it flew fewer passengers!

With the economic outlook increasingly grim, owners Rank decided to call it a day and on 5 May 1990 Novair closed down. G-GSKY/BJZE was eventually sold in America, where it was converted to a freighter and flew with Federal Express for another two decades.

The Aviation Photo Company

35: BRITTEN-NORMAN ISLANDER G-AWNR

Britten-Norman, a small company originally based on the Isle of Wight, has sold more than 1,250 BN-2 Islanders, a robust, twin-engine, nine-passenger airliner, and its bigger brother, the Trislander, which has three engines and can carry seventeen passengers. The Islander is still being made today. So why did the man from the Treasury, writing in December 1970 about the company to his boss, warn him: 'Be aware that another lame duck is on the wing'?

Britten-Norman, co-founded in 1955 by two brilliant innovators, John Britten and Desmond Norman, decided in 1964 to build the Islander, the aerial equivalent of a long-wheelbase Land Rover, after the two realised, following their own experiences in the Cameroons, that there was a demand for a small passenger/load carrier with good short-field performance: 'I'd always wanted us to build a simple aeroplane that would fill a niche,' Desmond Norman said in an interview published in *Islander News* December 2000, 'a plane with the simplest of instruments that kept maintenance to a minimum.' The first Islander flew in 1965 and almost immediately attracted worldwide interest. The challenge was to build them in sufficient quantities, and at a low enough price, from scratch. The government helped with launch aid and extra funding for production, all of which was subsequently repaid. Britten-Norman subcontracted building of the airframes, first to the British Hovercraft Corporation, later to a Romanian firm, but the company was underfunded and its finances were always precarious; hence the Treasury's

Orkney Photographic Archive

witty but unkind comments. To its credit the company has usually been able to dig itself out of a hole. Britten-Norman has gone through three receiverships in its long history. From 1972 it was owned by Fairey, a storied British aircraft manufacturer that had a production facility in Belgium where it built both Islanders and Trislanders in large quantities; the company continued to make Islanders in Romania as well.

Fairey went bust after too many Islanders were built, more than could be sold at the time, but Britten-Norman was then bought by the Swiss firm Pilatus, a worthy steward of the company for twenty years, from 1979 to 1998, which still made the aircraft in Romania and did much to develop non-airline, higher-value variants of the Islander. Wherever the airframes were built, they were always flown to Bembridge on the Isle of Wight for finishing and delivery to the customer. Production remained at a high level throughout the 1970s: 121 were built in 1971, 100 in 1975, 74 in 1974, then down to 54 by 1981; after that, from the 1980s only penny numbers appeared each year. Over the years, 517 were delivered from Romania, 411 built on the Isle of Wight, 267 at Fairey's plant at Gosselies in Belgium, and another 49 in the Philippines. Although a British success story, most of the aircraft were built abroad!

Among the earliest customers were two innovative airlines, Aurigny Air Services in the Channel Islands and Loganair in Scotland. Both airlines were kick-started by the availability of the Islander. Alderney, the third largest of the Channel Islands, was faced with the loss of its air links after the incumbent airline, British United Island Airways, served notice in 1967 that it could no longer sustain the financial losses of its de Havilland Heron services, which flew from the island to Guernsey, Jersey and Southampton.

Ron Roberts via Barry Friend

Sir Derrick Bailey, who had business and farming interests in England and South Africa, and a home in Alderney, used his charter company Glosair to help establish an Alderney-based airline, Aurigny, which took over the inter-island services in 1968, using three of the new Islanders. A fourth, G-AWNR, was added late in 1968; painted in a striking yellow, red and black livery with a heraldic lion rampant on its tail (the airline did not paint its name on its aircraft for many years), it was the thirtieth Islander to be built. For 1969 a fifth Islander was delivered to Aurigny, by which time operations were booming; the following year, 1970, the airline carried more than 100,000 passengers.

In 1971 the airline took over the Alderney–Southampton route and had begun to look for a larger aircraft, which it found in the Trislander. G-AWNR was handed back to

Britten-Norman in October 1971, following the delivery of its first Trislander in June of that year. Aurigny then standardised on the Trislander; the type stayed in service for more than forty years and the last one did not leave the fleet until May 2017.

Loganair stayed true to the Islander. Like Aurigny, Loganair's scheduled inter-island services would never have happened but for the aircraft. Before the war, Captain Fresson had flown between the islands of Orkney and also within the Shetlands, but these routes were suspended during the war and not resumed. For islanders wanting to make the trip to Kirkwall on the main island, known as Mainland, that often meant an uncomfortable boat journey. Loganair had begun using light aircraft for charter work and company transfers for Willie Logan's construction firm in 1962, and was looking for new business, which it found in the Orkneys. A deal with the local shipping company, Orkney Isles Shipping, allowed the airline access to Scottish Office funds, airfields on the islands were reconstituted and Loganair's Islander G-AVKC inaugurated the service from Kirkwall to Stronsay and on to Sanday and North Ronaldsay on 27 September 1967; the first sector took just eight minutes, the journey by boat two hours. Three years later Loganair started flying within the Shetlands between the main airport located at Sumburgh in the south and Unst in the far north.

G-AWNR was registered to Loganair in July 1972, in time to celebrate five years of inter-island services and 50,000 passengers carried on them. It spent time in both the northern isles and flew the first scheduled flight to Fair Isle, situated between Orkney and Shetland, in June 1976. In addition to regular services, the airline operated a considerable number of charter flights, most on behalf of the air ambulance, but also in response to the growing oil exploration in the North Sea.

By the time it left the fleet, at the end of 1977, it had flown 7,332 hours and made 24,260 landings, a punishing schedule, more than three an hour on some very rough airfields. Loganair's route network had expanded considerably; eight islands were served from Kirkwall, and the Shetland service now included a stop at Lerwick as well as Whaley and Fetlar on the way to Unst. In the Hebrides Loganair had begun taking over some of the island services from BEA, including the well-known and very photogenic route to Barra, where the aircraft still land on the beach at low tide. Just as photogenic, surely, is the magnificent image of G-AWNR passing the Old Man of Hoy.

Britten-Norman Aircraft Preservation Society

G-AWNR was sold in America, at first in Florida, later in 1985 to Panama and eventually in 1991 to Venezuela, to Aero Servicios Caicara. After that airline suspended operations, in 1997, the Islander was noted as destroyed in 2002.

Like the Land Rover, Islander sales suffered from the longevity of the product. Why buy a new one when there are plenty of second-hand models available in good condition? Although there have been changes to the design as production progressed and the interiors have been updated, the aircraft are still powered by Lycomings, although slightly more powerful now, and the dimensions of the basic BN-2 model have not changed. There have been variants: the Trislander, already mentioned; the turbine-powered BN-2T, popular with government agencies and the military, including the RAF, for surveillance work; and the stretched Defender 4000 model, like the BN-2T powered by Rolls-Royce Allison turboprops. Islanders are now being built at a facility across the Solent from the Isle of Wight, and the wings still come from Romania. Two Trislanders have been preserved in the United Kingdom, one at Duxford, the other on Guernsey. The latter, registered G-JOEY, is something of a cult aircraft and also spawned a number of illustrated children's books.

On the Isle of Wight Islander G-AVCN, the third one built, has been painstakingly restored after it was brought back from Puerto Rico. Only now, fifty years after the Islander first flew, has another manufacturer designed a replacement for the type, the Italian firm Tecnam. Despite the hiccups in Islander production, more Islanders were built than any other British airliner, and by some margin: in every way the achievement was heroic. Perhaps less sardonic commentary and more practical assistance could have been extended to help the company manage its cash-flow difficulties. No other country would have

left one of its most successful manufacturers to sink or swim. In the end Britten-Norman was able to continue swimming, but at the expense of lost opportunities; why should Pilatus, building aeroplanes in what must be one of the most expensive countries to do business, Switzerland, be selling robust utility aircraft and not a British manufacturer?

Maybe some of the Islander's pixie dust fell on the two airlines, Aurigny and Loganair, both of them still with us, unlike so many other of Britain's operators. Aurigny is now owned by the States of Guernsey, and flies ATR turboprops and jets from the island to the mainland, including London Gatwick, still in a distinctive yellow livery. The last Britten-Norman product has left the Aurigny fleet, and flights from Alderney are flown by Dorniers. But you can still fly from Kirkwall to Stronsay in a Loganair Islander and it will still take only eight minutes! Mind you, you will have to spend far longer checking in and going through security. Loganair went through some changes of ownership, and its route network has expanded and contracted. For a long time it operated as a franchise of British Airways, bringing the name of the former corporation back to the Highlands and Islands. That was an eerie reminder of the state airline, British European Airways, which had taken over the pioneering airlines of Scotland, Scottish Airways and Allied Airways (Gandar Dower) when they had been forcibly nationalised in 1948. Loganair is back flying under its own colours as Scotland's airline, serving the Highlands and Islands from both Glasgow and Edinburgh, and at a higher frequency than was the norm previously. My recollection of flying to Stornoway, when BEA plied the route with Viscounts, was one service a day with a stop at Benbecula; now there are four direct flights a day from Glasgow, and another from Edinburgh. And you can still land on the beach at Barra!

36: SHORT 330 G-BITV

There is a considerable gap between the early post-war Sunderland flying boats and the small airliners that Short started building in the early 1960s. Nevertheless the Northern Ireland manufacturer remained busy during this period, developing missiles and building aircraft for other manufacturers, including Canberra bombers and Britannias; it also worked on new designs. Out of the Britannia contract came the Belfast, a large air freighter ordered in 1960 for the RAF, which used the Britannia's wing design and was powered by Rolls-Royce Tyne turboprops; it was able to carry loads exceeding 11,000 cu ft and up to 35 tons in weight. Contrarily, Short was also considering a very small freighter that later evolved into the Skyvan. Its origins go back to the early post-war years and Miles Aircraft, builder of the Aerovan, a number of which flew with Ulster Aviation shuttling between the Miles factories at Reading and Newtownards near Belfast.

The Aviation Photo Company

The Aviation Photo Company

Although Miles Aircraft had closed down in 1947, it did not take long for Fred and Blossom Miles to bounce back, establishing F.G. Miles in 1951, which among its many other activities tested a version of the Aerovan, named the Caravan, which was fitted with a high aspect ratio wing. The long, thin wing proved to be as effective as most high-lift devices in achieving short take-offs and landings, but allowed a higher cruising speed; although, looking at the Skyvan's engagingly blunt profile, I wonder how relevant that was in practice! Short bought the design rights of the Caravan from F.G. Miles 'for further development and production' and made a fair fist of it, building more than 150 Skyvans between 1963 and 1985, mainly as freighters; a few were finished as eighteen-seat airliners, such as the example shown here that flew with British Airways for a few months in 1974.

Designs for commuter and regional airliners were constrained by American regulations that limited their carrying capacity to nineteen or twenty passengers. When these rules were revised upwards in 1972, allowing thirty-seat aircraft to be introduced, Short was first off the mark, offering a stretched development of the Skyvan, the SD3-30. The fuselage retained the Skyvan's attractive 6ft 4in cross section but was stretched 18ft, and larger windows installed; a freight door was added ahead of the wing on the port side. The Skyvan's Garrett turboprops were replaced by Pratt and Whitney Canada PT6As; a shapelier nose, air conditioning, a galley, toilet and overhead lockers were fitted. The SD3-30, later renamed the Short 330, retained the cantilevered twin-tail unit and smooth Redux-bonded double-skin lightweight structure of the Skyvan, but gained a retractable three-wheel undercarriage. Like the Skyvan, the thirty-seat Short 330 was unpressurised. Of interest is the amount of help Short received from other manufacturers in designing and building the 330, especially British Aerospace and Fokker.

Orders began to trickle in after the first flight in August 1974, and deliveries started to US and Canadian carriers in late 1976. G-BITV, the sixty-ninth Short 330 built, was the first to feature more powerful engines and was registered to Alidair in June 1981.

The Aviation Photo Company

Alidair was a Viscount charter operator that had started flying between Guernsey and Manchester through a subsidiary, Guernsey Airlines, in 1980. The trading name Inter City was adopted after Alidair acquired a certain notoriety following the forced landing in July 1980 of one of its Viscounts near Exeter after it had run out of fuel. G-BITV entered service in 1981 sporting small Guernsey Airlines markings; other flights were from East Midlands Airport to Edinburgh and Aberdeen, both important oil-activity centres, and to Brussels. Despite worthwhile oil-support contracts with Shell, and the promising Manchester–Guernsey service, Alidair had to call in the receivers in August 1983. The Viscounts, the oil contracts and the Guernsey Airlines subsidiary were

sold off; G-BITV passed to Air Ecosse, a Scottish charter and scheduled operator that had been established in 1977 by Biggin Hill's Fairflight. As well as a significant amount of charter work for the Post Office, Air Ecosse flew services from Aberdeen and Glasgow and the prestigious Dundee to London Heathrow route with a large fleet of Short 330s and Brazilian-built Bandeirantes.

G-BITV acquired the name *City of Aberdeen* and fitted into the fleet profile well, being used for the extensive scheduled service network that stretched from the north of Scotland to London's Heathrow and Gatwick airports. Things turned sour, however, when Air Ecosse was sold to a group of investors in December 1985; Fairflight retained most of

The Aviation Photo Company

the aircraft, leaving Air Ecosse with insufficient capacity to maintain its flying programme. In any case, G-BITV had temporarily flown the hangar early in 1985 and was now leased to Brymon, a West Country airline that was looking to develop services to and from London's new City Airport, and had also undertaken to operate a three-times daily service between Gatwick and Birmingham on behalf of British Caledonian. G-BITV was taken on for this flying and entered service with minimal livery changes.

At the end of the lease the aircraft was returned to Air Ecosse for a period, but the airline was in trouble and went

into receivership in January 1987. G-BITV headed south to Gatwick to join Connectair, a recently formed airline that had picked up the Gatwick–Antwerp route, which it flew as part of British Caledonian's Commuter operation, later followed by Manchester to Rotterdam. The airline then also took over the Gatwick to Rotterdam service previously flown by British Air Ferries. The seats were easy to remove and Connectair had some success with overnight mail, package and newspaper flights to Europe; as a result the airline achieved very respectable utilisation with its Short 330, well over 3,000 hours in 1988.

G–BITV stayed in service with Connectair for two years; it was replaced by the 330's bigger brother, the Short 360, which as its name implies, could carry up to thirty-six passengers in its lengthened fuselage, and sported a more streamlined tail. Connectair was bought in July 1988 by Air Europe and renamed Air Europe Express. After the collapse of Air Europe in 1991, the management team at Air Europe Express took over four of the 360s and the licences from Gatwick to Antwerp, Guernsey and Rotterdam under the name of Euroworld, eventually becoming a British Airways Express franchise operation under the name CityFlyer Express. This was a commercially astute operation that upended many previously accepted airline norms.

G–BITV had a new home to go to early in 1989, and as was now the way with these things, a new registration, G-OGIL. Gill Aviation had taken over the flight operations of Fairflight, a name previously linked to this aircraft, and used the aircraft on Royal Mail services and other charter work from its bases at Belfast, Cardiff, Edinburgh, Glasgow and Newcastle. Gill also ran a substantial maintenance and engineering organisation at Newcastle that specialised in Short 330 and 360 aircraft.

The Aviation Photo Company

The Aviation Photo Company

The new registration was not reflected in a change of livery! From 1989 the airline began to offer scheduled services, linking Newcastle with Aberdeen, Belfast, Jersey, London Gatwick, Manchester and Teesside, and many more secondary destinations; it went on to acquire Short 360s and the larger ATR42, built by a French–Italian consortium, eventually operating Fokker F100 jets under a franchise for Air France. But the airline was an almost immediate casualty of the terrorist attacks in America on 11 September 2001, coming soon after the company had restructured itself after entering administration in early 2000. G-OGIL had been withdrawn from service in July 1992 following a taxiing accident at Newcastle and the aircraft was donated to the North East Aircraft Museum, now part of North East Land, Sea and Air Museums in Sunderland, where it is on display.

Coincidentally, 1992 was the year Short closed down the production line for its twin-turboprops, having built more than 300 Short 330s and 360s. The boxy little planes belong to a gilded age of British airliner production, which also saw the Jetstream and BAe 146 enter service worldwide. Passengers may have been amused by the appearance of the Short airliners but appreciated the headroom and comfort of the cabin, superior to earlier regional airliners such as the Bandeirante and Twin Otter. The operating costs of the Shorts were not much higher than those smaller eighteen-seaters, but the Shorts carried many more passengers. Michael Bishop of British Midland (BM) was an enthusiast for the Shorts and it was reported in *Flight* magazine 'that the aircraft is the major single factor in putting BM Group airlines Manx and Loganair into the black: "The 360 has been the best aircraft we've ever operated – it has transformed routes from loss-makers to profit – particularly Loganair and Manx," says Bishop; however, he continues: "We have had problems with lightness of construction in the under-carriage and tail."'

Short continued to develop the 330 and 360, producing freighter variants, which were selected both by the US Air Force and US Army. A larger forty-eight-seat version, the 450, was proposed as a competitor to the ATR; it would still have been unpressurised but promised even lower passenger mile costs. Short shelved the project after it deemed the marketplace too crowded, and instead began building the Brazilian-designed Tucano training aircraft. The company was bought in 1989 by Canada's Bombardier and since then has built fuselage and wing parts for Bombardier subsidiaries Canadair and Learjet.

37: BRITISH AEROSPACE JETSTREAM 31 G-WMCC

Although it says British Aerospace at the top of the entry, this airliner was a Handley Page design, the last from that storied company, and if things had turned out differently, it could also have been Handley Page's most successful. Its airline activities go right back to the dawn of civil aviation; Handley Page used the large O/400 transports to shuttle mail and personnel between England, France and Germany during the Armistice at the end of the Great War, and started regular airline operations in 1919. Handley Page airliners flew with Imperial Airways before the Second World War, and Halifaxes, Hermes and Heralds contributed to Britain's post-war aviation development, if not exceptionally, at least competently. The company left its best idea to last, however.

Handley Page realised that specialists were modernising de Havilland Doves and Herons, and that there was an increasing number of small business jets on the market, but reasoned that a new design of twelve-to-twenty-seat turboprop would be more appealing than converted airframes, and cheaper to operate than a jet. The Jetstream was designed to carry eighteen passengers over relatively short distances in a third-level role; the cabin had 6ft of headroom, but for all that it was still cramped. In a more spacious ten-to-twelve- seat configuration, its range would be 1,000 miles. The engine chosen was the only one available at the time, the French Astazou, and its unfamiliarity may have hampered sales in America; later the company re-engined the Jetstream with the American Garrett TPE-331 for an aborted order from the US Air Force.

The first Jetstream flew in August 1967. Handley Page put some effort into the manufacture and marketing of the aircraft, appointing agents to help sell and finish the aircraft, building new factories at its Radlett plant and in Scotland, and using subcontractors including Scottish Aviation to help build the wings and tailplanes; that meant there was a lot of money going out but at this stage not much money coming in. The government gave some financial assistance but the development of the aircraft was protracted. It was overweight and a bit slow, and by the middle of 1969 when it was re-alised that further financial resources were needed, Handley Page had to appoint a receiver. This led to a six-month hiatus while Scottish Aviation and the American distributor ran the company, but that fizzled out too, and on 27 February 1970 Handley Page abruptly went into bankruptcy.

That could have been the end of the Jetstream. Around thirty-eight had been built and were now flying in Europe and America, and there were also twenty-one unfinished fuselages on the production line. But Terravia, the company that had been ferrying the Jetstreams to America, teamed up with Scottish Aviation to buy up all the spares and airframes, and to support the existing aircraft. Scottish Aviation bought out Terravia in 1972, at the same time successfully negotiating an order from the RAF for twenty-six Jetstreams that were needed to take over the multi-engine training role from the Vickers Varsity. Owned by the Laird Group, Scottish Aviation had a worthy ancestry, notable for building the Pioneer and Twin Pioneer short take-off and landing transports, and more recently, for rescuing the Beagle Bulldog trainer after Beagle collapsed in 1969. To build the RAF's aircraft the company repurchased two aircraft in the United States, then used unfin-ished subassemblies and later manufactured five new fuselages.

The Aviation Photo Company

Deliveries to the RAF started in 1973 and continued to trickle through to 1976, but depressingly the RAF had to cut back on its original training establishment and many of the new Jetstreams went straight into storage; fourteen of them were later transferred to the Royal Navy. And then early in 1974 there was a change of government and Labour was back in power, albeit with a very small majority.

The Labour manifesto had clearly stated that the party would nationalise both shipbuilding and aircraft manufac-turing; this directly affected the Laird Group, which aside from Scottish Aviation had shipbuilding and repair interests. Not surprisingly, Laird's interest in Scottish Aviation dissi-pated fast; there was no further investment in the company and over the five-year period no more Jetstreams were sold. The nationalisation Bill took an inordinate amount of time to make it through Parliament. After a false start in 1974 the

Bill had to be reintroduced in the 1975–76 session; it spent fifty-eight days in standing committee before a Conservative MP pointed out that it was the wrong sort of Bill anyway. The government eventually bulldozed its way through that barrier but in so doing caused much ill will; some readers may recall Shadow Industry Secretary Michael Heseltine picking up and swinging the Mace after the vote! The Bill was then rejected by the Lords on three occasions, which forced the government to modify it; it eventually passed into law in 1977.

The new nationalised entity British Aerospace (BAe) took a year looking at all the projects in its portfolio, before deciding to go ahead with the Jetstream in December 1978, relaunching it as the Jetstream 31. Powered by improved Garrett 331 turboprops and with an increased maximum take-off weight (MTOW) from 12,500lb to 15,000lb, the aircraft could carry nineteen passengers over 700 miles, cruising at 300mph. Undoubtedly the heft of this large organisation put the project back on course. BAe bought an existing Jetstream from an American airline and rebuilt it as the prototype, G-JSSD; its first flight was on 28 March 1980. The first production Jetstream 31, G-TALL, flew just under a year later, and was used on some significant sales tours to North America and the Far East.

By the end of 1985 more than 100 had been sold, and by the time production ceased in 1993 BAe had built 386 Jetstreams; at one stage American Eagle, United Express and USAir Express – all affiliated to major US carriers – flew almost 200 of them. An improved version, the Jetstream 32, was offered from 1988 with the MTOW increased to 16,000lb and a higher cruising speed. A further 104 of a stretched version, the twenty-nine-seat Jetstream 41, were built as well.

Shaun Connor

In Britain a new airline, Birmingham Executive, aiming for the business market, wanted to take over some of the routes out of Birmingham that had been recently abandoned by British Airways. Two Jetstream 31s were acquired, one of them G-TALL, which the company reregistered as G-WMCC. Operations began in June 1983 with flights from Birmingham to Copenhagen and Zurich, and later to Milan and Geneva. The aircraft was fitted with only twelve seats and much was made of the enhanced cabin service. Flight times were significantly longer than those of the previous jet service; the Jetstream took three hours to get to Milan as opposed to two hours fifteen minutes by BAC One-Eleven jet.

The Aviation Photo Company

The Aviation Photo Company

Regardless of their speed, the Jetstreams were really too small for the routes Birmingham Executive was developing, and the airline went through a difficult time trying to settle on a larger aircraft type before eventually buying second-hand Grumman Gulfstream 1s; seating twenty-two, the twenty-year-old former executive aircraft were powered by Rolls-Royce Darts. Late in 1985 the airline got a subsidy from British Airways to open four new routes out of Birmingham, but then got stabbed in the back by the same British Airways, which reintroduced its own jet services out of Birmingham to Switzerland. Having accumulated a deficit of £3.5 million, the backers of Birmingham Executive in 1988 accepted with some relief a takeover by a consortium named somewhat bizarrely The Plimsoll Line (TPL), which was owned jointly by British Airways and Danish airline Maersk (TPL already owned a stake in the West Country airline Brymon).

In March 1989 Birmingham Executive became Birmingham European; this did not mean much change for G-WMCC but in 1990 the fleet was enhanced by the addition of five One-Elevens from TPL partner British Airways. With the One-Elevens came a new colour scheme, replicated on G-WMCC.

The Gulfstreams were sold off but G-WMCC was granted a stay of execution, flying domestically to Newcastle and Southampton.

Of course, the marketing folks at The Plimsoll Line had to succumb to temptation and merge the two constituent airlines, Brymon and Birmingham European, adopting the utterly meaningless name Brymon European in October 1992. Brymon scarcely flew to Europe, and the Birmingham connection got lost in translation! G-WMCC had to go back to the paint shop yet again.

The Aviation Photo Company

The new paint job did not last long. Barely ten months later the backers of TPL decided to break up the loss-making consortium; British Airways took over Brymon, and Maersk got the Birmingham airline, which it renamed Maersk Air in August 1993. G-WMCC looks slightly down-at-heel in this photograph with its Brymon titling stripped off.

The aircraft did not keep its woebegone appearance for long. Almost immediately Maersk Air entered into a franchise agreement with British Airways to continue operating some of the Birmingham services, and that meant rebranding

The Aviation Photo Company

The Aviation Photo Company

in British Airways colours; G-WMCC faced another session with the paint brushes. The One-Elevens and Jetstreams were turned out in the sombre blue and grey British Airways Express scheme.

G-WMCC continued in service for another three years, before being withdrawn from use and later being donated to the local airport fire service. Maersk Air modernised its fleet at Birmingham, introducing Boeing 737s and Canadair regional jets, but by the beginning of the new millennium was losing money on its heavy investment. The airline was sold to its

management team, which relaunched the airline as Duo Airways after the British Airways franchise had been terminated in 2003, but Duo did not survive beyond May 2004.

A good try, the Jetstream, and credit to British Aerospace for persevering with it. It was replaced in due course by slightly larger jet regional airliners including the Canadair/ Bombardier jet mentioned above and advanced turboprops including the ATR. I was always surprised that more were not sold as corporate aircraft but I accept that it faced very strong competition from the Beechcraft Kingair 300/350 series that was launched in the early 1980s; with a narrower fuselage the Beech is somewhat faster. The Museum of Flight at East

Fortune in Scotland has preserved the prototype Jetstream G-JSSD in recognition of the airliner's Scottish heritage.

38: BRITISH AEROSPACE 146 G-BTNU

This small four-jet feederliner started as a Hawker Siddeley design. Hawker (and de Havilland before it) had been trying for some years to design a jet replacement for the many Fokker Friendships, HS 748s and Convairliners that were in service in 1960s and '70s but found it nigh on impossible as there were just no suitable jet engines available. The breakthrough came in 1972 when American engine manufacturer AVCO Lycoming announced a turbofan development of its T55 engine that powered the Chinook helicopter; the civil engine became known as the ALF 502 and was chosen by Hawker Siddeley for its projected HS 146 airliner and by Bombardier in Canada for the Challenger corporate jet. The name AVCO is a throwback to the automobile and aero engine manufacturer E.L. Cord, whose Lycoming engines had powered his splendid front-wheel drive cars in the 1930s.

In September 1973 Hawker Siddeley launched the 146, having successfully applied for government launch aid to the tune of £46 million, repayable through a levy on aircraft sales; the target price for the basic version was $4 million (aircraft prices are usually in US Dollars). The aircraft was not designed

to compete with larger jets such as the Boeing 737 or Douglas DC-9, but anything a HS 748 could do, the HS 146 could do better and faster. It came in two sizes, seating up to 71 and 102 passengers respectively, with superior airfield performance. The high wing allowed a low sill height, good for the carriage of freight, an important secondary function. The aircraft had four engines because it needed a minimum amount of thrust, and only four ALF 502s would provide it; also, in hot-and-high conditions the engine-out performance was degraded significantly less if there were still three performing! Although there were four of them, the engines were very quiet, a plus for night-time freight operations and an asset in an increasingly noise-conscious environment. The range was around 1,200 miles but the perceived requirement was for much shorter sectors; the 146 was designed to fly multiple sectors without refuelling, allowing quick turnarounds en route. Hawker Siddeley estimated that the size of the market would be 1,200 aircraft and expected to capture a third of it, around 400 units. The company was riding high on the success of its HS 125 executive jet, with more than 300 sold, many in the United States; Scottish Aviation was about to relaunch the Jetstream; Britten-Norman, under its new owners Fairey Group, was selling Islanders in significant numbers; and in Northern Ireland the Short 330 was about to be launched. It was a very positive time for British aircraft manufacturing.

But then there was a major hiccup. The Arab–Israeli war of 1973 had serious consequences after oil exports from the Middle East were curtailed, leading to a quadrupling of oil prices and severe economic recession in most of the Western world. Britain had a hard time of it; a three-day working week was imposed early in 1974, which was then followed by the miners' strike. Prime Minister Ted Heath called an election early in 1974, which he lost; or at least, the Labour party won more seats, and formed a minority government under Harold Wilson. In October Wilson went back to the country and this time the Labour party achieved a majority of just three seats. High on the manifesto was the nationalisation of the aircraft industry, not a prospect that enthused the manufacturers. Scottish Aviation lost interest in the Jetstream. Hawker Siddeley's reaction was stronger; it pulled the plug on the HS 146 programme after the government refused to undertake to pay the aircraft's future development costs, estimated to be £120 million. After pressure from its unions, and with some government money, the company agreed to keep the design function ticking over and retained the jigs, tools and drawings.

As recounted under the heading for the Jetstream, the bill to nationalise the aircraft and shipbuilding industries took a long time to make it into law, so there was a lengthy hiatus for the HS 146. It was not until July 1978 that the go-ahead was given for the 146 to be relaunched under the aegis of the nationalised British Aerospace Corporation (BAe). Other manufacturers participated: as well as providing the engines, AVCO (later known as Textron) built the wings; Saab in Sweden built the tailplanes; Short made the engine pods. There were no orders as yet; the relaunch was an act of faith. Launching costs had ballooned, along with the hideous inflation we suffered in the 1970s, to more than £250 million, although now that the manufacturer was owned by the government, that was less of a concern. The target sale price per unit had almost doubled; it was now between $7.5 million and $8 million. Finally, in June 1980 the Argentinian airline LAPA ordered three aircraft, and then cancelled them the following year. American regional carriers began ordering in penny numbers in 1981 and there was a breakthrough order from California's Pacific Southwest in 1984; the American regionals recognised the 146's ability to fly into noise-sensitive airports. After that sales picked up so that by the end of 1991 there were 222 orders for the 146. The eventual total built was 394, not that far from Hawker Siddeley's original projection.

Dan-Air ordered two in August 1982, financing them through Barclays Mercantile, which put down £15 million for the two aircraft, around $27 million; that is $13.5 million for each plane, another substantial hike of the target list price. They were not the first brand new planes that Dan-Air had ever bought – that honour belonged to Bristol Freighter G-APLH – but they were the first to be built specifically for the airline. Seating eighty-eight passengers, they entered service in 1983; Dan-Air was able to fly them into the small airport at Berne in Switzerland as well as using them for regional scheduled and charter services out of Newcastle. Dan-Air freshened the fleet as the type developed, usually fielding around three or four of the little jets and buying the larger 146-300 when it became available in 1990; this latter was 15ft longer than the original series 100, and accommodated up to 110 passengers in a six-abreast layout.

The Aviation Photo Company

G-BTNU, a 146-300, joined Dan-Air in August 1990 at a time when the airline was undergoing a metamorphosis, switching from its historic role as a major British charter airline to a repurposed scheduled-service airline for the 1990s, ready to take up the challenges of Europe's deregulated air services. Dan-Air had been flying scheduled services since 1956 but always in a subsidiary role to its charter operations. This was not because it necessarily wanted to, but the government would not allow the company to operate on any trunk routes, so Dan-Air had to make do with some pretty thin fare; Prestwick to the Isle of Man,

for example, or Newcastle to Kristiansand in Norway. The airline slowly developed a network over the years and even managed the occasional break-out route such as Gatwick to Aberdeen, but still relied for the bulk of its business and profits on its charter flying. That changed towards the end of the 1980s as Dan-Air, through no particular fault of its own, lost substantial amounts of its charter business; large tour operators, many of whom had been Dan-Air clients for years if not decades, started to invest in their own in-house airlines and, of course, put most of their flying with these new airlines.

Fortunately Dan-Air was well placed to take advantage of another trend, the opportunity as a result of deregulation to fly scheduled services to many more points in Europe, including many hitherto unobtainable trunk routes; it already knew how to operate scheduled services and had the systems in place. In its eagerness to take over the role of main Gatwick hub airline in the early 1990s I think Dan-Air rushed its fences; understandably, perhaps, following the collapse of rivals including Air Europe and British Caledonian. Nevertheless, scheduled services require enormous investment and in the end Dan-Air ran out of money. In 1992 the airline did achieve a major goal; it carried more scheduled passengers than charter, but in the process had been haemorrhaging cash. Sensible plans to standardise equipment on Boeing 737s and BAe 146s were not enough to save Dan-Air, which called it quits in October 1992 and sold out to British Airways.

British Airways had no interest in keeping the charter operation; instead it kept Dan-Air's new Boeings and tried to make a go of the Gatwick scheduled operations. The charter business evaporated after British Airways disposed of the charter jets, finding a willing buyer in Southend's British Air Ferries, which took over all eleven of Dan-Air's BAC One-Eleven 500s and for good measure in April 1993 took on G-BTNU as well, joining two other 146s already in its fleet.

British Air Ferries had recently changed its name. The original name goes back to Silver City, the Bristol Freighter car ferries, Freddie Laker and his Channel Air Bridge; after the two merged under the mantle of British United, the combined vehicle ferry became first British United Air Ferries, then British Air Ferries, which was sold on to 'Mike' Keegan, he of Trans Meridian repute. Keegan got bored with operating car ferries, so that business was closed down, and

the passenger scheduled services that had developed around them, together with the Heralds that had flown them, were sold off to Air UK. Instead Keegan bought old Viscounts and, with his engineering skills to the fore, rebuilt them and then either leased them out or used them himself on passenger, cargo and post office contracts; he sold the British Air Ferries business in 1989.

The new owner began buying jets, and in 1993 changed the name of the airline to British World Airlines. G-BTNU appeared in the new livery in April 1993. A major contract awarded at the time was from the Ministry of Defence to fly British troops and their families in the 146 between the UK and Germany, a service wrested from the previous incumbent, Britannia, which had held the trooping task since 1969.

Pictured taking off from Manchester, G-BTNU was also used on holiday charters out of Stansted, Manchester and occasionally Gatwick, alongside the One-Elevens; the carrier had some prestigious clients including the Travel Club of Upminster, and was able to offer a fairly relaxed schedule as there were not the same pressures to achieve high utilisation since the capital costs of the equipment were negligible. British World flew G-BTNU around five hours a day, enough for one daily rotation; the One-Elevens flew even less, barely managing two hours a day, and only flying at weekends. G-BTNU and the second 146 were returned to British Aerospace in 1996; the One-Elevens continued until 31 December 2000. British World went on to invest in Boeing 737s and BAe ATPs and began to concentrate on contract flying for other airlines, but was caught up in the aftermath of the severe business downturn following the terrorist attacks of 11 September 2001 and closed down in December of that year after more than fifty years of service.

Shaun Connor

G-BTNU went off the British register and flew with Aer Lingus for seven years before finding its way down to South Africa.

Before it quit the airliner manufacturing business, British Aerospace made one last effort to retrieve what it could from the dying embers of the industry now under its stewardship. Late in 1990 the manufacturer announced plans to revamp the 146 line, renaming the aircraft RJ Avroliners: the smallest 146-100 became the RJ70, intended for the American market with seventy seats in a five-abreast layout; the 146-200 became the RJ85; and the longer 146-300 was renamed the RJ100. The numbers reflect the passenger configuration; there was also a RJ115 that had a six-abreast layout. The engines were upgraded to the LF507, the cabin was tweaked and the new range was sold to some notable blue-chip airlines in Europe and America. The price had also risen, not unexpectedly, to around $17 million. After attempts to switch

production of the RJ series to China Taiwan came to nothing, British Aerospace combined its marketing in 1995 with the French-Italian combine ATR. Plans to re-engine the aircraft with Honeywell AS977 turbofans (it would still have used four of them) and rename it in the RJX series were stillborn after British Aerospace, now known as BAE Systems following the airframe manufacturer's merger with Marconi in 1999, cancelled the project in December 2001.

The last British-built airliner, a RJ85, was handed over in November 2003. In rapid succession BAE Systems, and British Aerospace before it, sold its business jet division to Raytheon in 1993 (from 1996 production was transferred to Kansas); terminated the ATP programme in 1996, and Jetstream production in 1997; closed down the 146/RJ line in 2001; and finally, for good measure, sold its 20 per cent stake in Airbus in 2006. BAE Systems is now a major defence contractor for the Pentagon.

39: BRITISH AEROSPACE ATP G-LOGC

The ATP (Advanced Turbo-Prop), derived from the Hawker Siddeley 748 and featuring a lengthened fuselage and new engines, is one of those aircraft that starts off doing one thing and ends up being quite good at something completely different; like the Comet, say, or the de Havilland Dove. The ATP was designed as a short-range, economical airliner, using efficient turboprops and filling a niche below the commonly used 130-seat passenger jets like the Boeing 737 and McDonnell

Douglas MD-83; its most successful user was a Swedish freight operator specialising in European package deliveries.

British Aerospace (BAe) positioned the seventy-two-seater ATP in the market somewhere between its smaller Jetstream models, with capacity for between nineteen and thirty passengers, and the jet BAe 146, which in its later guises could carry more than 100 passengers; the ATP was similar in size and performance to the Viscount, but used a third of the fuel.

The ATP received orders from prestigious names including British Airways, the Airlines of Britain Group, which included Loganair and Manx Airlines as well as British Midland, and US regional Air Wisconsin, flying as a United Express partner. Loganair had changed a lot since its pioneering days flying within the Highlands and Islands of Scotland in the 1970s, and had expanded its network to include trunk routes from Manchester to Edinburgh, Glasgow and Belfast; it also became involved in North Sea oil support work from Aberdeen. The aircraft progressed too, from Islanders to Twin Otters, Shorts, Friendships and leased Viscounts. In 1983 Loganair was sold by the Royal Bank of Scotland to British Midland Airways, which had been the launch customer for the ATP, ordering three in December 1985. Five more ATPs were ordered for Loganair and sister company Manx in July 1988.

The first, G-OLCC, was delivered in August 1989 and started flying schedules out of Manchester.

Its registration sequence follows two BAe 146s, 'CA and 'CB; G-OLCD was the second ATP. Both aircraft types represented a sea-change in Loganair's equipment and strengthened its ambitious route network out of Manchester, but in 1992 the 146s were returned to British Aerospace. The ATPs, five of them, became the main haulers in the fleet, accounting for just under half the total passengers carried by Loganair in 1992 and 1993. The ATPs were re-registered; G-OLCC became G-LOGC.

The early 1990s saw many changes and adjustments in civil aviation, none more so than the full implementation of European deregulation on 1 January 1993. Following the collapse of Air Europe and Dan-Air, both British Airways and British Midland endlessly reformulated their regional airlines in order to take advantage of the new freedoms that

David Lunn

The Aviation Photo Company

deregulation offered. British Midland took the decision in 1994 to restructure its airlines so that Loganair would return to serving Scottish internal routes only, and transferred its by now considerable Manchester operations to a new entity, Manx Airlines Europe, which took over the Loganair ATPs. G-LOGC was repainted in Manx colours.

But not for long! It was reregistered G-MANH in late 1994 to reflect its Manx ownership, and later that year Manx Europe signed up as a British Airways franchise, flying the same route network but now part of the British Airways timetable and booking system. It was time for another speedy visit to the paint shop.

In a further twist, Loganair became a British Airways franchise, too. But it did not end there. In 1996 British

Airways decided to withdraw from its remaining Scottish internal services, handing them over to British Midland's subsidiaries, which by now had been consolidated into a new airline, British Regional Airlines, whose logo can just be seen in the image of G-MANH; the newly named airline continued to fly as a British Airways franchise, and eventually in 2001 was bought out by British Airways. A splinter group had already broken away from the British Airways/ British Regional consortium in 1997 following a buy-out led by Scott Grier; it retained the Loganair name and took over the island routes in the north and west of Scotland, reverting to a Britten-Norman Islander operation. The 'new' Loganair continued as a separate British Airways franchise for another ten years, even taking over some of the routes in

The Aviation Photo Company

The Aviation Photo Company

Scotland that British Regional had subsequently relinquished! A feisty airline, Loganair, now operates under its own name throughout Scotland.

The new British Airways regional operation, which included the original Manx Airlines and West Country-based Brymon, was renamed British Airways Citiexpress, to which G-MANH was transferred. It continued to fly out of Manchester, but British Airways found it difficult to combine so many diverse operations into one profitable unit and began to do some trimming. Jetstreams and ATPs were culled, and in March 2004 G-MANH flew its last commercial flight from Manchester before going into storage.

Steve Ryle

The Aviation Photo Company

G-MANH's role now changed. The growth in the package express business led operators to look at all available aircraft hulls for conversion into freighters, and Sweden's West Air, already an HS 748 operator, had begun using ATP freighters, converted with a large freight door at the rear and able to carry 8 tons. British Aerospace began marketing the freighter, using the Romanian firm Romaero to perform the conversion work, and later in 2004 G-MANH was ferried to Bucharest for the work to be done. The following year it entered service with Atlantic Airlines, a sibling of Air Atlantique;

the latter operated its historic piston-engine fleet on cargo charters, while Atlantic Airlines flew the turboprops, Lockheed Electras, which were later supplemented by ATPs.

G-MANH joined Atlantic Airlines early in 2006. The photograph clearly shows the large freight door. Atlantic Airlines flew on behalf of DHL and the Royal Mail on night-time schedules, building up to a fleet of eleven ATPs that operated alongside Lockheed Electras. In Sweden, meanwhile, West Air continued to acquire more ATP freighters; by 2008 it and its Luxemburg subsidiary had a combined fleet of thirty-three. The West Air group joined forces with Atlantic Airlines in October 2008 and started operating under the new title West Atlantic. G-MANH received new colours, which it was still wearing in 2015 shortly before it was transferred to the Swedish register.

In total, West Atlantic flew forty-nine ATPs, a small number as passenger aircraft; the airline accounted for roughly three quarters of all ATPs built. The Swedish element of West Atlantic still continues to fly a sizeable fleet of ATPs in 2019; the British airline operates an all-jet fleet of Boeing 737s. In 2018 former G-MANH was sold in Kenya, where the aircraft is now stored.

It is puzzling that the ATP fared poorly in the market. The strategy should have worked. Fokker had re-engined its successful F27 Friendship and sold it as the F50, which was launched into service in 1985. The ATP followed in 1988 when the first aircraft of an order from British Midland was delivered: so a gap of three years. But the ATP was not only competing against the F50, it faced off against a vigorous newcomer, the French-Italian ATR 42, which had first flown in 1985. Originally built as a forty-eight-seater, the ATR was extended to carry up to seventy-two passengers and renamed the ATR 72, with entry into service in late 1989. And in a

Ian Tate

crowded marketplace, Canadian manufacturer de Havilland Canada also fielded an entry in this category, the Dash 8 series, which found its most successful variation in the Q400 version, able to carry up to eighty-two passengers. Sweden's SAAB built an advanced turboprop, the SAAB 2000, able to carry up to fifty-eight passengers, but like the ATP it suffered disappointing sales. Only sixty-three ATPs were built and operated, and coincidentally there were sixty-three SAAB 2000s.

The ATP line was uprooted to Prestwick and the type was even renamed the Jetstream 61, but to no avail. Production closed down after British Aerospace merged its twin-turboprop activities in 1995 with ATR, to concentrate on the more successful ATR airliners. As a point of interest, the ATP, ATR and DHC Q400 were powered by Pratt and Whitney Canada PW100 turboprops, the SAAB by Rolls-Royce Allison AE2100s. ATR sales have reached around 1,500; de Havilland Canada's Dash 8 series have exceeded 1,200.

40: BOEING 757 G-OOOB

First there was the Boeing 707. Pan American introduced the jet on transatlantic services in October 1958 but had to wait another year before it could start flying the true intercontinental version, the Boeing 707-320. The original 707-120 version, powered by 12,500lb-thrust Pratt & Whitney turbojets, was fine for domestic operations but still needed to drop into Gander in Newfoundland to refuel on transatlantic sectors. The intercontinental version had a fuselage 80in longer and could carry up to 189 passengers over 3,800 miles, using more powerful jets of 15,800lb thrust; even better was the 707-320B series, introduced in 1962, which had Pratt & Whitney JT3D turbofans, giving a range of 5,000 miles; best of all was the turbofan 707-320C, which had a large cargo door, strengthened floor and could carry 38 tons of freight, or up to 219 passengers.

The Aviation Photo Company

Lloyd International bought this fine Boeing 707-320C G-AZJM from Continental in December 1971 just months before the airline went bust; the aircraft went on to fly with both British Caledonian and British Midland. There was a Rolls-Royce-powered version of the Boeing, the 707-420, bought by BOAC, Cunard Eagle, Lufthansa and Air-India, which is described in the section relating to G-ARWD. A lighter, shorter version of the 707, the Boeing 720, entered service in 1960; when powered by turbofans it became something of a 'hot-rod' and was a strong competitor to the Vickers VC10.

Next in line was the Boeing 727, powered by three rear-mounted Pratt & Whitney JT8D turbofans; it looked like the Hawker Siddeley Trident. The 727 had the same fuselage width as the Boeing 707 and was designed for short- to medium-range routes, seating 129 tourist-class passengers; it entered service in 1964. Britain's Dan-Air squeezed in 151 seats, some of which had vertical backs that could not be reclined; it was one of the most uncomfortable configurations I have ever experienced. Here is Boeing 727 G-BAFZ in the last version of Dan-Air's red-and-black colour schemes.

The 727 had superior airfield performance thanks to its sophisticated wing design, and more than adequate range, allowing non-stop flights to the Canaries and Israel. The 727 was more fuel efficient than the Comet but still needed a three-man crew. A longer version of the 727, the -200 series, was introduced in 1967; it had 10ft fuselage plugs either side of the wing and could carry 155 passengers. Except if you were an airline called Dan-Air, which put in 187 seats when the 727-200 started joining its fleet in 1980.

The Boeing 737, smallest of them all, had only two engines but shared the same fuselage width as its siblings. Easyjet's G-EZYH is a Boeing 737-300 series delivered in 1998. The strapline on the forward fuselage is a waspish reference to the old British Airways boast that it was the world's favourite airline.

The Aviation Photo Company

The Aviation Photo Company

The Aviation Photo Company

The Boeing 737 entered service with Lufthansa and United Air Lines in 1968, beating the Boeing 747, at the other end of the scale, by just under two years.

Boeing's 747 was the first jumbo jet, mesmerizingly huge, the leading wide-body airliner, and it entered service with Pan American in January 1970. For decades Boeing had the market to itself. Lockheed and McDonnell Douglas also built large wide-bodied aircraft, as did Europe's Airbus Industrie, but the 747, which was continuously developed, was always the clear market leader: it even saw off the challenge from the Airbus A380. Over 1,500 Boeing 747s have been built.

I like the detail on Virgin's first Boeing 747 G-VIRG; the signwriter hanging perilously off his perch on the tail and the less than subtle name *Maiden Voyager*.

Which brings us to the Boeing 757 and its stablemate, the 767. The narrow-bodied 757 was optimised for short to medium distances, just 2ft longer than the Boeing 727-200 it was designed to replace but able to carry many more passengers, up to 233, with a flight-deck crew of two, and was powered by two large and economical turbofans; most Boeing 757s sported Rolls-Royce RB.211 engines. The 767 had a wider twin-aisle body and more range but very similar handling characteristics to the 757; pilots are type rated for both. American airline United launched the 767, British Airways and America's Eastern were the first to order the 757, which entered service early in 1983. British charter airline Monarch followed just months later; tour operator Thomson's airline Britannia preferred the bigger, longer-range 767, which entered service in 1984.

In a busy scene at Gatwick in August 1994, Britannia's 767 G-BKVZ is seen with two Air 2000 Boeing 757s, a British Airways Boeing 767 and a Caledonian 757; in the background a Virgin Boeing 747 is in the company of sundry British Airways Boeing 737s and the tail of a 747. Almost a full house for Boeing!

Roger Richards

Many tour operators owed their successful genesis and growth to Dan-Air, a flexible airline that offered outstanding commercial service, a varied fleet and departures from most major international airports in the United Kingdom. The trouble was that as the tour operators prospered and grew larger, they wanted to secure a reliable source of supply and to have more control of their airline product; now they wanted to turn away from a third-party provider and to keep the profits from airline operations in house. Intasun, entrepreneur Harry Goodman's cheap and cheerful tour operation, set up its own airline, Air Europe, in 1979, drawing ever more of its business away from Dan-Air as the new airline's fleet increased. In 1987, tour operator and seat broker Owners Abroad followed a similar course, forming Air 2000 in Manchester, which ordered Boeing 757s. Manchester was chosen because it was easier for a new airline to get slots there and because the distances flown were slightly longer, allowing the airline to achieve impressive utilisation rates; later the airline based aircraft at Gatwick and Glasgow. Owners Abroad at first specialised in providing flights for villa and apartment owners who wanted to fly cheaply to their holiday homes, but the business expanded to include more conventional hotel holidays; in addition the company built up expertise in selling wholesale blocks of seats on its flights to other, smaller tour operators.

Air 2000 chose the Boeing 757 because it was the best aircraft for its purposes by far, an unbeatable combination of economics, performance, range and durability. The aircraft were new, so financing was easier to obtain; they performed reliably thanks to their Rolls-Royce engines; even with 233 seats the interior was comfortable, spacious and bright; and the airline went out of its way to provide superior passenger service. To ensure consistency, meals were sourced in Britain and the inbound sectors with returning passengers were served with meals to the same standard and by the same caterer as those flying out; anybody who has had to cope with Spanish bacon will appreciate the significance of that! At 4,000 miles, the aircraft had more than enough range, easily able to fly a full load from Glasgow down to Cyprus; and there was enough payload to carry extra skis on winter charters and to pick up seasonal loads such as fresh fruit from the Canaries for some extra revenue. The range characteristics were a hidden benefit that the airline discovered when it started flying across the Atlantic to Florida.

G-OOOB was delivered to Air 2000 on 27 April 1987, the second 757 in the new airline's fleet.

G-OOOB looked fine in flight, but this 757 had a somewhat skittish relationship with Air 2000, finding itself more often than not in the service of other airlines. First there was a winter lease with British Airways during the winter of 1987–88, when the aircraft was used on domestic shuttle flights; livery changes were minimal.

The Aviation Photo Company

Then in December 1988 the aircraft began the first of a long series of winter cross-leases with its Canadian partner Canada 3000. In Canada the prime holiday season is during the winter months, the exact opposite of the situation prevailing in Britain. A number of British airlines had winter cross-lease arrangements but Air 2000 wanted to go one step further and have a stake in the airline to which it was leasing its aircraft. Unfortunately it was a step too far for the Canadian authorities, who objected, claiming that even with a minority shareholding the British airline would be in de facto control of the Canadian airline. It is difficult to get Canadian regulators to change their minds, so Air 2000 bowed out of the investment and its place was taken by a Canadian family with extensive aviation interests. But the cross-leases persisted, and Air 2000 in turn was able to use additional Canadian-registered aircraft of Canada 3000 during its peak summer season.

Author's Collection

In all G-OOOB, temporarily registered under Canadian marks as C-FOOB, spent a total of nine winters in Canada flying holidaymakers down to Mexico, Florida and the Caribbean from Toronto and other Canadian airports. On its return to Air 2000 for each summer season the aircraft resumed its British registration, except in 1995; on that occasion the aircraft remained on the Canadian register even when it was returned to the UK, which allowed the airline to use Canadian flight-deck crews.

A new name had appeared alongside the familiar Air 2000: First Choice. Owners Abroad had been rebranded as First Choice following a change of management in 1994. At first the Air 2000 name remained although the airline was subjected to an aircraft livery change; the new design purported to reflect a tapestry of colours and shapes associated with the destinations to which the the airline was flying.

On the next page G-OOOB displays a profusion of different typefaces as it takes off from Palma in Majorca in August 2000. Of course, the arrival of the new millennium raised questions as to the ongoing suitability of the Air 2000 name!

And indeed in 2004 the airline's name was changed to First Choice, G-OOOB briefly displaying First Choice titling before it was eased out of service in December 2004, after eighteen years and 70,000 hours of flying. First Choice Airways continued for another three years, increasingly flying long-haul sectors, before it amalgamated with Thomson's Thomsonfly, formerly Britannia Airways; that was a consequence of the merger between German operator TUI, which now owned Thomson and First Choice.

G-OOOB had some years of life left in it before facing the ordeal of an expensive and time-consuming D Check, and the aircraft entered service almost immediately with a

The Aviation Photo Company

The Aviation Photo Company

Kevin Colbran

new British airline, Astraeus, which had been started in 2002. When I say new it was new in name only; the team behind the project, as was so often the case with British charter airlines, were veterans with years of practical operating and commercial experience. Chairman Brad Burgess has an impeccable record establishing new airlines, with a portfolio that included Connectair, Air Europe Express, Euroworld and CityFlyer. Commercial Director Jonathan Hinkles has been in civil aviation all his life and now heads up Loganair in Scotland.

Astraeus was a niche charter airline that could fly for other airlines, other tour operators and undertake more specialist missions including oil support flights to Algeria and Equatorial Guinea. As holiday flights began to extend beyond the Mediterranean, to Egypt, India and West Africa,

Tony McGhee

the Boeing's excellent range characteristics and useful pay-load were put to good use. Fitted out with 186 seats, later revised to 202, which included a number of convertible club-class seats, G-OOOB found itself visiting Agra in India (for the Taj Mahal), Djibouti in East Africa and Freetown in The Gambia, Egyptian Sinai and many of the smaller isles of Greece, where its superior airfield performance allowed non-stop return sectors.

After three years with Astraeus it was time for G-OOOB to face up to its increasing age, and the aircraft left the airline in October 2007 for a new home in America. After a lengthy conversion to freighter configuration, and registered N822PB, the 757 entered service with Arrow Cargo, an airline with a huge past going back to Miami's George Batchelor and Arrow Air. But its time with Arrow was short-lived. The airline ceased operations in 2010; the aircraft was at first stored, then broken up in 2013. Astraeus had a somewhat rocky experience after it was taken over by Icelandic interests in late 2006. The new owners decided to focus on contract work, principally leasing its aircraft to other operators, and pulled out of the specialist tour and charter operations. The end came in 2011 when business opportunities began to dry up, leaving the airline high and dry.

Boeing built more than 2,000 767 and 757s, in roughly equal numbers. Many 757s found further work as package carriers for FedEx, UPS and DHL. Others remain in front-line service with transatlantic carriers such as American, Delta and United. The British took to this Rolls-Royce powered aircraft: more than 150 were bought by UK carriers. The biggest operator was British Airways, with forty-five aircraft. Britannia (later Thomson Airways) and Thomas Cook

The Aviation Photo Company

accounted for another forty-six; Air 2000 (later First Choice) fielded nineteen, Air Europe sixteen. Monarch, which introduced the type to charter airline fleets, had ten. At least another ten British airlines flew a further twenty Boeing 757s. It will not be an easy aircraft to replace, although the Airbus A321 in its various guises comes closest, and longer-range developments of this type will eventually surpass the Boeing 757's admirable performance.

As a young salesman I grew up working with Bristol Britannias, and I always like to draw comparisons between the Britannia and the 757; they were both equally viable over short- or long-haul routes, carrying passengers or freight, flying scheduled services or happy holidaymakers to the sun.

COMPARATIVE PERFORMANCE OF BRITISH-REGISTERED AIRLINERS

airliner designation	DH.84 Dragon	Shorts Sunderland Hythe	Avro York	Avro Tudor 4	DH.89B Dragon Rapide	DH.104 Dove	Douglas DC-3	Vickers Viking I	Bristol Freighter Mk. 21	HP Halifax Halton	HP Hermes 4
engine type	DH Gipsy Major	Bristol Pegasus	Rolls-Royce Merlin	Rolls-Royce Merlin	DH Gipsy Queen 3	DH Gipsy Queen 70	P & W Twin Wasp	Bristol Hercules	Bristol Hercules	Bristol Hercules	Bristol Hercules
number of engines	2	4	4	4	2	2	2	2	2	4	4
payload (number of passengers)	8	24	50	32	8	8	32	36	36	12	68
normal cruising speed (mph)	109	165	160–210	218	115	179	160	190	163	210	276
range with full payload (st. miles)	460	2,350	2,700	2,700	578	500	1,500	1,000	500	2,530	1,300

airliner designation	Douglas DC-4	Canadair C-4	Airspeed Ambassador	Vickers Viscount 701	L049 Constellation	Douglas DC-6A	Bristol Britannia 102	DH.114 Heron IB	Douglas DC-7C	Bristol Britannia 312	Vickers Vanguard 953
engine type	P & W R-2000 Twin Wasp	Rolls-Royce Merlin	Bristol Centaurus	Rolls-Royce Dart	Wright R-3350	P & W R-2800 Double Wasp	Bristol Siddeley Proteus	DH Gipsy Queen	Wright R-3350 Turbo-Compound	Bristol Siddeley Proteus	Rolls-Royce Tyne
number of engines	4	4	2	4	4	4	4	4	4	4	4
payload (number of passengers)	86	82	55	63	82	102	112	17	105	139	132
normal cruising speed (mph)	204	250	240	301	275	315	362	165	355	357	420
range with full payload (st. miles)	2,140	1,860	550	990	2,290	3,005	3,450	805	4,605	4,268	1,830

DH de Havilland
HP Handley Page
P & W Pratt & Whitney

airliner designation	DH.106 Comet 4	DH.106 Comet 4B	DH.106 Comet 4C	Boeing 707-420	Vickers Viscount 831	Avro 748 Series 2	HP Dart Herald 201	ATL.98 Carvair	Vickers Super VC10	BAC One-Eleven 408
engine type	Rolls-Royce Avon	Rolls-Royce Avon	Rolls-Royce Avon	Rolls-Royce Conway	Rolls-Royce Dart	Rolls-Royce Dart	Rolls-Royce Dart	P & W R-2000 Twin Wasp	Rolls-Royce Conway	Rolls-Royce Spey
number of engines	4	4	4	4	4	2	2	4	4	2
payload (number of passengers)	109	119	119	189	80	48	56	23 plus 5 cars	163	89
normal cruising speed (mph)	503	532	503	604	351	266	270	184	580	548
range with full payload (st. miles)	3,225	2,500	2,650	4,330	1,275	930	700	2,070	4,720	1,430

airliner designation	HS Trident 1E-140	BAC One-Eleven 509	Boeing 737-200 Advanced	Douglas DC 10-10	Britten-Norman Islander	Short 330	BAe J31 Jetstream	BAe 146-300	BAe ATP	Boeing 757-28A
engine type	Rolls-Royce Spey	Rolls-Royce Spey	P & W JT8D	General Electric CF6	Lycoming O-540	P & W Canada PT6A	Garrett Airesearch TPE331	Lycoming ALF-502	P & W Canada PW126	Rolls-Royce RB211-535E4
number of engines	3	2	2	3	2	2	2	4	2	2
payload (number of passengers)	126	119	130	345	9	30	19	110	72	233
normal cruising speed (mph)	604	541	480	574	145	180	302	460	272	530
range with full payload (st. miles)	1,800	1,570	2,000	3,500	620	544	700	1,400	712	4,000

BAC British Aircraft Corporation
BAe British Aerospace
DH de Havilland, HS Hawker Siddeley
HP Handley Page
P & W Pratt & Whitney

INDEX

IF YOU ENJOYED THIS TITLE FROM THE HISTORY PRESS

978 0 7524 3696 8

Aquila Airways, British South American Airways, Silver City and a host of other airlines tend to be forgotten in the telling of British aviation history as everyone remembers the big names: British Airways, BEA, and BOAC. Guy Halford-MacLeod's three-volume series on the history of independent airlines in Britain after the Second World War redresses the balance in telling the stories of the independents.

978 0 7524 4276 1

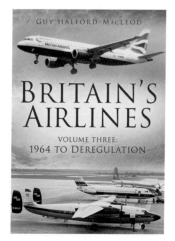

978 0 7524 5499 3

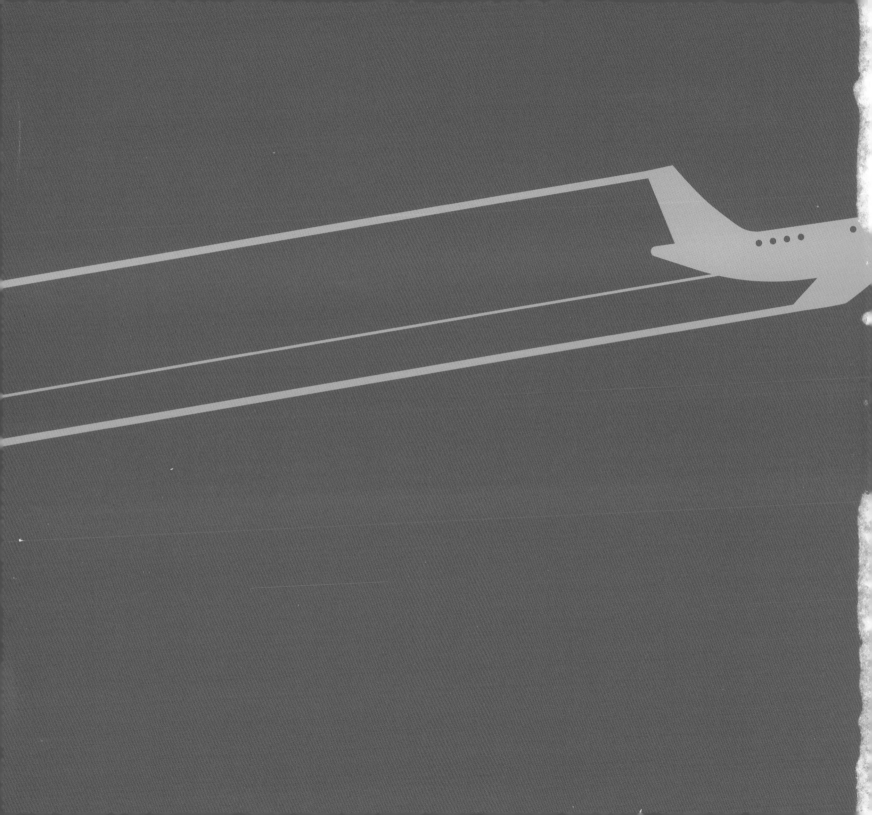